Past Event and Present Salvation

Past Event and Present Salvation

The Christian Idea of Atonement

PAUL S. FIDDES

Westminster/John Knox Press
Louisville, Kentucky

First published in 1989 by
Darton, Longman & Todd Ltd.
89 Lillie Road, London SW6 1UD

First American edition

Published by Westminster/John Knox Press
Louisville, Kentucky

PRINTED IN THE UNITED STATES OF AMERICA

2 4 6 8 9 7 5 3 1

Library of Congress Cataloging-in-Publication Data

Fiddes, Paul S.
  Past event and present salvation.

  Includes bibliographies.
  1. Atonement. I. Title.
BT265.2.F53 1989   232′.3   88-33935
ISBN 0-664-25036-X

Contents

TO F. W. DILLISTONE
wise teacher, gracious friend

Preface

This book is not written for skilled theologians, though it does seek to engage all those who want to be theologians in the root sense of being 'talkers about God'. I have aimed to provide an *introduction* to the Christian theme of atonement, and so in writing it I have not presumed the reader to have any previous acquaintance with academic theology. I hope it may be used not only by students in departments of theology and religion, but by all people in the churches of Christendom who want to think seriously about the meaning of their faith in the modern world. The title, however, also draws attention to an aspect of the idea of atonement that is often glossed over. How can a particular event in the past have an effect upon our experience of salvation today? My aim of keeping this question in view throughout the study may still interest those for whom the basic information in this book was new long ago.

The advanced theologian, should he or she read this book, will notice that I have not scrupled about using a broad brush-stroke where the composition of the picture demands it. I have not felt obliged to support every argument with reference to previous scholarly work, though I trust that the way I have written makes the fruits of that work available. In one case, however, I have provided a slightly more detailed study. The thought of the twelfth-century monk Peter Abelard has been enormously influential during the last century, even upon those who fail to acknowledge him or apparently discard him. His insights have been formative in my own reflections, and so I thought it right to give rather more than a sketch of his understanding of the cross of Jesus Christ.

The dedication acknowledges another debt, to F. W. Dillistone, a scholar who was once my teacher and is now a personal friend. His own book, *The Christian Understanding of Atonement* (1968), has a beauty of writing and depth of perception that makes it a theological classic of our age, and an enduring witness to the faith.

Regent's Park College   P.S.F.
Oxford
Michaelmas 1988

Part I

Issues

1

Introduction
Atonement and the human predicament

'During my stay with you the only knowledge I claimed to have was about Jesus, and only about him as the crucified Christ.'[1] On first hearing, this may seem a rather limited programme of teaching for an apostle faced with the startling range of human problems exhibited by the Christian church at Corinth. Visiting this great sea port and commercial centre in the first century of the Christian era, Paul found the many problems of the society reflected in the church. There were tangled sexual relationships, social divisions between rich and poor, and the in-group snobbery of those who thought themselves wiser than others. Yet Paul, it seems, confined himself to the theme of 'Christ nailed to the cross'. This does not mean he was always repeating himself, or preaching the same sermon. The point he is making, as he reflects upon his troubled stay among them, is that he proclaimed the cross of Jesus as occupying the centre of all life. The many strands of human experience run through the cross-roads of the cross.

The Christian doctrine of atonement affirms this extraordinary significance of one *particular* event. Human beings have always been in quest of 'salvation', or a making whole of what is broken in existence. 'Salvation' is an idea which has the widest scope, including the healing of individuals and social groups and even the conserving of a natural world ravaged and polluted by human greed. The quest for salvation is the search for authentic life, and many people hope for it beyond death as well as here and now. The idea of 'atonement', however, has a narrower focus. It insists that salvation depends upon the restoring of a relationship between human beings and God, who are estranged from each other. The English word 'at-one-ment' spells out this 'making at one'. In his early English version of the New Testament (1526), William

3

.s the first to apply it to the Greek word meaning
tion',[2] and in succeeding translations it was widely used
Hebrew word in the Old Testament which expresses the
ciling effect of sacrifice.[3] 'Atonement' thus also implies that
the divine–human relationship can be repaired only through a
specific act or event; in ancient Israel the critical act was the ritual
of sacrifice, and for Christian believers atonement happens because
of the death of Jesus in a Roman execution one Friday afternoon.

The Christian view of salvation thus moves, in what may seem
a scandalous manner, away from general truths about the nature
of existence to a very particular moment within it. Salvation, or the
healing of life, issues from atonement, and this in turn has its basis
in the cross of Christ. All roads lead, not to Rome, but to a mound
of earth outside the walls of a Middle Eastern town in a remote
corner of the Roman Empire. We must, of course, be careful not to
lock atonement into that one place in time and space, sealing it into
the past; what matters, according to Christian understanding, is
that atonement *depends* upon that moment. In this sense the cross
stands at the centre of life, and is relevant to all patterns of experience. It does not simply express and reveal the extravagant love of
God in bringing about atonement, but is the decisive point of that
love, from which all else stems.

It is the nature of this *link* between present salvation and past
event that I want to explore in this study of atonement. The connection perplexed C. S. Lewis before he became a Christian; as he
wrote in a letter to a friend, he could see how people might be in
a hopeless condition 'unless something quite beyond mere natural
help or effort stepped in' but 'what I couldn't see was how the life
and death of Someone Else (whoever he was) 2000 years ago could
help us here and now.'[4] Finally Lewis came to see that 'a man can
accept what Christ has done without knowing how it works' and
that 'the thing itself is infinitely more important than any explanations the theologians have produced.'[5] This is certainly an
important warning to bear in mind at the outset of this study. That
the effect of the cross can never be fully or properly explained is
witnessed to by the wide range of images and metaphors created
through the ages to express it; atonement has been portrayed in
pictures drawn (among many others) from the temple, the battlefield, the law-court, the slave-market, courtly love, family life and

medicine. Though the Christian church has been in no doubt that 'God was in Christ, reconciling the world to himself', it has never made any one understanding of the atonement official or orthodox. Creeds and councils have pronounced upon the nature of the Trinity and the Person of Christ, but have never tried to pin down the exact meaning of the atonement.

At the same time the creation of many images shows that the experience of salvation can be enriched by thinking responsibly about it. Doctrine too is a kind of worship, a celebration by the mind, returning words in praise to God who is himself the supreme word-crafter. Curiously, however, theories of atonement do not always explicitly address the question of how a past event can affect our present existence; the issue underlies all the images, but it is often simply assumed that if something important happened in the relationship between God and his estranged world at one point in time, it is bound to affect us now. In this study it will be my aim to highlight the link between past event and the renewal of life in the present, both as we explore the traditional images of atonement (Part II) and as we see how these relate to some important areas of individual and social experience (Part III).

The sheer variety of images and concepts for atonement is also evidence that Christian faith *has* found that the event of the cross touches life at many points. The church has failed to exhaust the meaning of the cross because it makes contact with a human need which is many-dimensional. Different images of atonement have gripped the imagination at different periods of history, because the understanding of the basic human predicament has changed from age to age. John A. T. Robinson tells of once seeing on a church notice-board the announcement, 'Christ is the answer', and scribbled next to it 'Yes, but what is the question?' This ironic query reminds us that each generation seeks a picture of Christ that will answer the great human questions of its time, and Robinson shrewdly points out that this need not mean reducing Christ to one who is palatable to the contemporary taste. Rather, to allow Christ to come as the answer to the questions of the day can be 'to remove obstacles in order that the real "offence" of Christ and him crucified, can be exposed rather than overlaid'.[6] The cultural conditioning of theology can thus have the positive effect of *locating* where the 'mystery in our midst' is to be found. So Christian faith has affirmed

5

that 'Jesus saves', and the scribblers of the age have rightly asked, 'from what?'

When the Christian faith calls the world 'fallen' it is taking a realistic view of a situation in which the distortions of life run deep. Whatever the sensibility of the age, we may identify at least three constant factors in people's awareness of the human predicament. First there is a sense of alienation or estrangement. It is a typical human experience to know oneself to be divided from other people and at odds with one's own inner being; finally this feeling extends to a sense of estrangement from reality itself, a not being at home in the world. It is no great step from the Wanderer of the eighth-century Old English poem, who laments a 'loneliness at the dawn of each day', to the Outsider of Albert Camus' novel in the twentieth century who greets 'the benign indifference of the universe', even though the modern writer accepts the condition as inevitable. The Christian faith identifies this situation as a loss of contact with the ultimate basis of life, and calls it a separation from God; typical biblical terms for the experience are being 'lost', or 'straying' or 'afar off'. Second, we are continually aware of failing to fulfil our potential as human beings. As the philosopher Jean-Paul Sartre puts it, we have an 'unhappy consciousness' of reaching out beyond ourselves to what we always lack.[7] From a Christian perspective, St Paul interprets this experience as a 'falling short of the glory of God'. Since we have failed to measure up to our destiny of sharing in the life of God, this loss of potential is also a kind of estrangement – a falling away from our true being.

But where secular observers of the human scene can speak of alienation and failure to reach potential, the Christian believer also finds a third dimension in the human predicament, underlying the other two. The religious term 'sin' indicates a failure in personal relationships between human beings and their creator, due to a rebellion from the human side. The biblical terms 'disobedience', 'unfaithfulness' and 'breaking of covenant-agreement' point to a human refusal to accept God's purpose for his creation and a setting up of our own project in its place. Looked at from another angle, unfaithfulness is a failure to *trust* in what is offered to us in the midst of our predicament. Sin is unbelief, a lack of trust in the friendship offered to those who are estranged, and a refusal to open ourselves to the fulfilment of potential that a partnership with God brings. The world is, in Emil Brunner's memorable phrase, 'a theatre of revolt'.

These three constant elements in the human predicament – estrangement, loss of potential and rebellion – will, however, take on a different shape and colour in different times and in different cultures. As the expression of the human predicament alters, so there will likewise be a shift in the way that salvation is expressed. Thus as time passes there develops a whole kaleidoscope of images of atonement, none of which can be complete in itself, each of which remains to overlap with the next, and all of which contribute to the pattern of God's act of reconciliation.

In the period of the New Testament church, for example, sin was often pictured as a kind of impurity or uncleanness, tainting life. Human beings were shut out (estranged) from the sphere of 'the holy' or the sacred in which God dwelt because they were defiled and not fit to enter. Atonement was thus frequently portrayed as *sacrifice*, in which the blood of Christ was an agent of cleansing, wiping away the defilement of sin. Images of washing, sprinkling, bathing and fresh clothing cluster around this idea of salvation. Though a picture from the rituals of the ancient world, this way of expressing a sense of disruption in life still persists deep in our consciousness today; we speak of 'a dirty trick', 'foul language' and 'a clean driving licence'. After a particularly unpleasant experience a person may say, 'I had to take a bath because I felt unclean all over'. We also understand the state of mind of Shakespeare's Lady Macbeth who found that 'all the perfumes of Arabia will not sweeten this little hand'.

In the age of the early Church Fathers, the human predicament was frequently understood as that of being oppressed by hostile powers. People lived in fear of the baleful influence of astral deities or of demons who inhabited the natural world, and their own sin either prevented them from overcoming the enemies or pushed them into their grasp. The world felt alien to people because they had lost control over it, manipulated as it seemed to be by supernatural forces. Thus the victory of Christ over the devil and all the powers which threaten the life and health of humankind, while already celebrated in the New Testament, became the most popular way of understanding atonement. There is no need to underline at this point how this sense of predicament remains with us today, as people feel helpless before powers of various kinds, not least before the machinery of the state and bureaucracy.

As philosophy weakened mythology in the following centuries, another view of the human predicament which had been already present became more prominent. The problem was widely understood to be the great difference between an immortal soul and the body in which it was imprisoned. Under the influence of Platonic philosophy, people felt alienated from a world of mere shadows in which they dwelt. According to the Christian view of creation, the material body was certainly not evil in itself, but it was still seen as hampering the soul and thwarting its ascent to the true spiritual world because sin was believed to have worked its greatest havoc in the physical areas of life. Sin caused mortality, corruption and death which held back the soul destined for eternal life. Thus the atoning work of Christ was understood to be his renewing of the image of the immortal God in the whole human being, flesh and spirit. Salvation was divinisation, in the sense of raising humanity to share in the life of God. We cannot any longer accept a view of the soul as a kind of separate 'survival capsule' within the body; modern insights into the nature of the self confirm the ancient Hebrew view of the profound unity of body and mind. But the idea of the frustrated destiny of the soul did express the potential that we feel for transcending (going beyond) ourselves. The Christian faith interprets the call 'to voyage out on to distant seas' (Nietzsche's phrase) as a restlessness for our proper home in God.

In the Middle Ages the problems of society were seen in terms of a disturbance of order, and particularly of feudal obligations. Chaos ensued when loyalty and honour were no longer paid to the overlord by his vassals, and order could only be restored if the debt of honour were paid – either by compensation or by penalty inflicted. In this cultural context the human predicament before God was seen as failure 'to render to God his due', and atonement could be understood as settling a debt which human beings could not repay. This hierarchical view of reality is ours no longer, and we must always be alert to the way that an appeal to order can suppress rightful protest and new thought; nevertheless there is an order and harmony in creation to which we must also be sensitive, and which we have harmed with our exploitation of the world's natural resources. There is a social harmony which we damage when we abandon mutual respect in favour of the brute deity of competitiveness.

In the early twelfth century, in the years immediately following the emergence of this theory of satisfaction, there began what one scholar has called 'one of the greatest revolutions in feeling that Europe has ever witnessed'.[8] A new intensity of emotion erupted and was expressed in the secular poetry of courtly love, and in religious lyrics which involved the reader imaginatively in the sufferings of Christ or the sorrows of Mary. Indeed the secular and sacred merged in poetry which addresses Christ as 'my lemmon (lover) swete',[9] in which Christ pleads for the mercy of humankind as the courtly lover begs mercy of his lady, or where he jousts with death for the sake of her love. When the human predicament is felt to be a loss of love the corresponding concept is of the cross as a mighty demonstration of the love of God, turning human hearts back to love. This did not, however, become the dominant image of atonement at this time; except in the thought of the much maligned Peter Abelard it supplemented other concepts, such as the satisfaction of divine honour. It was when the Romantic movement of the nineteenth century placed a new emphasis upon the individual and his emotions, that the ability of the cross to evoke feeling was fully appreciated as a power of salvation.

The period of the Reformation laid new stress upon the central place of law in human society. In an age of political turmoil and social upheaval it seemed that the only security lay in the absolute claims of law to guard rights and punish offenders. Moreover, in a world emerging from the medieval period when the rule of monarchs had often been despotic and arbitrary, Protestant thinkers found it essential to assert that even kings and emperors were subject to the laws of God. While the 'godly ruler' was to be allowed some latitude in the framing of human ('positive') law, he must never contradict the laws God had established in nature and revelation. Thus the estrangement of human beings from God was understood in terms of their being law-breakers, summoned to receive condemnation at the divine bar of justice. Atonement, correspondingly, was a matter of satisfying not so much the honour of God as the demands of his Law, with Jesus punished as a substitute for guilty humankind. In our age we shall want to take a more flexible view of the function of law, but we neglect at our peril the insight that there is a 'structural justice' in life, so that certain consequences follow naturally from wrong-doing.

The age of Enlightenment brought a new confidence that reason alone could discover those truths about the world that God had implanted in creation. Even when not taken to 'deistic' extremes, there was a widespread suspicion of any notion that help was available from beyond the human mind. Religious experience was interpreted as experience of the moral life, rather than any direct encounter with God. The human problem therefore was seen as a falling short of those ethical standards to which the mind bore witness, and salvation lay simply in repentance; the real need was a change in human beings, not the placating of any supernatural authorities. For those who took this track of thought, there seemed to be no place for a concept of atonement. It took two giants of nineteenth-century thought – Schleiermacher in Germany and Coleridge in Britain – to show that while the age of Reason had properly located salvation in repentance and the transforming of human attitudes, this could not come about without the influence of the Spirit of the Redeemer. A power to mould the human spirit was at hand because direct intuition of the being of God *was* possible; there was another mode of knowing besides rational argument, an awareness of God that owed much more to elements of imagination and feeling. A symptom of distortion in human life was the blurring and confusing of this consciousness of God, though it could never be completely suppressed.

In modern times, as we reflect upon the disruption in the human condition, we are greatly influenced by the perceptions of the new human sciences of sociology and psychology. The literal meaning of salvation as 'healing' (from *salvus*, 'healed') has thus acquired a new importance. The image of healing has become predominant among concepts of atonement, overcoming an alienation which has its base in the fragmenting of the personality and in friction between social groups.

In particular, alienation in human existence is often diagnosed as arising from the situation of being caught between various tensions in life, the root tension being that between our freedom and our limitations. On the one hand we enjoy a freedom that the rest of the animal kingdom does not; while a forest animal is bound to his habitat, the person born in a forest does not have to make his career of wood-cutting. We are free to transcend the present moment, backwards in memory or forward in hope, free to transcend ourselves in reflection upon who we are, free to transcend our environment by shaping it for our own purpose, free even to leave our small planet for other worlds. But on the other hand we are also limited, conditioned by all the pressures and 'hidden persuaders' that psychology and sociology reveal to us. We are shaped by bad housing conditions, broken families, unemployment, advertising, the media, our own inner complexes and the inheritance of our genes. Finally death stands as an unavoidable boundary to all the possibilities of life. In the tension between our freedom and our finiteness, or between the possibilities and actualities of our lives, we become anxious.[10] The result, as John Macquarrie aptly defines it, is 'an existential imbalance'.[11] In our anxiety we fail to hold the balance between the two poles of our existence, and we tip over to one side at the expense of the other; we either ignore our limits and posture as gods, or we give away our freedom and succumb like animals to the forces that squeeze and determine us. The result is the alienation from ourselves, others and the whole of reality that we have already noticed.

This description of the human predicament is widely shared today. For psychologists in the school of Freud, a person is torn between the ego which makes reasoned decisions, and the complexes in his unconscious mind, which retain the fantasies and impulses of his infancy. Some existential philosophers find the tensions of life witness to the sheer absurdity of human existence. Like Sisyphus in the Greek myth we are bounded by our fate of continually rolling the boulder up the mountain, only to watch it crash down to the bottom again, and yet we are free because we are conscious of our limits and can scorn them.[12] Such thinkers urge us to recognise that we *are* alienated from the universe, that there is no intrinsic meaning in reality, and that human beings are a cosmic joke. Only on this realistic basis, they suggest, can we start to make our own freedom and our own meaning: as Sartre concludes, 'Man is condemned every moment to invent man.'[13] For a Christian thinker, however, these very tensions are a witness that we are persons in the making, that our self is not complete but is being formed into the image of God. The tensions of existence are not the whole of our story; there is also help ('grace') offered to us as a gift in the midst of them.

11

Sin is the refusal to trust in the resources that are offered from *beyond* ourselves or, to change the image, to neglect the support that lies at the *depth* of existence; Paul Tillich aptly speaks of sin as a 'turning away from the infinite ground of our being'.[14]

Rather than coping with our anxiety by trusting in God, we thus try to create our own solutions by making some object or person within the world our absolute security. Here Reinhold Niebuhr draws attention to the ancient lure of idolatry, in which a person 'lifts some finite element of existence into the eminence of the divine', using it as 'the ultimate principle of coherence and meaning'.[15] So we make idols for ourselves and place our trust in them. We may use them as a vehicle of pride, hiding from our limits, or as a means of escaping from the dizzy challenge of our freedom. A career, a hobby, a work of art, an organisation or an ideology becomes our 'ultimate concern', and then because we must have it, begins to dominate us. The very works of our hands become alien to us, exercising a demonic power over us.[16] Thus idolatry leads to a sense of estrangement, not only from God who is the source of our being but from the world that we should be controlling and governing.

The Marxist analysis of society agrees with the Christian one at least as far as observing that, in an industrial age, we have been caught in our own machinery. We have lost our names and become a string of digits in a computer memory. Marxism too recognises the alienation of working people from the works of their hands, though it attributes this entirely to the class struggle. It claims that because one class has appropriated the wealth of capital for itself, the objects produced by labour are alienated from their producers. In the view of Marx, the belief that we are alienated from God is therefore only a myth, a projection of the alienation we suffer within society.[17] A Christian recognises that all economic systems – whether capitalist or Communist – can become oppressive and demonic; but this is a symptom and manifestation of sin, not the *whole* reason for the experience of alienation in human existence.

In a modern study of the doctrine of the atonement such as this, we are bound to reflect these preoccupations of our present age. The atoning work of Christ will be understood as meeting the questions of our day, which are directed to the fragmenting of personality and loss of social relationships. Of course, the various ideas of atonement I have listed cannot be confined within the particular historical moments to which I have loosely attached them. They represent response to *types* of human experience that can be found in every age; they all, for instance, have some grounding in the New Testament documents. There are periods in human culture where certain images come to the fore and seem most relevant, but they persist, overlap and re-form into different combinations, and all express a dimension of human experience that remains valid for us here and now.

When we come to explore each of these images in more detail, we shall need to be alert to something fundamental about the tensions within which we live. We experience the predicament of being torn between the preservation of our individual identity with all its integrity on the one hand, and our involvement in society with all its corporate demands on the other. As with other tensions, we attempt to quieten our anxiety by stressing one aspect or the other, and in our present age this tends to be individualism. Yet to be truly a 'person' does not simply mean being a separate ego but living in relationship with others. We often wrongly speak, for example, of 'personalising' some possession with our initials, when we really mean 'privatising' it. Meeting this predicament is a certain concept of salvation: when God reconciles persons he brings them into community in a new way. St Paul affirms this by using the complex metaphor of sharing in the 'body' of Christ (1 Cor. 12:13): we encounter the risen personality ('body') of Christ as members of one 'body', the church, and this transforming relationship is focused in sharing the 'body' of the Eucharistic bread. So in surveying the great images of atonement, we should ask how well they express the healing not only of individuals but of groups and structures in our society. Implied in this enquiry is a view of the church as a visible sign of the rule of God which is present in a hidden way in the wider world, and yet still to come in its fullness.

In the Christian understanding of atonement the cross of Jesus Christ thus occupies the centre of all human experience. The old market crosses of English towns were well situated, standing where the main streets intersected, where people met to gossip, where justice was often done and in whose shadow went on the business of buying and selling.

2

Salvation as event and process

Salvation happens here and now. It is always in the present that God acts to heal and reconcile, entering into the disruption of human lives at great cost to himself, in order to share our predicament and release us from it. This may seem obvious, and if we examine the hymns of popular piety we can often detect just such an appeal to a present experience of atonement, expressed in phrases like 'Jesus *saves*'. It is ironic, however, that when this devotion has been translated into sermons it has often emerged as more equivalent to 'Jesus *saved*'. For there is a great deal of difference between believing that God 'saves' through Christ, and believing that we simply claim the benefits of a salvation that has already happened, a deal that has already been concluded. Salvation in the present tense has frequently been depicted as if it were merely picking up a ticket to paradise which was issued long ago, and which has been waiting through long ages on the counter of a celestial travel agent. But a transactional view of atonement like this is highly impersonal. If salvation is the healing of a broken relationship between persons, then it must actually happen now; it must involve the human response as an intimate part of the act of atonement. As the characters in Shakespeare's play *Love's Labour's Lost* perceive, where love is concerned, any single moment is 'time . . . too short/To make a world-without-end bargain in'.[1]

The restoring of relationships

To believe in a saviour God is to affirm that he is always saving, always participating in the pain of an estranged world to win back rebels. Salvation is a continuous process. If, as Christians believe, the focal point of salvation is the cross of Jesus Christ, then the cross is a contemporary event as well as past history. A first clue which points towards this insight is the one at which I have already been hinting, the nature of the realm of personal relations. Therapy using psychological analysis has made it abundantly clear that to restore a relationship requires the deepest cooperation of the one who is alienated, even if one had failed to realise this from the everyday experience of family life. A healing of relationship and personality cannot be accepted like a package, a ticket or even a contract. It must be created anew through the meeting of persons. Applied to a doctrine of reconciliation between God and humanity this means that human response must actually be part of the act of salvation, not merely a reaction to it afterwards. This principle is perhaps demonstrated most vividly in the experience of forgiveness, and although I shall be making a more detailed study of this later, some grasp of the dynamics of any act of forgiveness is fundamental to an understanding of atonement.

The record of early Christian preaching in the Acts of the Apostles associates the death of Jesus with 'the forgiveness of your sins' (Acts 2:38), and this is also at the heart of Paul's preaching of the cross of Jesus. Even though Paul rarely uses the actual term 'forgiveness', the concept of 'justification' carries the same content of having a relationship with God restored, and being accepted by him.[2] It is tragic then that this profound experience of forgiveness has often been reduced in Christian doctrine and preaching to the idea of a mere legal pardon. Popular evangelistic preaching has often, for example, depicted a prisoner languishing in a condemned cell on the eve of execution, and then suddenly receiving a free pardon from the monarch or president. All the prisoner needs to do, it is urged, is to accept what is offered. But this legal illustration (as well as being out of date in societies today such as Britain which no longer have capital punishment) loses the personal nature of forgiveness, and when transferred to God it evacuates love from his activity. The picture of a pardoned criminal fails to communicate the painful relational experience which lies at the heart of forgiving and being forgiven. The mere issue of a notice of pardon cannot touch a person deeply; in life a prisoner can accept a pardon and go free, hating the authorities who gave it and the judge who sentenced him – or perhaps laughing at them. Such a legal transaction comes close in tone to the words of the poet Heine as he lay dying that God would of course forgive him, for 'it's his business'. But forgiveness is no business, even a legal business. Much more profound is the insight of the theologian H. R. Mackintosh, that:

> We are constantly under a temptation to suppose that the reason why we fail to understand completely the atonement made by God in Christ is that our minds are not sufficiently profound . . . But there is a deeper reason still. It is that we are not good enough; we have never forgiven a deadly injury at a price like this, at such cost to ourselves as came upon God at Jesus' death . . . Let the man be found who has undergone the shattering experience of pardoning, nobly and tenderly, some awful wrong to himself, still more to one beloved by him, and he will understand the meaning of Calvary better than all the theologians in the world.[3]

Forgiveness is no mere business; it is a 'shattering experience' for the one who forgives as well as for the one who is forgiven. This is because forgiveness, unlike a mere pardon, seeks to win the offender back into relationship. Nor is forgiving simply forgetting about an offence done; in order to reconcile the person who has hurt him, the forgiver must painfully call the offence to mind. Reconciliation is a costly process because there are resistances to it in the attitude of the person who has offended; the one who sets out to forgive must aim to remove those blockages and restore the relationship. Forgiveness then involves an acceptance which is costly.

The question is sometimes asked about the Christian doctrine of atonement, 'If God forgives us, why doesn't he simply announce it from heaven? Why is there this whole complicated affair of the cross?' The question may be put both by those who think there is no need of an atoning act, and also by those who cannot believe that divine forgiveness is the whole meaning of the cross of Jesus. But forgiveness is not simply an announcement, a notice of pardon; it seeks to reconcile the person who is hostile to accepting forgiveness, or who is so anxious that he cannot believe he *is* accepted. Forgiveness as an act creating response is therefore bound to be expensive in time and effort, requiring mental and physical anguish. The illustration of the prisoner receiving a royal pardon once again

16

falls short here. Often a preacher, using the illustration, will hammer home to his hearers the incredible foolishness of a prisoner who would not accept a pardon offered him; the argument runs that if any prisoner in his right mind would accept it, why should people refuse to accept God's pardon? But human lack of response to the grace of God is not so astonishing when we realise that it is actually forgiveness we are talking about. It *is* hard to accept forgiveness, whether from God or other people; there is so much in human emotions and reactions that resists it.

The unity of creation and redemption

A reflection upon the realm of personal relationships and in particular the experience of forgiveness, tells us that salvation must be a present event, and so atonement can be no transaction sealed in the past. This accords with a second clue towards the present tense of salvation, the insight found in the Old Testament about the oneness of God's activity as creator and redeemer. We often think that the idea of a continuous transforming and renewing of creation is a modern one, deriving from scientific views of evolutionary development. But as early as the Old Testament we have a perspective upon the world in which we cannot divide creation from the ongoing process of redeeming human life and overcoming its disharmonies. Christian theology has often cast the drama of history into a strict three-act sequence of old creation, redemption and new creation. But the faith of ancient Israel tended to bring creation and redemption together into the same focus, whether they were recalling old event in the past or hoping for a new kind of event in the future. So powerful had been their experience of God's redemptive acts in their history, and especially in the exodus from Egypt, that their poets and priestly theologians depicted creation itself as an act of redemption.

A frequent way of portraying God's creation of the world was as a deliverance from the hostile forces of chaos, setting it free from the oppression of disorder into a life of order and harmony. To express this idea of creation as a victory over chaos, the Israelites used a myth found elsewhere in the ancient Near East, the victory of God over the dragon or chaos monster:[4]

17

> By his power he stilled the sea;
> by his understanding he smote Rahab.
> By his hand the heavens were made fair;
> his hand pierced the fleeing serpent.
>
> (Job 26:12–13)

The smiting of the dragon is closely associated here with the curbing of the unruly sea, whose constant threat to overflow the cultivated land and spread havoc made it a ready symbol of chaos. Elsewhere the sea is still a symbol of disorder, even where the sea-monster (called variously Rahab and Leviathan) has dropped out of sight:

> Or who shut in the sea with doors,
> when it burst forth from the womb . . .
> and said, 'Thus far shall you come, and no farther,
> and here shall your proud waves be stayed'?
>
> (Job 38:8–11)

In creation, then, God conquers the sea and liberates the land.[5]

There are, of course, parallels to this picture in the mythologies of other ancient cultures; the Babylonian sea-monster Tiamat is slain by Marduk, the Canaanite sea-God Yam and his dragon Leviathan are defeated by Baal. But there is a significant emphasis in the Israelite accounts: when God's creation of the world is portrayed as a matter of conflict and victory, it rarely stands as a theme on its own, but is usually related to the redemptive acts of God in Israel's national life.[6] The breaking of the heads of the dragons on the waters, and the regular coming of summer and winter since then, are counted among the 'saving acts' (Psalm 74:12–17). Order is brought out of chaos in primeval and recent event; victory in creation and redemption in history are brought together in one image, never to be dissolved. The two kinds of event were, it seems, celebrated as one at the greatest festival of the year, the festival of the New Year in autumn.[7] As the people acknowledged the kingship of Yahweh over creation, which was witnessed to in his provision of harvest, they remembered also the victories of God in redeeming the nation; stilling the sea of Chaos, bringing the chosen people into the Promised Land and elevating David to a powerful kingship all merge into one:

18

Thou dost rule the raging of the sea;
when its waves rise thou stillest them.
Thou didst crush Rahab like a carcase,
thou didst scatter thy enemies with thy mighty arm.

(Psalm 89:9–10)

This merging of images of creation and redemption comes to a
climax in the thought of Isaiah of Babylon, as he faces the national
crisis of Exile in the sixth century BC, and seeks to raise the people
out of their despondency into faith in the power of God. He promises
that the God who 'makes a way in the sea, a path in the mighty
waters' will make a way in the desert. In a remarkable fusion of
imagery, the curbing and dividing of the hostile waters at creation
and in the crossing of the Red Sea are seen in one focus; at the
same time a new exodus, bringing God's people out of Babylon, is
compared with both these past victories over the sea-monster:

Was it not thou that didst cut Rahab in pieces,
that didst pierce the dragon?
Was it not thou that didst dry up the sea,
the waters of the great deep;
that didst make the depths of the sea a way
for the redeemed to pass over?
And the ransomed of the Lord shall return,
and come to Zion with singing.

(Isa. 51:9–11)

God is redeemer at creation, exodus from Egypt, entrance into the
land, founding of the royal House of David and return from exile
in Babylon, but not only at those points. Because images of creation
and redemption have shaped each other, both are presented as
ongoing processes; creation belongs to the flow of history where
redemption has happened, and redemption in history is as
constantly present as creation. In the rainbow sign the priestly
theologians of Israel found assurance that God was continuing to
hold back the waters of chaos (Gen. 9:12–17); at the autumn festival
they celebrated his redemption in the yearly harvest and in their
continuing survival as a nation in the face of attacks from their
rapacious neighbours (Ps. 68:7–14).

19

The Psalms also speak of a continual redemption from death in the life of the individual; when in illness God holds back the forces of death and restores health then he is liberating from the power of the underworld (Sheol), a threat which is depicted as taking a grip on the sufferer's throat like the monster of chaos, stifling him with the weight of a great flood of water:

> He reached from on high, he took me;
> he drew me out of many waters.
>
> (Ps. 18:16)

The image of water also appears when the psalmist speaks of God's delivering him from social oppression – from those who show malice, who falsely accuse him, and who lay traps for him: to be wrongly accused of stealing is like sinking up to the neck into water or being swept away in a flood (Psalm 69:1–5). If it is correct to find the ritual experience of the king, as representative of the nation, at the centre of some of these psalms, this only underlines the fact that redemption as an individual and as a nation are both continual events and are intimately connected.

In a rich range of life, then, Israelite faith found that God's creative and redemptive activity was continual and inseparable. The instances we have been considering are, of course, to do with God's delivering of his people from oppressions of a physical and political kind; indeed the concept of 'redemption' belongs almost entirely to this context in the Old Testament, as does the term 'salvation' itself. The Hebraic outlook held such a view of the worth of physical life here and now that they naturally conceived of God's care being expressed in salvation from the forces that spoilt its wholeness – whether the spoilers were enemies, famine or illness. We must avoid so spiritualising this experience of salvation that we miss the political and social implications of exodus and return from exile; this is a point made strongly by recent 'liberation theology'.[8] But we should also not neglect the spiritual dimension within it; the relationship with God, often expressed as 'covenant' was central to the whole of life and gave it final meaning. When people thought explicitly about this level of life they realised that there was something else from which to be delivered, an uncleanness of a ritual and moral kind that resulted from a neglect of God's will, an impurity or 'sin' which had devastating consequences upon the health of the community. Release from this threat through sacrifice and repentant obedience seems at first glance to be a different realm of thought altogether from the creative–redemptive process of which we have been thinking, and in fact the term 'redemption' is almost never applied to it. Later we shall be making a more detailed reference to sacrifice and atonement in Old Testament faith. But here we should not miss the obvious point that the vehicle of atonement or purification was, like the occasion of redemption, something which was provided in creation; the animal or cereal offering, and the very time of the feast-day itself, was part of God's creative work.

The priestly theologian makes this clear when he describes the whole sequence of creation as ending with the Sabbath, or the day of worship and occasion for sacrifice. Creation finds its proper fulfilment in worship. In a humorous piece of de-mythologising the priestly writer explains the result of splitting the chaos monster in two: the upper part makes a firmament across which move the stars, which are not (as in Babylonian religion) astral deities but a liturgical calendar for reminding God's people of the days of festival and worship (Gen. 1:14). Thus here too creation and redemption are inseparable; God as creator provides the ram for an offering (Gen. 22:13) just as he uses that offering as a means of wiping out sin. There is a merging of focus here between creation and redemption which is made even more intense in the sacraments of the Christian church; the fruits of the earth – bread and wine – become the occasion for continuous participation in a historic event of redemption, an event in which God acted decisively to deliver his creation from all the hostile forces that threaten to spoil it. We share in redemptive history through small pieces of creation, material objects that focus God's work in the whole of the physical world.

Thus in different areas of Old Testament faith – wisdom literature, Psalms, prophecy and priestly theology – creation and redemption from oppression are brought together into one ongoing process. From a perspective of Christian theology, the idea that a redemptive event in history is part of the whole story of creation seems clear enough to grasp. But what, conversely, can it mean to speak of creation as a victory over hostile forces, a defeat of the forces of chaos? If God creates 'from nothing', there can be no eternally

21

existent opposite principle to God, as there is in dualistic systems of thought where forces of good and evil are for ever balanced against each other. The Old Testament itself does not ask such abstract, philosophical questions, but we may surely say that the picture of redemption from chaos (Gen. 1:1–3) means that creation involves God in cost and pain from the very beginning.[9] God is always sustaining his creation and keeping it from falling into nothing. In creation God gives freedom to something over against himself; he limits himself by the freedom of others, his creatures, and becomes vulnerable to their decisions. In the very act of creation then, he must preserve it from wilfully drifting away into nothingness and the void. From the act of creation onwards he faces the tragedy of death, and seeks to win his own creatures into free and joyous fellowship with himself.

The continual suffering of God

This affirmation brings us to a third reason for understanding salvation as always being an event in the present, that is, a belief in the continual suffering of God for humankind. Actually the classical thinkers of the Christian church in the past were very cautious about saying that God suffers, insisting that he could not be moved or affected by the world. This meant that, strictly, he could not feel any emotions, and so his love was purely a matter of doing good to his creatures. However this kind of approach was due less to biblical pictures of God than to a Greek Platonist philosophy in which God was understood as the very summit of pure being, totally unlike the state of becoming or change in which the world existed. Thinking along these tracks led to the belief that the humanity of Jesus was the means through which the unchanging and invulnerable divine nature could, though indirectly, endure turmoil and death. It was affirmed that God entered into the suffering of the world once only, through the uniting of the divine Son with a human nature that *could* suffer in Jesus Christ.[10] Salvation then had to be simply a past event, because it was at one point in the past that this had happened.

Recently however, having thrown off the cultural chains of this world-view, theologians have not found the same difficulty in conceiving of a sovereign God who *freely* chooses to suffer with and for human beings in their predicament. Martin Luther protested long ago that if it was the whole person of Jesus who suffered for us, as the church had always affirmed, then suffering must have penetrated not only his human but his divine nature.[11] From this insight we must now surely go on to think of the divine personality as feeling in *all* ages the pain that is caused by human sin. Truly personal love involves the sharing of experience, so that an awareness of the plight of another will always mean *sympathy* in its literal sense – a 'suffering with'. The prophets of ancient Israel were in fact already highly sensitive to how much it cost God to share in human life. As they entered with sympathy into the pain of their nation, hurt by oppression from without and torn by social divisions within, they understood their experience as nothing less than a fellow-feeling with God's own suffering for his people.[12] Similarly the Old Testament historians, looking back to the redemptive event of the exodus, speak of God's bearing with the complaints of people as he travelled with them across the desert. Later Jewish mystical theology even spoke of the going of God's own glory into slavery as he went with his people into the agony of their exile in Babylon and joined their wanderings.[13] In allowing a disaster which was the natural consequence of social and spiritual decay, God was sharing in the pain of his own rightful judgement upon a rotting society.

Thus it is that God is always accepting the cost of redeeming a world fallen from his purpose, always entering with sympathy and divine grief into all situations of human desolation, whether caused by people's own sin, or where people are tragic victims of the sins of others. It is such an insight to which François Mauriac appeals in his highly personal foreword to one victim's (Elie Wiesel's) first hand experience of the Nazi extermination camps:

What did I say to him? Did I speak of that other Israeli, his brother, who may have resembled him – the Crucified, whose Cross has conquered the world? Did I affirm that the stumbling block to his faith was the cornerstone of mine, and that the conformity between the Cross and the suffering of men was in my eyes the key to that impenetrable mystery whereon the faith of his childhood had perished? ... This is what I should have told this Jewish child. But I could only embrace him, weeping.[14]

Faith and openness

Mauriac's awareness that, in the face of unspeakable human suffering, no mere argument could create faith, not even faith in a suffering God, gives us a hint towards a fourth reason for placing God's saving activity in the present. The New Testament presentation of faith in the crucified Christ makes it clear that this is a step of openness and risk in response to the proclamation of cross and resurrection. The message of atonement calls for a movement of the hearer into a new and disturbing future, a willingness to leave behind all the securities by means of which *we* attempt to give meaning to our lives. Response to God's act of atonement is the opening of a new horizon, an acceptance of the reversal of all worldly values which the message of a crucified Messiah produces. As the apostle Paul perceives, if God has made a crucified man lord of the universe, then all the securities by which we live and all the achievements by which we justify ourselves and give ourselves esteem, are shown to be hollow (1 Cor. 1:18–25). God 'puts down the mighty from their seats', as Mary exults in the song recorded by Luke; God turns the human, prudent view of events upside down. Now, such a shift of perspective upon the world can only happen here and now in the present; salvation cannot be a mere contract or arrangement made and sealed in the past – it is a transforming of all human words and thoughts by the divine word in the present.

A decisive event of salvation?

But in saying all this, perhaps we seem to have been moving away from the point with which I began, that our salvation is somehow dependent upon a particular event in the past. What is the place of a cross outside a city wall, if God is indeed always initiating the process of healing human lives in a formative act of forgiveness? What is the importance of one event, exactly located in time and space, if God is always redeeming life as part of his ongoing work of creation, as a continual act of suffering and as a call to an open future? In short, why speak of *an* act of 'atonement' as well as the activity of 'salvation'? Of course the belief that divine salvation is

24

a process does not in itself mean that there can be no place for moments of crisis within the process, high points in the drama. After all, ancient Israel had herself increasingly begun to look forward to a final or decisive act of redemption. Under threats from new enemies, as the empires of Greece and Rome replaced the faded empires of Egypt and Persia, Israel began to expect God to act in a radical way to save her from oppression and from the dilution of her religious life by successive conquerors. So the apocalyptic litera-ture written between the Old and New Testaments depicts a final victory in climactic terms, with the shadowy figure of God's ideal King and Redeemer emerging in many forms. Of this apocalyptic vision we have a few pieces in the latest parts of the Old Testament, such as the second half of the Book of Daniel, and this significant fragment which re-uses the imagery of the sea-monster: 'In that day the Lord with his hard and strong sword will punish Leviathan the fleeing serpent, Leviathan the twisting serpent, and he will slay the dragon that is in the sea' (Isa. 27:1).

Such expectations of a high point of salvation had, claimed the early Christian believers, been fulfilled in Jesus Christ, though admittedly in a surprising way. Redemption was not to be in the salvation of one nation but in a new kind of reconciliation between peoples, and between people and God. Since the victory over the chaos monster was embodied in Christ, they depicted Christ as the one who walked upon the waves of the troubled sea and subdued them, and as the one whose lordship would bring about the age of cosmic harmony, when there would be 'no more sea'.[15] Yet we notice that these Israelite hopes for a decisive redeeming act, and the Christian beliefs that the hope was fulfilled in Christ, do not in themselves altogether explain the kind of significance that traditional Christian confession has given to the event of the cross of Jesus. Such a decisive event might be no more than a high point in the continual movement of the reconciling Spirit of God in the world. It is one thing to find critical moments in the ongoing process of salvation, and quite another to claim that the process somehow depends upon *one* of those moments.

Of course it must be true that the cross of Jesus is a sublime example of what God is always doing in his creative–redemptive work; it is a clear window into the whole scenery. But traditional Christian belief has wanted to venture even further than this. It has wanted to affirm the cross of Jesus as more than one sharply focused moment among others in salvation, viewing it as *the* focal point of the whole picture, without which the composition would fall apart. It is this kind of belief that I want to hold together with the equally important belief that salvation is an ever-present experience. We must try to do justice to salvation as present process and to atonement as past event, reducing our understanding of atonement neither to a mere past transaction nor to a mere example of what is always true. As the poet Gerard Manley Hopkins expresses it, the 'stroke and stress' of salvation both 'rides time/Like riding a river' and also 'dates from day/Of his going in Galilee'.[16]

Objective and subjective dimensions in atonement

Now, we cannot begin to discuss this question carefully without familiarising ourselves with a pair of technical theological terms. The descriptions 'objective' and 'subjective' have often been used in thinking about the nature of the atonement, and they are a convenient piece of shorthand that we shall be returning to many times. In the first place an interpretation of the atonement may be said to be 'subjective' when it describes salvation as a process in present human experience. It is 'objective' when it locates salvation in a past event, outside our experience and feelings. Obviously then, no theory of atonement can be entirely subjective or objective, but there will be a shifting balance between the two elements in different understandings of atonement. The more that salvation in the present is believed to be dependent on a past event, the more objective it becomes, and the greater is the danger of regarding present experience as a mere appendix to a completed act. But conversely the heavier the stress laid upon present experience, the greater the danger becomes of regarding salvation as a merely subjective matter of human feelings. The question then is not whether a view of atonement is objective *or* subjective, although much fruitless argument has been spent on this by Christian thinkers in the past; the question to be asked is how well it *integrates* the two elements. All theories of atonement, however culturally determined they have been, have at least tried to bring the elements of past and present, event and process, together. It is a piece of

special pleading when Bishop Aulen, in his famous study of atonement as the victory of Christ, claims that this interpretation is
'quite different' from either the objectivity of the 'penal view' or the
subjectivity of the 'moral view'.[17] Not only does his insight have
both subjective and objective elements, but it also fails to escape
from tipping the balance one way, as we shall see later.

A second set of 'subjective' and 'objective' elements is often
simply, and misleadingly, equated with the balance between past
event and process. This is the polarity of act and response. If the
first polarity puts the past and the present in tension, the second
relates the divine and the human. Objectively salvation is an act of
God; since human beings are trapped in a predicament from which
they cannot extricate themselves, God must take the initiative
himself in providing a release. The apostle Paul sums up the matter
when he says, 'God shows his love for us in that while we were yet
sinners, Christ died for us' (Rom. 5:8). Subjectively salvation must
include the human response for, as we have seen, it needs two to
make a meeting. We must take thought, however, not simply to
identify the past event of salvation with the *divine* act, and the
present process with the *human* response. While God has certainly
acted in the past event of the cross, he goes on acting in the process
of salvation, taking the initiative in entering the lives of human
beings and luring them into response. On the other hand, at the
heart of the past event is the human response of Jesus, in open
obedience to the Father, fulfilling human destiny where other men
have failed. However, while these two sets of subjective and objective elements are not identical, views of salvation which lay most
stress upon a single act in the past also tend to stress the action of
God at the expense of human reaction.

The movement between action and response leads us to a third,
and even more profound polarity between objectivity and subjectivity in salvation. Traditional, strongly 'objective' doctrines of
atonement have proposed some change in God resulting from the
atoning work of Christ. More 'subjective' accounts have laid the
stress upon the power of the cross to produce a change in human
attitudes. Now clearly, salvation requires a change in human minds
and emotions, described in biblical language as 'repentance'.
Human attitudes of pride, fear and anxiety create blockages between
God and humankind, and as a saviour God sets out to remove these

in a sacrificial way. But some views of atonement have suggested, in effect, that there are blockages to reconciliation in God's own nature; while affirming that there is no reluctance on God's part to forgive and accept, it has been suggested that God's justice requires to be satisfied before he can put his forgiving love into effect. Because man is a guilty sinner, it is maintained, a debt has to be paid to justice before he can be forgiven. Highly 'objective' views of atonement have thus conceived of a change in God in the sense that his righteous wrath is satisfied through some kind of propitiating act. More 'subjective' views of atonement insist that the only problem lies in human hearts and minds; while God is always willing to accept his creatures, the problem is how to remove the hindrances to acceptance in *them*, and how to persuade people to respond to God's offer of forgiveness. In a later chapter I wish to argue that the view of a 'barrier of justice' in God's nature is misconceived, though it points to important aspects in the human and divine situation. However, the notion of a 'change' in God ought not to be quickly dismissed as 'too objective'. If we are to speak at all seriously about suffering in God, then this must involve change of some kind, for suffering is always a movement from one state of being to another. If, then, there is some change in God's experience of the world from one moment of human response to another, we begin to see how one particular moment could be more intense and critical than others. Though we may not think of God's changing from wrath to love, if God did enter into the human predicament in a decisive way in the cross of Jesus then he must have been exposed to something 'new' in the divine experience of the world and himself. We shall be exploring later the way in which this divine movement in experience is central to atonement, and it is a factor that is rightly to be called 'objective'.

The cross of Jesus as an enabling event

We must admit that no understanding of the atoning work of Christ is going to integrate subjective and objective dimensions in a completely satisfying way. Theories of atonement are, after all, conceptual tools with which we try to grasp a mystery in the divine–human relationship. I drew attention in Chapter 1 to cultural conditioning of our understanding of 'atonement', and I intend to show in later chapters how such models as sacrifice, justice and victory have in fact shifted from an objective to a more subjective colouring in recent years. Earlier theories of atonement (with the partial exception of Abelard's) tended to begin at the objective end of the spectrum of understanding with some kind of transaction, and then added a subjective appendix. Modern ideas have tipped the balance the other way; they tend to begin at the subjective end with the present human response to God, and then to affirm an objective focus for response.[18] This, I believe, is basically the right orientation for Christian thinking today. If we are to serve our age and our culture – though this includes being prepared to challenge it at some points as well as being shaped by it – we must learn from insights of the human sciences into the nature of relationships and personality. We are bound to understand reconciliation by analogy with the process of healing rather than by analogy with a legal or commercial transaction. Using traditional terms this might be called 'subjective', but it will work hard at understanding the 'objective focus' of God's activity, both in past and present events. This means, I believe, understanding the cross of Jesus as an event which has a unique degree of power to evoke and create human response to the forgiving love of God. An event of power like that goes far beyond an 'example' or 'window into God's love', important descriptions though these are.

There is a whole range of ways in which we can begin to comprehend the objective, creative power of the cross of Jesus. From an existential viewpoint we can think of the power of a disclosure of something new in human experience, prompting repetition of it. From a viewpoint of narrative theory we can begin to appreciate the power of a story to create new experience within the hearer. From a viewpoint of social dynamics and the power of groups, we can begin to see the effect of a community which has lived through the ages under the cross and which links us now with the earliest discipleship. With the help of psychological theory we can glimpse the power of an event outside ourselves to break open a self-enclosed ego. A proper doctrine of the Holy Spirit will help us to speak of the personality of Jesus as a present reality, with an influence which is more than historical recollection. Above all, a doctrine of God which takes his suffering seriously will link our present experience of God with the past event of the cross. In all these ways we can begin to grasp the truth that an event two thousand years ago can actually enable people here and now to recognise the offer of divine grace and mercy, and then to respond to it. In a closer study of the traditional understandings of atonement as a sacrifice, a victory, an act of justice and a revelation of love, we shall see that these 'models' of thought can alert us to such objective dimensions in atonement as those I have mentioned, and others too.

The power of future salvation in the present

Throughout this chapter we have been thinking of salvation as 'riding time' from the past to the present, but salvation has a future tense as well. The New Testament writers profess the hope that 'we shall be saved',[19] when all hostile powers will submit to the cosmic lordship of Christ, and the whole universe will enter upon the 'freedom of the sons of God' (Rom. 8:21). Hope in a new creation need not be a form of escapism from uncomfortable reality, for hope can have a transforming effect upon the present. Just as the past event of atonement works forward into the present, exercising a creative power to change it, so the future event of fulfilment works backwards, having a powerful influence upon things as they are now.

Indeed the fact that future salvation affects the present through its creative influence upon it confirms the discovery that influence is also the mode by which a past event changes the present. Here hope and memory, expectation and recollection fuse in present experience. Once again the sacraments of the Christian church provide a focus for this process; the Eucharist, for example, celebrates the three tenses of salvation. There is remembrance of God's redemptive act in the past, an encounter with the crucified and risen Christ who shares table-fellowship with his disciples in the present, and a longing for the final coming of the kingdom of God, expressed in the words of institution that the celebration is to continue 'until he comes'.[20]

The kind of hope which challenges and changes the present is no mere forecast of the future. There is a good deal of 'futurology' around today which is simply a calculation of what is likely to happen, based upon present trends;[21] computer models or graphs are used to project present data forward into the future – for example statistics about the birth rate, world hunger or nuclear proliferation. But this kind of exercise will only confirm conditions in the present, and may even support the status quo. Hope from a Christian perspective is hope in the 'desirable future' rather than the 'calculable future', to use a distinction helpfully made by the theologian Jürgen Moltmann.[22] Recent so-called 'theology of hope' has therefore begun with hope in a future which is radically different from the present, rather than merely being an extension of it. It begins with hope in God's purpose of a new creation which will fulfil his intention for the world, a redeemed cosmos of justice, love and peace. It trusts that despite present appearances God has such a future, that he is Lord of this future and that hope in it is 'evidence of things not as yet seen'. God is the free Lord who does the new and unexpected thing, and his future does not simply depend upon the present. The future consummation, though hidden from view, exhibits its power now in that those who trust the promise find a stimulus to change the present. For if we hope in a God who can do something altogether new and unpredictable in future salvation, we shall be alert to the new possibilities he offers here and now. Future salvation 'contradicts' the present, liberating us into new attitudes and actions. Those who have hope refuse to regard any structures as final or sacrosanct, in church or society. They have a holy discontent that is always breaking open old structures and institutions to find new life.

The event of future salvation thus has a liberating effect upon the present, rather than merely being a projection of it. There is a further parallel here with the past event of salvation in the cross of Jesus, whose effect, as we have seen, does not simply come from a projection of memory backwards from the present. The past event exerts a greater power than memory gives it, just as the future event has a greater power than calculation can give. This is because past and future belong to the God who is himself always present to save. There is an objectivity about both past and the future event which evades the control of our present experience, and so remains a protest against our view of things, based as it often is upon a worldly search for false securities. God is transcendent or 'other' than the world in being free to do new things *within* it, and he uses both past history and future promise to face us now with the challenge of his free actions. So the past event of the cross of Jesus is an offence to the present world. By choosing to reveal himself fully in a crucified man God contradicts all notions of what it means to be 'divine'; by becoming weak and a prey to death God makes foolish the wisdom of this world which understands power to be the ability to inflict suffering, or at least to escape from it. The resurrection of Jesus continues the theme of God's freedom; God gives new life in the midst of human history in a way that escapes all human tools of enquiry, whether scientific or historical. Then, by promising a future liberation of the whole of creation, God contradicts the powers which sustain themselves by oppressing others. In the name of the coming Lord Christians will engage in movements for the liberation of the oppressed, refusing to tolerate any dehumanising methods of authorities in the present world, and contradicting them with the contradiction of the Spirit of God. A doctrine of atonement thus leads naturally into political engagement, as we shall see in greater detail later.

Moreover if the past event can only be grasped through images or 'models' (such as sacrifice and victory), it is even more true that the future salvation can only be proclaimed in symbol. This is not only due to the limits of cultural conditioning to which all human language is subject. Since God's future has the quality of the new and the incalculable about it, it cannot be forecast or exactly described, though it can be proclaimed in the great symbols of faith. God fulfils promises, not predictions, and is free to fulfil them in unexpected ways; he has purposes, not blueprints for his world. Even the resurrection of Jesus promises the future rather than predicting it, for though it has happened as an objective event in our history it eludes scientific description. But it gives us a language of faith and image with which to anticipate the final destiny which God intends for the personalities he is creating. His purposes for future salvation can be celebrated then, in such metaphors as resurrection of the body, the golden city of Jerusalem, the river and the tree of life, and the holy mountain where the lion lies down with the lamb. As we celebrate what we cannot map, we become impatient with the evil and oppression that spoil present life, and we are opened to respond to God's offer of healing here and now. In the festivity of worship, and especially in the sacraments, we use imagination and 'play' to experience the fulfilment of all things ahead of time, and this builds up an intolerance towards the cramping conditions of the present.

In worship we live in the vision of a saved world, and this leads to actions which will liberate both inner personal lives and the life of society. The Black theologian James Cone has pointed to the way that Negro spirituals, with their images of freedom from Egypt and the journey to the crystal city, were not only songs about future salvation and the redemption of the individual sinner; they were also building up a resistance to physical slavery in the present, and were giving expression to a demand for freedom that would finally have to be satisfied in social justice.[23] Still in Black worship today, 'The moan, the shout and the rhythmic bodily responses to prayer, song and sermon are artistic projections of the pain and joy experienced in the struggle of freedom.'[24] At the same time we must not forget the need for personal liberation, a freedom from the chains of guilt, rebellion against God and fear in the life of the individual; without such redemption society can never finally be free. Here the image of future resurrection of the body alerts us to the possibility of transformation which touches every part of our own existence.

If true hope is directed to a 'desirable future', then it is the task of Christian faith to expand the imagination of a society which is imprisoned within a sense of what is merely 'feasible'. Hope means having a love for the future of things and people, able to take daring steps of seeing their potential within God's purpose. Harvey Cox laments that our society today has 'a surplus of means and a shortage of visions', and a notable lack of the prophets and seers who were 'spinners of visions' in times past.[25] But if Christian people are to foster their prophetic spirit, it will not be by making a forced effort to spin webs of images of the future. Again we return to the relationships between past, present and future in the process of salvation. It is not just that there is an interesting parallel between the past event of atonement and the future hope of completed salvation. Each unlocks the meaning of the other. From the viewpoint of God's final purpose for creation we can see what atonement 'is for'. But since the future is a matter of promise and surprise, we need to be pointed in the right direction. The signpost, as the saying about the 'sign of Jonah' in the gospels reminds us, is nothing else than the descent of Jesus himself to death and his resurrection to a new sphere of life with God (Matt. 12:40).

Christ then is the sign of future hope. Because there are elements of the new and the unexpected about the future, we can know our future only indirectly, through perceiving the future of Jesus. What it may mean to experience 'resurrection of the body' can only be known through reflection upon the raising of the one who was crucified. So, in exploring the past event of salvation, with the help of the great images of faith which have emerged in the Christian community, we shall be released in imagination to celebrate the future too. Recalling the past and expecting the future in this way will enable us here and now to respond to the God who draws near in forgiveness. This is the Saviour God who is 'Lord not only of the dead but the living.'

3

Faith and history

'Crucified also for us: suffered under Pontius Pilate', *Crucifixus etiam pro nobis: sub Pontio Pilato passus*. The stabbing chords with which Beethoven sets these words in his *Missa Solemnis* jolt upon our ears like the hammering of nails into the cross. In the midst of worship the composer will not allow us to escape the reality of this death, just as the phrase itself does not allow those who repeat the Creed to escape from the arena of history. 'Suffered under Pontius Pilate'. Within the church's confession of faith in God the Father, Son and Holy Spirit there appears the name of a rather minor Roman commandant, the representative of the occupying power in Jerusalem, to make clear that God's saving act has happened right in the middle of the human politics of power and fear. As an early Christian witness insisted, the crucifixion of Christ and what followed it 'was not done in a corner'.[1] The name of Pilate roots us in history, in the messy and confusing events of public life.

It may then seem odd that a great deal of Christian thought this century has wanted to detach the story of salvation from the facts of history. What really matters, it is often urged, is our belief in Christ as the Lord of all life, and our experience of his presence here and now, transforming human existence and opening up hope in the future. Talk about the actions of God in our world belong, it is said, on a totally different plane of reality from that which a historian can record.[2] While a historian might be willing to tell us about a prophet from Nazareth who was crucified, he can tell us nothing about the atoning act of God through this man; thus, the conclusion is drawn, while Jesus was certainly a figure of history, historical investigation cannot be of assistance to faith. It is not so odd that many Christian thinkers take this view when we consider the problems of history to which they draw our attention. However,

35

I believe that to each argument for retreat from history a valid reason for returning to history can be opposed, and that a doctrine of atonement positively *needs* the help of historical enquiry.

No retreat from history

A major reason advanced for detaching faith from history is the evident fact that the documents which record the life, death and resurrection of Jesus are highly interpreted accounts. The gospels are written from the perspective of the belief of the early Christian community, and the stories and words of Jesus have been shaped to make a particular point in preaching about Christ. 'In the beginning was the sermon', says one scholar, and much of the gospel material is angled to meet the needs and problems of particular Christian groups, or to meet the challenge of mission in new cultures. In describing the crucifixion of Christ, for example, Mark tells us that Jesus cries out with the lament 'My God, why have you forsaken me?' and then utters a loud cry of agony before dying (Mark 15:34,37). The evangelist is writing to a community that is bewildered by the harsh persecution inflicted upon it, and is assuring them that even the Messiah himself had to suffer. In contrast, the fourth evangelist interprets the last cry as a triumphant claim that 'it is accomplished'; the work the Father gave Jesus to do is completed (John 19:30). One of the aims of this evangelist is to root Christians more deeply in their faith, to help them realise what it means to have received a new kind of life from Jesus. The one who can give life is the true Son who has come from the Father; through death Jesus returns to the Father and so is 'lifted up' in glory as well as pain upon the cross, to draw all people to him. The insights of these two evangelists do not contradict each other, but draw out some of the wealth of meaning which lies in the event.

Given the nature of the gospel material, some Christian thinkers have concluded that it is hopeless to try to say anything about the actual Jesus of history. All we have is 'the Christ of faith'. But we should not forget that all writing of history involves interpretation; all historians write from the angle of their own view of the world (even if they do not notice what they are doing), and seek meaning from event. There is no such thing as a bare, uninterpreted fact.

36

The approach of the gospel writers then should not, in principle, rule out our making *some* discoveries about what was happening in the historical life and death of Jesus, even though we ought to be aware that the results can only be called probabilities; after all no historical enquiry can yield certainty. Moreover this quest is actually demanded by the fact that so many meanings have been found in the death of Christ. Throughout the ages of the church different theories have been developed to explain *how* the death of Christ brings about atonement. No historical enquiry can prove one theory to be 'the right one', but finding out something about the actual event of this death in its social and political context should lay down some boundaries for interpretation. Some pictures or concepts, as we shall see, fit better with the events than others.

I have already agreed that no historical investigation can of itself find an act of God. If it could, then God would be reduced to an object of human study; the living and incomparable Lord cannot be pinned down under the microscope of scientific investigation. It needs the eye of faith, and the power of the Holy Spirit to bring matters into focus before we can say that 'God was in Christ, reconciling the world to himself'. But this is a no more adequate reason than the previous one for abandoning history. If God has really become flesh in our world, in the very marketplace where Pilate struts with his petty power, then an investigation of the scene on which God has acted is bound to be relevant to faith. A historian can only tell us about the worldly setting for God's mighty acts, but this must throw light upon the meaning of the event as faith perceives it.

This relationship between history and faith helps us to understand why the 'lives of Jesus' written in the last century were such failures. The quest for the historical Jesus undertaken by Christian thinkers at that time ended in producing a figure who, as Albert Schweitzer pointed out, appeared to be remarkably like themselves.[3] They looked into the well of history and found only their own reflections; the 'Jesus of history' turned out to be an urbane teacher of morals and an upholder of liberal values. He fell considerably short of 'the biblical Christ', the Lord of the cosmos exalted to God's right hand to whom the early church bears witness. This failure to find within history the Christ who 'can be understood only by contact with his spirit which is still at work in the world'

(Schweitzer)[4] thus provided a further reason for turning away from history altogether. But the quest failed because the searchers expected to find the *whole meaning* of Jesus through scientific historical enquiry.

The whole meaning of Jesus cannot emerge from past history; indeed what it means for the risen Christ to be saviour in the world today will go on expanding until the end of time. I am suggesting that we should be placing historical fact (that is, probability) *alongside* the insights of faith. When we ask *who* is this 'spirit at work in the world' (Schweitzer's phrase), the answer cannot avoid reference to the Jesus who suffered under Pontius Pilate. As the 'liberation theologians' rightly point out, a lack of interest in what Jesus was actually doing for the poor and oppressed around him leads to theories of salvation which make no contact with the real needs of those who suffer under the Pilates of today.[5] The theories float away from this world into another 'spiritual' realm. Historical enquiry can thus *shape* faith, giving content to such abstract words as salvation.

Yet a further reason often urged for a flight from history concerns the nature of faith itself. On the one hand faith is a personal step of risk and trust, not assent to evidence. Reliance upon facts of history would, it is said, thus destroy the very character of faith. But I have not been suggesting that we should look to history to *prove* faith; rather, belief that certain events have happened will shape and educate a faith that comes from encounter with Christ today. On the other hand, it is urged that faith has its own kind of certainty; the believer *knows* God in a direct way which is not hedged around with the uncertainties of history. What then can faith have to do with mere probabilities of what might have happened? In answer, we may return to the insight that faith is a matter of risk and commitment. When we believe that God has committed himself to the hazardous enterprise of becoming flesh in our history, and becoming identified with a powerless people in one small part of the world, we are also ready to take the risk of having a historical faith. We are prepared to look at the evidence, to probe it with all the critical tools that historical research can offer, and then to commit ourselves to the belief that Jesus probably did say and do certain things, and that other things probably happened to him. This is not to look to these probabilities to verify our faith itself but to be willing to let these discoveries shape the content of faith; to inform us about what it might *mean* to confess Christ as the one in whom our world is reconciled.

Concepts and images of atonement are thus open to history. At the same time the traffic of thought and experience moves the other way too; we have to admit that our view of what can be called 'historical' will be shaped by a world view in which God's act of atonement plays a central part. This brings us to a final reason why some Christian thinkers have wanted to abandon history. At the centre of Christian faith is the belief that God raised Jesus Christ from the dead and exalted him to be Lord of the universe. The resurrection, it may seem, is not an event that a historian can examine, since his method of investigation depends upon being able to compare his own experience of what is objectively real with what is claimed to have happened in the past. He has no experience of resurrections in the present from which to work. A rigid view of history, which tries to reduce human events to scientific laws (positivism), would go further and conclude that the resurrection *could not* have happened because it is not a regularly recurring event, and so we cannot perceive and examine it with our senses. However there is no reason why we have to accept that history is totally regular. As Wolfhart Pannenberg observes, natural science can only express the 'general validity of laws of nature' and anyway 'conformity to law embraces only one aspect of what happens'.[6] While we must not expect the historian to verify the resurrection of Jesus, we can ask him not to rule *out* the event of resurrection as an impossibility, as long as there are good reasons in what he *can* examine to make him cautious.

In support we can appeal to such historical evidence as the birth of the Christian community, and ask what kind of event could have turned frightened and despairing disciples into courageous witnesses who were willing to face death for the sake of a Christ whom they believed to have risen from death. We can point to the phenomenon that people claimed to have witnessed an 'appearance' of the risen Christ when, far from expecting any such thing, they thought his work had come to a disastrous end. We can reflect on the fact that the authorities did not produce the body of Jesus when the early disciples claimed the tomb was empty. But these facts fall short of *proof* that Christ overcame death in a way that no human being had ever done before, and that his whole being (including his body) was somehow transformed and raised to communion with God. Other explanations can always be found. I have suggested that historical enquiry can tell us only about the secular setting of God's activity, and these circumstances surrounding the resurrection are likewise open to study. But the actual raising of Jesus from death is not open to historical examination or scientific explanation, since it is an act of God.

As the work of God in our world, the resurrection is like the atoning act of God through the cross; it needs eyes of faith to perceive it. But as an event in itself the crucifixion is not at all unusual; thousands of victims were crucified by the Romans, and that a man called Jesus suffered this kind of punishment is, in principle, open to proof. By contrast, in the case of the resurrection the event that happened in the world is no more open to historical proof than the activity of God within it, and it is this which has led Christian thinkers to remove it from the stage of history altogether. However it is quite consistent to believe that the resurrection is an event within history, and yet not open to historical proof. The New Testament presents the resurrection of Jesus as an event of the new creation which has happened in the midst of the old. There were strong Jewish expectations that people would be resurrected at the end of the world, when God would act to renew and transform the whole of the physical universe, raising it to a new level of being. The astonishing claim of the early Christians was that in the case of one man, this had already happened.[7] What was expected to happen in the far distant future had taken place on a recent Sunday morning.

Now, as an event of the new creation, the resurrection cannot be analysed with the tools of the old one. It escapes our methods of doing history, and so we cannot describe exactly what happened. In the resurrection of Jesus, God protests against the world as it is. From the viewpoint of the new creation he contradicts an order of things which lies under the shadow of death. He thus provokes us to question the existing structures, making us restless and unsatisfied with the injustices of the present world. It is essential, then, that we maintain the resurrection to be a historical event; if we remove it from the arena of history we have defused it of its shocking impact upon us, and lost its challenge to the way the world is. The raising of Jesus from among the dead is the work of a God who is free to do new things, and who is not bound by the status quo.

The risen Christ is the crucified Jesus. Their encounter with the risen Lord compelled the early disciples to look again at the meaning of the cross, and to find a surprising act of God in what seemed to be failure. On the other hand, the atoning work of God in the cross looks forward to resurrection for its completion; the submission of God to death is followed by his conquest of it. The movement of God from humiliation to triumph makes a story that can only be read from the book of history by those who have eyes of faith; but the story which all *can* read throws light upon the other. This is because they are both God's story.

History shapes faith: the conflict with law

There can be no serious doubt that Jesus came into conflict with the religious authorities in the Israel of his time. There is every reason to accept the record of the evangelists that Jesus was tried before the Sanhedrin or Privy Council of the High Priest, on which sat both major groups of religious leaders – Pharisees and Sadducees. It would likewise be odd to deny that part of the friction between Jesus and the religious establishment was a difference of attitude to the Torah, the code of laws for directing the whole of life which was believed to have been revealed by God through Moses when the nation was founded. The gospel narratives have certainly been coloured by later problems, when Christianity had to face Jewish opposition from outside, and the question from inside as to whether new Christians must first be asked to obey the Jewish law. But the theme of Jesus' conflict with the guardians of the law is too deeply rooted in the gospel stories to be entirely a reading back from the situation in the early church. What is not so clear, however, is the extent and nature of the conflict, and in what sense it was a factor that led to his death. New Testament scholars such as E. P. Sanders have rightly protested against pictures of a bigoted establishment of legalistic Pharisees opposing root and branch the preaching of God's grace by Jesus.[8] It is this kind of crude portrayal that has done so much to spoil relationships between Christians and Jews.

Following the approach explained above, I intend to take the risk of describing what I believe to be the probable situation that the ministry of Jesus created, and of letting these conclusions have an impact upon the meaning of atonement for us today. Although my outline does, I believe, reflect a wide consensus of agreement among New Testament scholars, my concern here is not to defend it, but to admit the way that my commitment to a certain picture of the historical Jesus shapes the whole approach to the doctrine of atonement that I am adopting in this study.

In his 'conflict' with the religious law of his nation, Jesus was probably not making a point of rejecting the Mosaic code but simply adopting a sublime freedom with regard to it. In his ministry he was creating a new *climate* of understanding about the way that God deals with people, placing the emphasis upon God's free offer of forgiveness for sinners, rather than upon a style of life shaped by the keeping of regulations for right living. In stressing that God offers forgiveness to those who repent, his offence was not to say something which was alien to the piety of the Pharisees, but to press it in a way that they must feel was dangerously out of all proportion. When, later on, the former Pharisee Paul proclaims that Christ is the 'end' of the law (Rom. 10:4) he thus takes the whole momentum of the ministry of Jesus to its natural conclusion. The lifestyle of Christ is the 'end' of law in the sense of being its goal (*telos*), or what the law was really aiming at all the time.

Any impartial historical study of the activity of Jesus of Nazareth is likely to take it as reasonably 'certain' (within the limits of any historical verdict) that he was announcing the near arrival of the kingdom of God. The rule of God that was already breaking in with his own ministry would shortly come in a fuller way.[9] This need not mean that he expected the literal end of the world; like the prophets of ancient Israel he was proclaiming that God was about to break into the life of the world, doing something so new and decisive that things would never be the same again. In this longed-for moment injustices would be righted and the whole creation would enter upon the harmony so long denied to it. In the light of the immediate crisis, Jesus was calling for trust in himself as the final agent of the kingdom; those whom he welcomed into his company would be received by his heavenly Father and would escape judgement when the kingdom came. The stress of his

42

ministry, then, was upon having trust in the Father who welcomed all to his house and banquet, and trust in himself as the Father's representative.[10]

The gospel accounts, for example, portray his fellowship with the 'common people' or 'the poor', and his ready welcoming of them into the kingdom of God. Now we must be careful not to confuse 'the poor' with the group of social outcasts called 'the sinners' (or 'the wicked ones') with whom Jesus was also constantly accused of consorting. It would be quite wrong to suppose that the Pharisees thought all the common people ('the people of the land') were automatic rejects from the kingdom of God because they were too ignorant and uneducated to keep the Law properly. They certainly 'sinned', but they were not regarded as a class of hopeless 'sinners'. After all, they shared in the atoning sacrifices made in the Temple, whose validity the Pharisees did not deny. Morever, though the 'common people' must often, in the eyes of the Pharisees, bring impurity upon themselves, they could cleanse themselves through ritual bathing, commended by the Pharisees as thoroughly in line with Old Testament scripture.[11]

It is likely then that the majority of Pharisees would have allowed that the common people were potentially worthy members of the kingdom of God. It would be a travesty to say that they were shocked by the mere fact that Jesus offered forgiveness of sins to the 'poor'. But we are concerned with the momentum of different styles of life. However much Pharisees proclaimed the grace of God, offering forgiveness to all those who repented, the result of giving a central place to law was to create a whole massive structure of secondary laws to interpret and apply it. The impression must then be given that the common people could only be accepted into the kingdom as a kind of concession, as last-comers who had just squeezed through the door and only through constant repentance and satisfaction for their many lapses. Jesus, by contrast, made it clear that God actually had a bias to the poor and humble who were 'weary and oppressed by many burdens'. His ministry was 'good news to the poor', for 'the first shall be last and the last shall be first'; those who had performed many good works, admirable though this might be, would have no preferential place in the kingdom above late-comers who had not time or means to do so, and riches would actually make it extraordinarily difficult to enter it at all.[12] Moreover Jesus appears not to have been the kind of preacher of national repentance that John the Baptist was; it seems to have been enough to admit one's need of God's grace and to have trusted in Jesus as the agent of the coming kingdom. Repentance was understood by the Pharisees as entailing the much more exact requirements of the law, namely a sacrificial offering made in the Temple, strict restitution to those who had been wronged and a resolve to keep the law in future.

The momentum of this ministry, running into inevitable collision with the way of law, becomes most acute in the scandalous acceptance by Jesus of 'tax collectors and sinners'.[13] The title 'sinners' seems to have been attached to those whose behaviour or job involved a deliberate and persistent breaking of the religious law; chief among these were tax collectors (quislings of the Roman occupying power who gained their living by extortionate demands), prostitutes and money-lenders. Jesus offered these outcasts too the forgiveness of God and a place in the kingdom of heaven, sharing the fellowship of the meal table with them as a sign that they would sit down with him in the coming Messianic banquet. Once again we must be careful not to make a crude parody of the situation; E. P. Saunders is convincing when he suggests that the Pharisees would have been only too delighted if Jesus had succeeded in converting these notorious sinners into upright citizens of Israel, showing repentance in the approved manner that the law required.[14] There is no reason to suppose that they thought the 'sinners' to be beyond the scope of the grace of God under *any* conditions. The scandal seems to have been that Jesus assured them of his Father's welcome on the grounds of a more simple kind of repentance altogether – namely trust in himself as the representative of the kingdom and a following of his way of life. Thus Jesus outraged the religious establishment by eating with sinners while, in their view, they were *still* sinners.

The bias of God towards the outcasts, as well as to the poor, is revealed in the scathing comment of Jesus to the scribes and Pharisees, that 'the tax collectors and prostitutes go into the kingdom before you'. Moreover, while the 'poor' should not be simply confused with the 'sinners', there was no doubt a sliding scale between the two in the minds of the Pharisees. Some occupations sat uneasily on the boundaries, such as shepherds, whose animals constantly strayed on to other people's land so involving them in breaking the law of trespass, and whose hours of work made it virtually impossible for them to attend synagogue or Temple.[15] The shepherds on Christmas cards of today may be a picturesque detail for us, and a bonus to the card manufacturers, but Luke the evangelist is making a shocking point by including them in the birth scene; from the beginning of his life Jesus welcomed the poor and sinners.

Jesus, then, shows a remarkable freedom from anxiety about keeping the law, whether written or oral. His concern was to relieve the poor and the sinners of the burdens they carried, even the burden of onerous repentance. He turned upside down the system of values that favoured the wealthy and the educated, and challenged the roles that society thrust upon the weak. He welcomes women openly to his company, when custom would have kept them in seclusion, and announces that under-age children are nearer to the kingdom than adults:[16]

> He has brought down monarchs from their thrones,
> but the humble have been lifted high.
>
> (Luke 1:52)

The extension of the ancient written code into a mass of extra sub-rules (the *Halakah* or oral law) was inevitable if life was to be guided by law, since it was the only way of making an ancient document relevant to daily life in the present. A notable example was the fantastic spinning of a web of petty instructions about keeping the Sabbath free of work (which in later rabbinic teaching was even held to forbid the wearing of false teeth on that day). Jesus rejects the weaving of intricate oral laws about the Sabbath, allowing his disciples to make themselves a snack from the cornfields and healing on the Sabbath even where life was not endangered,[17] because such law prevents the fulfilling of the greatest commandment – to love.[18] He follows the great Rabbi Hillel who, fifty years before, had remarked that the sum of the Torah was 'do not do to another what seems to you to be hurtful', but he makes it even more positive: 'love your enemies, and do good, and lend, seeking nothing in return'.[19]

That the remarkable freedom of Jesus with regard to law extended

45

even to the written Torah, is shown fundamentally (as we have seen) by his attitude to repentance. A similar freedom is shown in the saying that 'there is nothing outside a man which by going into him can defile him' (Mark 7:15); though in itself this probably does not amount to asserting that all foods are clean it is hardly surprising that the evangelist draws this meaning from it for the life of his church, since it does at least place a question mark against the Old Testament laws about clean and unclean animals. Again, while the Old Testament commanded that oaths should be kept and that revenge should not exceed the strict right of an eye for an eye, Jesus forbids both swearing and retribution altogether.[20] These sayings should not be taken as either a making of the law more strict or a blatant contradiction of it, but rather an imaginative pressing behind the written text to the intention of God. Most revealing here is Jesus' comment on the law of divorce, that 'For your hardness of heart [Moses] wrote you this commandment. But from the beginning of creation, "God made them male and female . . . so they are no longer two but one" ' (Mark 10: 6–8). Jesus quotes one piece of Torah (Genesis) against another (Deuteronomy) to conclude that written law is only a temporary provision, not a final and absolute statement of the will of God but a form of it suitable for a particular time and culture. In turn, this should warn us not to take Jesus' own words about God's creative intention for life-long union as a new law. The point is that, though the brokenness of human relationships may require divorce, it must never be taken as God's final purpose for human life.

Similarly the radical instructions gathered together in the Sermon on the Mount are not evidence that Jesus gave a new law to replace the old. The command to turn the other cheek and to give away one's shirt are little cameo pictures of what living in the kingdom of God is like. They portray what love might demand in its boundless way; the point is not that we must always act like this, regardless of circumstances, but that love *may* require *even* this. We are not to draw the limits ourselves, but to let love make its own demands upon us. Alongside the demand of love is the crisis of the breaking in of the kingdom; the urgency of responding to the demands of the kingdom might require a person even to break a law that seems to be supported by common decency and the deepest human feelings: the disciple may not be able to wait to bury his parents.[21] The

46

divine forgiveness which Jesus offers certainly requires a change of life, but it is response to the call of the kingdom which can seem scandalous.

Whether or not the saying of Jesus that he 'came to fulfil the law'[22] is from his own lips, it sums up his approach of 'filling out' the written law in his own personality. The way of love and forgiveness incarnates the intention of moral rules in flesh and blood, as a skilful speaker of a language fills out the aims of the rules of grammar in his speech – and often sits loose to the letter of the rules the more beautiful and effective his speech becomes. We recall Paul's phrase that 'Christ is the end (or the goal) of the law.'

Jesus cannot be pinned down in either the simple category of a law-supporter or a law-breaker. He escapes our labels, and 'fits no formula'.[23] The whole thrust of his ministry was to cut through the maze of moral rules, even of the highest quality, in order to offer forgiveness and the acceptance of the Father. Even if the phrase 'but I say to you' is not from Jesus himself, he clearly laid claim to an astonishing authority, assuming that the rules could be waived for those who accepted him as the agent of the kingdom. There is no need to set up the scribes and Pharisees as either hypocrites or unbelievers in the divine mercy in order to explain the conflict between them and Jesus; the question was who was right about the way that God was acting. In the parable of the prodigal son there is no suggestion that the elder brother was a moral hypocrite, or that he thought it impossible for his rake of a brother to be forgiven under any circumstances; he just failed in sympathy with the outrageous generosity of the father.

A commitment to this sketch of what Jesus was doing in his life's work must have a shaping effect upon a doctrine of atonement. Some scholars, after careful historical enquiry, may well find Jesus less in conflict with the Jewish law than I have described, and others may find him to be even more so. The risk of making a decision on the evidence has to be taken if faith is exposed to the hazards of history, and the outline I have adopted leads me to several conclusions about the meaning of atonement that are funda-mental to this study. Since the act of atonement on the cross sums up and completes the whole course of Jesus' life, the controlling aspect of any doctrine of atonement must be the forgiveness and acceptance of God. As Jesus showed a sovereign freedom over the way of the law, so a doctrine of atonement must be free from any notion of a 'transaction' which somehow satisfies the demands of a divine law code. It hardly makes sense that the Jesus who declined to give law any final importance and who was certified as being in the right about this when God raised him from among the dead, should have died as a means of satisfying law. At the same time, as we shall see, the theme of a conflict with legalism in the name of love helps us to re-use and remake several of the ancient images of atonement for the present day.

Did the conflict with legalism actually bring Jesus to his death? It seems highly probable that one charge against him in his trial before the Sanhedrin was that he had blasphemed,[24] but it is much less easy to see what the 'blasphemy' was thought to be. Jesus claimed to be a spokesman for God, announcing the divine forgiveness, but this in itself was hardly to be counted as blasphemy. The priests laid claim to be the official spokesmen for God, and though they were not pleased when prophets arose among the people and claimed to speak for God, there is no evidence that they usually suppressed them. However in the case of Jesus his presumptuousness was compounded by his wayward attitude to the law and his acceptance of sinners into the kingdom. Probably then his by-passing of the law of Moses was seen as a kind of blasphemy since the law had been given by God and was the channel through which he communicated to his people.

But it is unlikely that this in itself would have been enough to condemn him, or even perhaps to have had him arrested. It seems that a *number* of factors must have accumulated to bring Jesus before a hostile Sanhedrin, seeking his death. Here we must notice the charge at his trial that he threatened to destroy the Temple in Jerusalem; although this is judged by the evangelists to be false witness against him, they themselves record he warned that the Temple would *be* destroyed in the near future.[25] It seems most likely that he was announcing that God himself would sweep away the old Temple when the kingdom broke in, and would replace it with a new building fit for the new age. Since he believed that he would play the key role in the coming of the kingdom, the form of accusation at the trial is understandable even if strictly untrue. A threat made against the Temple would be deeply offensive not only to the religious leaders but to the whole population, and would probably be reckoned as 'blasphemy' since the Temple was revered as God's dwelling place.[26] The dramatic incident in the last week of Jesus' life, when he overturned the tables of money-changers in the court of the Gentiles and forcefully cleared out the clutter that was blocking its use for worship was no doubt a symbolic action, threatening that God himself was shortly to overturn the whole Temple.

Even the provocative act in the Temple might not, as an act of blasphemy, have led to arrest and prosecution. But when it became clear, underlined by this incident, that Jesus would have to be dealt with as a threat to imperial order and the safety of Jewish life, then the accusations of blasphemy against God's law and Temple would add weight to the desire to remove the disturber. We really cannot separate out the political and religious elements from Jesus' proclamation of the kingdom of God, and in this sense it is true to say that his conflict with the institutions of legalism brought him to his cross, even if the immediate cause was political.

History shapes faith: the political disturbance

Jesus was crucified under the Roman prefect Pontius Pilate by a Roman form of execution. The Jewish Sanhedrin handed Jesus over to a Roman trial and death sentence. This must mean that the imperial powers regarded Jesus as a political disturber and a threat to orderly rule, a fact confirmed by the charge pinned up over the cross: 'The King of the Jews'. It seems that the charge that Jesus was making himself a king also surfaced in the trial before the Sanhedrin, and this may well reflect the fact that he saw himself as playing the prominent part when the kingdom of God finally came. Here it is quite possible that Jesus also identified himself with the figure of the 'Son of Man' who appears in the book of Daniel as the champion of heaven overcoming the forces of bestiality and chaos.[27] Even if the 'triumphal entry' of Jesus into Jerusalem was a demonstration on a rather smaller scale than the gospels suggest, perhaps restricted to a small group of his close followers, it must have implied a claim to kingship *of some kind*.

However it seems certain that neither Jesus nor his disciples expected this new world order to be brought about by force of arms, but rather by an act of God; the kingship of Jesus was no part of the power games of this world. Although Jesus had one known Zealot in his company of disciples and was crucified between two more, all the evidence is against his taking such a path himself.[28] There is, for instance, the fact that no attempt was made to arrest the followers of Jesus along with him, showing that the authorities considered him to be a limited danger.

This does not mean that Jesus was crucified as the result of a misunderstanding over words like 'king'. The Roman priority was order, and any disturbance which agitated the populace was unwelcome and possibly dangerous. Crowds were unpredictable, easily moved to violence against the occupying powers, and Jesus had been drawing crowds through his powers of healing and pithy teaching. No sharp line could be drawn between religion and politics. Jesus was arousing enthusiasm for a new kingdom which God alone could bring in, but this still amounted to criticism of the Roman rule since Caesar would not be reigning there.[29] He was calling for a spiritual renewal of the nation, but this would mean sweeping away the present religious establishment in Jerusalem, whose appointment had been sanctioned by Rome. The fate of John the Baptist had already shown that even a preacher of repentance and righteousness in the old prophetic style could become a threat to the structures of power; as the Jewish historian Josephus interprets John's execution, Herod had become alarmed because 'eloquence which had so great an effect on mankind might lead to some form of sedition, for it looked as if [the people] would be guided by John in everything they did'. Thus, comments Josephus, Herod 'thought it much better to strike first'.[30]

Jesus, with his announcement of the kingdom, was much more disruptive than John. The Jewish religious authorities, headed by the High Priest Caiaphas, were anxious to prevent any demonstrations of riots that could give the Roman powers an excuse for savage retaliation; thus in the interests of safety it was 'expedient that one man should die for the people'.[31] The Pharisees and Sadducees lived under a truce with their Roman rulers, that as long as the political authorities committed no grievous outrage against their religious sensibilities, such as installing images of the Emperor in the Temple, they for their part would make sure that their religious teaching did not infringe the rights of the occupying power to collect taxes and maintain law and order. Jesus, however, was just not as 'careful' as this in his announcement of the rule of God. As he showed an outrageous freedom in matters of religious law, so he allowed nothing to qualify the claim of God upon the whole of life. The famous saying 'render to Caesar the things that are Caesar's, and to God the things that are God's' (Mark 12:17) does not at all exclude matters of faith from politics. Rather, it leaves as an open question what the things *are* that are God's. The listener is left to make the decision as to what obedience to God will mean in any situation, including political affairs.[32]

To make the historical judgement that Jesus represented a disturbance on the political scene, which Jewish and Roman authorities collaborated to remove, is not at all to fasten the portrait of a modern freedom fighter upon him. But his proclamation of the kingdom of God raised expectations, and made demands upon the hearers, which cut across any neat boundaries of religious and civic life. If we allow history to shape faith, a doctrine of atonement cannot therefore address the situation of an individual alone; it must affect the health of the society. Jesus was crucified because he called the ultimate claims of human power 'there and then' into question, insisting upon the final demands of the rule of God. If we believe that through this death God was bringing salvation, this must have relevance for the situation of those oppressed by human powers 'here and now'.

The true Son of God

Any historian, whether or not he had any faith in God, could accept that a man called Jesus believed that the kingdom of God was about to dawn, that he shocked the establishment by promising admission to the outcasts, and disturbed the Roman peace by arousing expectations of a new age among the masses. But how are we to interpret these events? Does the God whom Jesus called Father actually exist at all? If so, were the Pharisees or Jesus right in their view of the place of law in life? Were Jesus or the Roman authorities right in their view of where true power lies? It takes a leap of faith to answer these questions by saying that in all this God was at work, declaring Jesus in the right through raising him from the dead, and making the cross a means of reconciling the world to himself. No historical

51

enquiry can in itself find an act of God, but I have been wanting to show that historical conclusions do *affect* our interpretation; they shape our understanding of what it *means* to say, in faith, that God was atoning for sin through the life and death of Jesus.

To speak of atonement is to affirm that God was himself acting in Christ to deal with the human predicament where human beings are helpless. The enquirer is not compelled logically to take the step from the event to this interpretation, and yet there is a continuity between history and the insights of faith. But in what sense was God present and acting in Christ? How deeply was God involved in these worldly happenings? These are questions about the true identity of Jesus Christ, and we would expect historical enquiry to be relevant here too, although we could not expect any historical account to be able to express the whole truth about Jesus.

When we find the gospels presenting Jesus Christ as 'Son of God', we ought to be aware that the title was widely applied to human individuals in the time of Jesus. It indicated that a person was thought to have a special relationship with God, and that he acted as God's representative in some way. Among others reckoned to be righteous or wise and so 'sons of God', a charismatic preacher named Honi who was a near contemporary of Jesus is said to have prayed 'like a son of the house'.[33] Much earlier the promise of adoption as a son had been given to kings of ancient Israel at their coronation: 'You are my son, today I have begotten you.'[34] Yet they had often failed to represent their Father as true and obedient sons, as the historians of the Old Testament make all too clear. Israel as a whole had also failed in its vocation of sonship, so that the prophet Isaiah articulates God's lament: 'Sons I have reared, but they have rebelled against me.'[35] The New Testament writers thus portray Jesus as the truly obedient Son that other Israelites had failed to be; in the fourth gospel Jesus tells the little parable of 'the Son (who) always does what he sees the Father doing'. The picture is of a son in his father's workshop, learning his trade by faithfully copying the workmanship of the father. At his baptism in the Jordan, according to the other gospel writers, the heavenly voice recalls the coronation promise of old, pronouncing 'you are my beloved son; with you I am well pleased'.[36]

The early Christian church clearly believed that Jesus, open in total obedience to God, had acted on his Father's behalf in a unique

52

way. As the final agent of salvation, he had had authority to invite outcasts and sinners into the kingdom that was already dawning. The title 'Son of God' was apt to express this, and they found his sonship to have been greatly enhanced by his resurrection from the dead as God put his seal of approval on his representative, exalting him to be Lord of the universe: 'appointed Son of God by resurrection from the dead'.[37] Jesus was thus 'one' with the Father in *function*, since God revealed himself through this man, acted through him and encountered others through him; in this sense he was 'Immanuel, God with us'. Looked at from another angle Jesus was the new Adam who was the obedient son that Adam had signally failed to be. As the agent of the Father, all his actions and teaching were inspired and empowered by the Spirit of God, the dynamic power of God himself reaching out and affecting people; indeed two of the gospel writers affirm that his very birth was overshadowed by the creative power of the Spirit, so that he can be reckoned Son of God from the very beginning of his life.

It will be essential, for a doctrine of atonement, to recognise that within the time-span of the New Testament church a shift began to occur in the meaning of the title 'Son of God'. But even the earliest use of the name, within the context of Jewish ideas of human 'sons of God' as I have described it, is of course an interpretation of the historical event of Christ. No historian could make the judgement, strictly as a historian, that Jesus actually *was* open to God or acting for him. No relationship with God is a matter of scientific enquiry. But it is not unreasonable to find this interpretation fitting into something in the ministry of Jesus that a historian *can* in principle comment upon, namely the sense of sonship that Jesus himself possessed. Here the New Testament scholar James Dunn is surely right to affirm that a historian ought not to regard it as a hopeless task to penetrate into the self-understanding of a historical individual, 'otherwise history would be nothing more than a dreary catalogue of dates and documentation'. The historian can inquire after motivation and intention, and 'though he can never be certain that he is right . . . he would not be worthy of his profession if he did not expect to provide a plausible and convincing character study of his chosen subject'.[38]

When we take the risk of making this kind of enquiry, I believe we can discover from the source materials in the gospels that Jesus had an acute sense of his own relationship as son to God. It seems to have been characteristic of his prayers to address God with the intimate word 'Abba' (Father), and though it is overstating the case to claim that no other Jewish persons of his time would have prayed in this way, it is clear that it was an unusual and daring form of address. Most would have regarded it as too much a word of the close family circle to be suitable for prayer. Certainly there is no parallel at all for the *regularity* with which Jesus used 'Abba', and the fact that Paul later explains the Christian habit of crying 'Abba' in prayer as due to a sharing in the Spirit of Jesus (Rom. 8:15–16) shows that it could not have been a common usage within the Jewish faith.[39] Indeed it is probable that Jesus himself saw the sonship of his disciples as somehow dependent upon his own, since he teaches them to address God as 'Abba' in the prayer he gave them.

For Jesus, it seems then that the nearness of the kingdom was bound up with his own awareness of the nearness of the Father to himself; his sense of being a 'son of God' was unique, related as it was to his sense of vocation to bring other sons into the kingdom which was breaking in, at the climax of God's purpose for his people. He was the son who was acting on behalf of his Father in an unprecedented way. When the gospel writers explain the charge of blasphemy at the trial of Jesus as relating to a claim to be 'the Son of God' they are probably short-circuiting the accusation. Given the widespread use of the title, this in itself could not have been regarded as blasphemous; but, as we have already seen, the priests and Pharisees might well have regarded as blasphemously arrogant the authority he assumed because of his sense of sonship.

It is of course a matter of interpretation to say that Jesus was right in the way he understood himself. It is a still further step of faith to follow the early Christian church to a more far-reaching conclusion it gradually reached – that the sonship of Jesus has eternal significance for the nature of God. As we have seen, the three earliest gospels (Mark, Matthew, Luke) and the earlier letters of St Paul understand the sonship of Jesus as a 'functional' oneness with God: Jesus is one with the Father in action and relationship, acting for God and being totally open in obedience to him. However in some later parts of the New Testament we find a shift of thought: if there was a son on earth in perfect relationship with the heavenly

Father, then God must always have enjoyed such a relationship. If on earth there were an agent of the Father, acting in perfect harmony with him, then the Father always had such a son to express his purpose. The endpoint of this process of thought was to be reached two and a half centuries later at the Council of Nicaea, with the credal formula that the Son was 'of the same essence (*homoousios*) as the Father'. That is, the sonship was not merely a matter of *doing* but *being*; if Christ was one in action with the Father he was one in being with him. Even the latest parts of the New Testament writings do not employ such a philosophical concept as 'one in being', but they do begin to experiment with words, breaking open the old wine-skins of language, straining to express a half-grasped insight that the sonship of Jesus has implications for the very life of God.

This shift of thought was most assisted by Jewish ideas of the wisdom of God. In Old Testament and later Jewish writings, the skill and purpose of God in creating the world and ordering human life was sometimes presented poetically as a person. In Proverbs 8, for example, the wisdom of God is portrayed as a young child playing in the presence of God as he creates the universe. Though the wisdom of God is personified here, it seems clear that the writer thought of Wisdom as a power of God's mind, an extension of his own personality, not actually as a distinct person. As time went on Jewish religious thinkers began to ask where they could find this wisdom of God which they needed to impose order upon the chaotic world and to grasp the perplexing pattern of their lives. The wisdom of God seemed hidden, far away: 'no man knows the way to it' (Job 28:13). The answer which they arrived at was that God had made his wisdom available in the Torah, the scriptures of the Law and the Prophets. The key to all reality, the plan of God for the universe, was embodied in a book. New Testament writers such as the apostle Paul were familiar with this answer, and reply that the real place to find the wisdom of God is not the law, but Jesus. The hidden purpose of God for the world and human life is incarnate not in a book but in a person: 'in him lie hidden all God's treasures of wisdom and knowledge' so that (like the Wisdom of Proverbs 8) 'in him everything in heaven and earth was created' and 'all things hold together in him'.[40]

This identification of Jesus with divine Wisdom lies behind other playful experiments with talk about him: in Hebrews 1 he is the 'outshining of the glory' of God, sustaining the universe, and in John 1 he is the Word spoken by the Father. Now, if Jesus Christ were the Wisdom that was with God from the beginning, then it followed that Christ too must in some sense have always been 'with God' (John 1:3). Conversely it followed that this Wisdom of God must be not merely a poetic personification but a distinct person. Thought moved on from the belief that God's wisdom is fully expressed through a person in our history, to the belief that there must eternally be a son in relationship with the Father. Thus, when the fourth evangelist actually portrays Jesus as aware of a pre-existent life with the Father we must understand that he is drawing out the meaning of the sonship of Jesus from the viewpoint of faith, rather than recording the inner mind of the earthly Jesus. Jesus could be more than he knew himself to be.

My concern here is not directly to expound a doctrine of the Trinity, but to admit the way that a certain picture of the historical Jesus will shape a doctrine of atonement. I am taking the historical 'risk' of affirming that Jesus had a unique sense of being related to God as a son, and that from this awareness he drew his authority to accept the poor and sinners into the kingdom. While his message was the nearness of the kingdom, it was the nearness of the Father that he communicated through his deeds of accepting love. Any doctrine of the atonement which is in continuity with the ministry of Jesus will therefore make the involvement of God in human life the central factor. Through Jesus, God participates in the situation of those oppressed by every kind of sin and evil. While we could certainly affirm this if we understood the commitment of God to this 'son of God' to be a merely functional one, the level of identification would be infinitely deeper if God united himself with Jesus in his very being.

I am basing this study of atonement on the conviction that in Christ God participated to the utmost in the human predicament, and has never journeyed farther into the depths of his creation. That is, I believe the church to be right when it came to believe that God had identified himself with this man without reserve and with his whole being. Early Christian thought moved from a 'sonship of function' to a 'sonship of being' with the help of Jewish ideas of wisdom. In our age we might reflect upon the meaning of persons, and the artificiality of dividing 'being' from 'doing'. Persons are not ready-made products but become what they are because of their relationships and actions; if there really were someone who was completely open to God in trust as a son, and who was totally transparent to the loving activity of God, then such a communion would be so close that we could not think of the being of God without this person. As Pannenberg says concisely, 'Such personal community is at the same time essential community.'[41] If, then, there were a oneness of being between God and the human son Jesus, there must always be something 'son-like' in the being of God himself; for God to commit himself in this way to a human son, he must already live in a relationship which we can only say is like that of a father and a son. In the movements of God's personal being, there is sonship as well as fatherhood.

The communion of Jesus with the Father was so central to his task that his mission was inseparable from his own person. It was those whom he accepted into his fellowship who would be welcomed into the kingdom, not those who vowed to live by some code of teaching. This makes the cry of Jesus on the cross the more horrific: 'My God, why have you forsaken me?' Unlike a religious teacher who could contemplate his death with the satisfaction that his wisdom would go on lighting the minds of succeeding generations, Jesus understood his mission to be dying with him. He was facing the yawning abyss of failure. It seems highly improbable that the early church would have invented this shocking cry which Mark and Matthew record in all its starkness, especially since Luke deliberately omits it, but the sense of forsakenness that Jesus must have felt does not finally depend upon the exact words used.

A historian could accept that Jesus *felt* forsaken by his heavenly Father, that his special relationship as son seemed to be denied in the face of death; it is a step of faith to say that this was actually happening, and that God finally vindicated him by raising him from the dead. But the historical 'forsakenness' of Jesus does have a decisive effect upon a doctrine of atonement. When Jesus is recognised as the Son of God, the cross must mean that the alienation and brokenness of the world enters right into the relationships that form the being of God. The cross reveals the nature of God, not as an invulnerable Absolute, immune from all suffering and change in our world, but as a Father who suffers the loss of his son, a son

57

who is forsaken by his Father, and the Spirit of love and self-giving that moves through this event. There is no other God than the one who is unveiled here. The doctrine of the Trinity, as Jürgen Moltmann has said so well, is a conceptualising of the event of the cross.[42] The doctrine of atonement, we may add, explains *why* God suffers this breach in the harmony of his own life.

If historical enquiry tells us that Jesus felt forsaken, and a doctrine of atonement tells us that this was in order to bring the forsaken back to the Father's house, is there any closer continuity between these two stories? Did Jesus know that his death was atoning? He must, by the last weeks of his life, have sensed that death was a likely outcome of his challenge to the authorities, and it seems most probable that Jesus came to see his death as the surprising means by which the kingdom would come. His holding of the Last Supper, with his use of powerful symbols of sacrifice, shows that he was able to fit his coming death into the whole process of the dawning of the kingdom. Perhaps he saw his death as extending the time for response to the offer of God's grace; because of his death, in some way, God would go on offering acceptance to sinners until the kingdom finally broke in. Certainly he seems to have expected that after his death he would be shown to be in the right in his view of God's purposes. St Luke's interpretation of his last cry as a trusting committal of his Spirit to God perhaps then reveals the attitude with which he went into the dark valley of death; he submitted himself to all the uncertainties of death, looking for vindication, and we may say that God fulfilled his promises in a totally unexpected way by raising him from the dead. That death was a place of real uncertainty is, however, shown in his actual experience of it as a shattering and numbing forsakenness.

The testimony of history is that the experience of sonship was basic to the work and hopes of Jesus. If we let this shape our faith, we must understand atonement as the bringing of many human sons and daughters into the fellowship of God's own life. This confirms once again that atonement is something that happens here and now. The creating of children of God can be no mere conferring of a label and a status through an arrangement made in the past, but the opening of the human self to God in trust.

Part II

Images

4

The point of sacrifice

Words can play tricks on us. We may fail to notice that their meaning has been changing with use through the years, though poets like T. S. Eliot are certainly aware that the words they work with:

> Crack and sometimes break, under the burden,
> Under the tension, slip, slide, perish,
> Decay with imprecision, will not stay in place,
> Will not stay still.[1]

It is not hard to notice the 'slipping' of a theological word when a car manufacturer advertises its new version of an old model as 'a born-again Volkswagen'. But we may fail to perceive that the word *sacrifice* has not 'stayed still', or we may mistake the way in which it has moved, from the time when the early Christians used it as a way of understanding the effect of the death of Christ in their lives. 'Sacrifice' was probably the first image by which the Christian community interpreted its experience of salvation, and it is properly the one with which we begin our survey of images of atonement.

The final sacrifice

The word 'sacrifice' is certainly in current use today, even though the ritual sacrifice of animals or crops is not part of our living culture. In a secular context, 'sacrifice' carries the meaning of making a costly gift for the sake of others. Journalists write about pensioners making a sacrifice by giving money for famine relief, of Black people in South Africa being willing to sacrifice their jobs

61

and livelihood as the cost of imposing trade sanctions on the government, and of soldiers making the supreme sacrifice in conflict with terrorists. We easily make a shift into a religious meaning of sacrifice if we believe that such costly gift-offerings as these are being made to God in obedience to his purposes in the world, and the widespread feeling that sacrifices are being made for the sake of a principle of truth or justice marks a transition stage from secular to religious use.

This modern emphasis upon the 'gift' element in sacrifice is actually a slippage from the ancient usage of the term, which formed the context for early Christian reflection upon the death of Christ. It is important therefore not to misunderstand the *way* in which the meaning of sacrifice has changed. It is certainly not the case that an understanding of sacrifice as a gift offered to God was unfamiliar to the ancient world; this type of sacrifice was widespread in Jewish, Greek and Christian cultures. The 'whole burnt offering' in ancient Israel, where the entire sacrificial animal was consumed in fire upon the altar, was an extravagant expression of praise, thanksgiving and obedience to God.[2] Though the gift-offerings in Greek religion (the 'votive offerings') were often less a matter of thanksgiving than a bribe to the god to be favourable, sacrifices of praise were certainly part of festival days celebrating the foundation of the city-states by their patronal gods.[3]

We might then be inclined to say that there has been a change of meaning over the years from the 'literal' sacrifice of things such as animals, to 'metaphorical' or 'spiritual' sacrifices of the heart. But the slippage of meaning is not really to be found here either. The gift-offerings in both the Jewish and early Christian traditions were already spiritualised, and the line between 'literal' and 'metaphorical' is very hard to draw in the case of sacrifice anyway. In the Old Testament it is required of the worshipper that gift-offerings be accompanied by a thankful and contrite attitude which is felt to be as 'real' a sacrifice as the burning of flesh or flour and the spilling of blood or wine.[4] There was a long prophetic tradition of protest against conducting the ritual of sacrifice when it was not matched by moral behaviour, such as the giving of justice to the poor.[5] When the Temple at Jerusalem was finally destroyed, and animal sacrifices were no longer possible, the rabbis could call fasting a gift-offering because the essential element of giving up something for God was still there. The early Christian church also urged its members to offer 'spiritual sacrifices', in such forms as prayer and a life of service to God and others, and it is clear that these were regarded predominantly as gift-offerings: 'Through him [Christ], let us continually offer up a sacrifice of praise to God, that is, the fruit of lips that acknowledge his name. Do not neglect to do good and to share what you have, for such sacrifices are pleasing to God' (Heb. 13:15–16).[6]

The context of this appeal from the letter to the Hebrews makes clear that Christian gift-offerings are to be made in response to the sacrifice which Christ made in his death. The early Christian martyrs who looked on their deaths as 'whole burnt offerings' of praise to God certainly saw themselves as imitating Christ.[7] So, although the New Testament writings do not explicitly identify the sacrifice of Christ as a precious gift-offering, it is a natural conclusion to drawn. It *is* said that Christ gave up his life as an act of obedience to his heavenly Father (see Heb. 10:5–9), and the picture of Christ exalted in heaven is easily understood as the presenting of a perfect human life in homage to God. When Origen, a Christian theologian writing in the second century, portrays Christ as the High Priest in the heavenly sanctuary, it is in terms of his offering himself there as a gift to the Father.[8]

In all these ways the modern idea of sacrifice as a gift seems thoroughly in line with advanced ideas of sacrifice in the ancient world. The saving work of Christ can thus be understood as a sacrifice of homage and obedience to God in which we can join, making his act our own. As he gave himself away in love for God and humankind, so we can give ourselves for God, for our friends and our enemies. However, in the light of our previous discussion about 'subjective' and 'objective' dimensions of atonement (pp. 26–8) it will readily be seen that this is a highly subjective view of the death of Christ, and it is here that the slippage in the meaning of sacrifice is to be truly located. The element of 'gift' in sacrifice is an important insight into the meaning of atonement, but it needs to be balanced by something more objective if salvation is an act of God for us. In fact when the New Testament writers speak of the death of Jesus as a sacrifice they have another dimension of sacrifice to the forefront of their minds; they refer to the type of sacrifice called a 'sin-offering'. In the early church the gift-offerings of Christians were mainly understood as being a response to the *sin*-offering of Christ, rather than the copying of a larger *gift*-offering, and it is at this point that the system of sacrifice in the ancient world may begin to strike a modern person as strange and alien.

In the sacrificial rituals of ancient Israel some sacrifices were understood to be a means of dealing with the problem of sin. They were an act by which it was believed that God overcame the human predicament of estrangement from himself, removed guilt, and freed his people from the threat of just punishment which lay upon the whole community. In the technical term which occurs some ninety times in the Old Testament, 'atonement' (translating the Hebrew verb *kipper*) was made for sin.[9] The New Testament references to the death of Christ as a sacrifice mostly draw their images from this kind of sacrifice, and notably from a Jewish festival where the dimension of sin-offering was prominent, the Day of Atonement held in autumn. The letter to the Hebrews depicts the death of Christ in the colours of this major annual ritual, when the blood of a bull was offered as atonement for the sins of the priests, and the blood of a goat as atonement for the sins of the people. The picture of the sin-offering has made so powerful an effect upon Christian imagination that the English word 'atonement' is usually reserved for it, though the word has the much wider sense of 'being set at one', and sacrifice is anyway only one image by means of which Christian belief has interpreted the cross as an event in which God reconciled the world to himself.

The aspect of atonement in sacrifice was very common by the time of Jesus. It seems that the instructions for the Day of Atonement as we have them in the book of Leviticus date from fairly late on in Israel's life, probably from the period of the exile in Babylon when the priestly theologians were acutely aware of the failure of their nation to obey God and to follow his way of living.[10] So the idea of sin-offering is central to the 'Day', which became the most important of all the Jewish festivals. Though it is likely that some sacrifices were considered to be sin-offerings before the catastrophe of Israel's exile, the sense of national failure and repentance certainly led to a stress on this kind of sacrifice from then onwards. It has become conventional, in studying the sacrificial system of ancient Israel, to categorise sacrifices into three classes: gift-offerings, communion-offerings and sin-offerings.[11] This classification is useful enough, but

Lamb Sacrifice as a gift.

the types should perhaps be regarded as aspects of sacrifice rather than absolutely distinct rites. As G. von Rad suggests, 'whenever sacrifice was offered, several motives were involved'.[12] If they had ever been neatly divided into types, the instructions in the Book of Leviticus show that by the post-exilic period the priests had become expert in producing combinations and mixtures for every need, and the element of sin-offering tended to be included on most occasions.

This needs to be remembered when we consider the imagery for the death of Christ drawn by New Testament writers from the Passover Festival, the second major event in Israel's calendar of worship. At the time of Jesus the sacrifice of lambs in this spring festival was not basically a sin-offering, but a gift-offering of praise and thanksgiving to God for his deliverance of the nation from slavery. Whatever the actual origin of the rite might have been when Israel's ancestors were wandering herdsmen, the liturgy recorded in the Book of Exodus makes clear that it had early become a memorial of the escape from Egypt; the story was told of how blood had been smeared on the door-posts to avert the attentions of the angel of death who smote their enemies (Exod. 12:24–27). However, the element of atonement was not absent from the festival, since it commemorated not only the Exodus but also the making of the covenant between God and his people at that time, and this covenant had been sealed by a sacrifice that the Jewish rabbis regarded as purifying the people from sin (Exod. 24:6–8). Moreover the prayers at the festival looked forward in eager anticipation to the future redemption of Israel from her oppressors, and this would probably include the hope of a new national purification.[13] Thus ideas of atonement were present in historic remembrance and in future hope. When Christian believers followed the initiative of Jesus himself at the Last Supper and identified Christ with the Passover lamb, they were asserting that the new covenant relationship had *now* been made with God through his death. 'Christ our Passover has been sacrificed for us' (1 Cor. 5:7). The new covenant had been sealed with a blood-offering, and so it was natural to associate this with atonement for sin. Above all this connection is made by the writer of the fourth gospel: 'Behold the Lamb of God who takes away the sin of the world' (John 1:29). The first three evangelists arrange the timetable for the Last Supper so that the

65

Passover lambs are slain in the Temple on the day when Jesus breaks the bread and pours the wine, while the fourth evangelist arranges things so that Jesus dies at the very moment when the lambs are killed.[14]

Because the early Christians were so familiar with animal sacrifice as a sin-offering, sacrifice had a strongly objective aspect for them. It expressed the will of God to reconcile his sinful people to himself, and so (to anticipate a technical term to be discussed later) it accomplished the 'expiation' or wiping out of their offences. When Christian believers reflected upon their experience of being restored to fellowship with God through the death of Jesus, the idea of sacrifice was therefore immediately illuminating. 'It's just like a sacrifice,' they said, assuming that this comparison was self-explanatory. But this is no longer our cultural setting, and our view of sacrifice has therefore shifted; the natural meaning of sacrifice has become the rather rational idea of a gift, where in the ancient world this was only one element, and in Jewish and Christian thinking was subordinate to ideas of sin-offering and expiation. Accordingly when the Christian experience of salvation is described in images of sacrifice the subjective meaning of self-giving comes immediately to mind today.

Again we can see that this slippage of meaning cannot be accurately described as a move from literal to metaphorical concepts. It was not only because the practice of *animal* sacrifice was commonplace that the early Christians found ideas of atonement in the cultural air around them. They were also familiar with a whole range of *spiritual* sacrifices that were understood as expiating sin and effecting atonement, and these too provided a backdrop of meaning for the death of Jesus. In the Jewish tradition the highest perceptions of sacrifice among the priests, as well as in prophetic faith, had always insisted upon the repentance of the worshipper to make the sacrifice valid. An offering to atone for sin was no automatic mechanism but required the spiritual sacrifice of a 'broken and contrite heart' to accompany it.[15] Later the rabbis continued this spiritualising tendency as they had to cope with the many scattered Jewish communities in the Graeco–Roman world who could not come to the Temple in Jerusalem to sacrifice, and after the destruction of the Temple in AD 70 they had to adjust to the impossibility of any blood-sacrifices at all. In a revealing rabbinic exchange the Rabbi Joshua lamented, 'Woe to us, for the place wherein the sins of Israel were expiated is destroyed,' and Rabbi Johannan ben Zakkai replied, 'We still have a means of expiation of equal value – the practice of kindness, for it is said, "I will have kindness and not offering." '[16] Of even more direct relevance for interpreting the death of Jesus was the death of a martyr, which was considered in both Jewish and Gentile traditions to be a kind of spiritual sacrifice, having power to atone for the sins of others. Among the stories told in the books of Maccabees about Jewish heroism under persecution, one martyr prays at his death: 'Be merciful to thy people, and let my punishment be sufficient for their sake. Make my blood an expiation for them, and take my life as a ransom for theirs.'[17] Such martyrs died in keeping faith with the law of Moses, but this kind of sentiment can be paralleled in Gentile stories of heroic death for the mother country. As related by the Roman writer Lucan, the young Cato dies affirming that 'This my blood will ransom all the people; this my death will achieve atonement for all that the Romans have deserved through their moral decline.'[18] As Martin Hengel aptly remarks: 'These words help us to understand why the earliest Christian message made sense in Rome.'[19]

The accepted environment of atoning sacrifice enabled the early Christian church to affirm not only that the death of Christ was a means of dealing with the predicament of human sinfulness, but that it was the final sacrifice, dealing with all the sins of the world. The salvation offered in Christ was thoroughly objective; it was an act of God from beyond them, achieving what they could not do, and it was also a 'once-for-all' event in the past. In the words of the writer of the letter to the Hebrews, 'Christ had offered for all time a single sacrifice for sins' (Heb. 10:12). The commonplace practice of animal sacrifice gave them the words to speak about decisiveness; they could say that there was no need for further sacrifices after this one. Mere animal sacrifice was redundant if the Christ, God's Messiah or final representative on earth, had himself been sacrificed. Such a message communicated, even if its content was also shocking. Part of the shock lay in the reason given for the uselessness henceforth of animal sacrifice. It was not just that blood-sacrifice should be spiritualised into heart-sacrifice, as Jewish rabbis and Gentile philosophers were increasingly teaching. In the popular

Greek philosophies of the time there was a reaction against what were felt to be crude concepts of deity implied by blood-sacrifices, and though such sacrifices were rarely rejected completely there was a tendency to put prayer and moral living in their place.[20] But Christians gave another reason for dispensing with animal sacrifice: the *true* blood-sacrifice had taken place, and something had happened upon which all experience of God afterwards somehow depended.

In this study we are acknowledging that salvation is a present event; it happens here and now as broken lives are healed by God. But at the same time we are trying to be true to the Christian conviction that present salvation depends somehow upon a particular historic event, the cross of Jesus. To use the convenient terms, we must keep 'objective' and 'subjective' dimensions together. We can see that the early Christians were attempting to do exactly this when they spoke about the death of Jesus as the final sacrifice. They found that the cross of Jesus had been the decisive act of God in dealing with the problem of human sin, and the picture by which they could most readily understand this was sacrifice. The experience of forgiveness and reconciliation came first, and then they interpreted it by saying 'It's like a sacrifice' and 'yet it's for all time.' For us now the question arises as to how far we can move the direction of thought back the other way, unpacking the inner meaning of sacrifice in order to resolve some of the issues with which a doctrine of atonement confronts us. First can the idea of sacrifice itself throw light on *how* sin and guilt can be destroyed in human lives by an event outside ourselves? Second can it explain *how* the human predicament could be so decisively altered by *one event*? Finally can such enquiries be any more than a historical reconstruction of what Christians believed in the first five centuries? That is, can the image of sacrifice still be useful in its objective as well as subjective sense?

Sacrifice and expiation of sins

The Old Testament offers no proper theory as to *how* the act of sacrifice could remove sin and guilt from the community or from individuals within it. Perhaps the strongest hint about the mechanism of sacrifice is given by the priestly theologians of ancient Israel in Leviticus 17:11, presenting an utterance of God: 'The life of the flesh is in the blood; and I have given it for you . . . to make atonement for your souls; for it is the blood that makes atonement, by reason of the life.'

The declarative form of this text points to God as the one who effects the atonement *through* the ritual of sacrifice, suggesting that sacrifice was regarded as a performative action, like the visual symbols which the prophets often gave to underline a word of promise or threat.[21] So the ritual act gave the assurance that God would surely accomplish what the sacrifice portrayed; it was *he* who broke the link between sin and its otherwise inevitable consequence of calamity. As the widespread image of purification indicates, through the sacrificial death God was believed to 'cleanse away' or 'cover over' the uncleanness of the sin that lay upon the lives of his people. This in itself does not explain why sacrifice should be the appropriate medium for God's act, but a hint is given here when blood is described as containing life. The idea seems to be that the tainted and unclean life of the offending community is renewed by the pouring out of the fresh life present in the blood of the animal. But this rationale is not repeated as clearly elsewhere, and falls short of an Old Testament 'theory' of sacrifice. Indeed in later times the rabbis saw a positive advantage in the fact that God's people were sacrificing in 'blind obedience', suggesting that the action would be less meritorious if some reason could be given for it![22]

But the early Christian thinkers *did* look for a coherent account of how sacrifice effected atonement. The extraordinary claim that the death of one human person had been a final and universal sacrifice made an explanation more necessary, and we may add that the alien character of sacrificial ritual to us today makes explanation more urgent still. While the author of the letter to the Hebrews was content simply to affirm that the sacrificial blood of Christ purified human life from sin, the Fathers of the Church went beyond this. They produced two main answers – either the sacrifice propitiated God, or it averted the threat of the devil. Both these explanations, however, move away from the central point of sacrifice, the first into legal categories and the second into the area of warfare and victory over evil powers. We shall have opportunity later to consider these images of lawcourt and battlefield in their own right; here I simply want to make clear that they do not illuminate the image of sacrifice, and so do not succeed in remaking the meaning of a 'sin-offering' for us.

The belief that God is 'propitiated' by the death of Christ may take several forms. The early theologian John Chrysostom represents the straightforward belief that the death softened the anger of God against sin, and won him over to us.[23] Athanasius feels the conflict between the love and wrath of God that seems to be involved in this kind of appeasement, and suggests that the death satisfied the integrity of God; since God had declared that death should be the reward for sin, Christ took on human nature in order to suffer death and so pay the debt to God's truthfulness on everyone's behalf.[24] Finally, Calvin maintained that Christ paid a debt to the justice of God by taking the punishment which the law of God demanded from those who breached it (a view usually called 'penal substitution').[25] Athanasius and Calvin thus insist on the atonement as a strategy of the divine love, and effectively propose that God is propitiating himself, satisfying the demands of his own truth or justice. The attraction of this kind of theory to the Christian mind has been that it does appear to explain how the death of Christ is a final and decisive event; after this death the anger or truth or the justice of God never needs to be propitiated again. Henceforth, it seems, human beings can be accepted by him.

But we notice that 'propitiation', however sensitively it is stated, is all about dealing with the reaction of God against sin, not about the taint of sin in human life itself. Later I shall be critical of the theory of penal substitution from the viewpoint of the nature of God; here we observe that any theory of propitiation fails to explain how one event can decisively alter the state of human personalities. Sin is a disease, a distortion of existence which alienates persons from God and from each other. A doctor might be said to 'hate' disease as God hates sin, but the first aim of medicine is to remove the disease and heal the patient, not to placate the anger of the doctor. An understanding of sacrifice as propitiation, whether it be of the ritual in ancient Israel or the death of Christ, is too objective and not subjective enough. It does not enter the actual sphere of human sin and lack of response to God, which is our present situation. Salvation must heal broken lives here and now. Now, it is this assault upon defilement in human life itself, or expiation of

70

sins, which the biblical image of sacrifice so powerfully presents. Sacrifice, according to the Israelite and earliest Christian conceptions, is not something human beings do to God (propitiation) but something which God does for humankind (expiation). The point at issue here is not just that theories of propitiation misunderstand the biblical view of sacrifice, but that in doing so they miss the value of the image and fail to identify the experience that underlay it.

In his letter to the Romans, Paul uses the imagery of sacrifice when he affirms that God has set Christ forth 'as an expiation (*hilasterion*) by his blood' (3:25), and similar expressions are used in two other places in the New Testament (1 John 4:10, Heb. 2:17). Although the word *hilasterion* certainly means 'propitiation' when it is used in other Greek texts of the period, our understanding of its meaning in the New Testament cannot be decided by mere appeal to a dictionary. The New Testament writers are challenging established ideas of religion in the world around them, and they do so by drawing upon the Old Testament. The Greek version of the Old Testament (the Septuagint) had already translated the Hebrew verb 'to atone' (*kipper*) by the Greek verb *hilaskesthai*, from which the term *hilasterion* comes. In line with this, the way that the New Testament writers use forms of the verb *hilaskesthai* corresponds to the Old Testament idea of atonement as expiation; God is always the subject of the process and never the object. He acts to deal with sin, to root it out, so that Christ became 'a merciful and faithful high priest . . . to make expiation for the sins of the people' (Heb. 2:17).

The religious experience that underlies this idea of expiation is well expressed by the priestly writers in ancient Israel who concluded sadly that God's people had proved unable to obey him. Other religious leaders in Israel, such as the writers who gave us the Book of Deuteronomy, were hopeful that people could obey God if he made things easy for them by setting his purpose down clearly and simply in a law book (Deut. 30:11–16). But after many years in which Israel continually rebelled against the will of God, the priests came to the conclusion that God himself had to provide a way to deal with the dangerous contagion of sin. He had to provide a way of atonement, if people were to be restored to fellowship with a holy God. So the priestly writers retold the story of Israel's earliest days; their contributions to the first four books of the Pentateuch lay stress upon God's gracious provision of the way of sacrifice. In the books of Leviticus and Numbers they collected together all the instructions for making sacrifices that had grown up over several hundred years, and by presenting them as a revelation to Moses they make clear that the seed of this sacrificial ritual had been given to Israel while the nation was in its very infancy, wandering in the desert. Even more fundamentally, in telling the story of the creation of the world as a seven-day event, they make clear that the climax of creation is the Sabbath; so at the beginning of everything God had provided a day for his people to gather as a worshipping and sacrificing community.[26]

It is such experiences of faith as this that really tell us what the Old Testament writers meant by using the Hebrew word *kipper*, just as the later New Testament writers use the parallel word *hilaskesthai*. They meant that the God who set up the way and place of sacrifice acted there himself to blot out human sin. The linguistic origin of the verb *kipper* is not clear; it may come from word-roots meaning 'to wipe away' or 'to cover'. But the fact that sacrifice was understood to expiate sin in the sense of 'wiping it away', or 'covering it over' by divine mercy, is clear not from linguistics but from the very idea of sin itself. The Old Testament often pictures sin as uncleanness, a patch of dirt and disease that needs to be cleansed away.[27] Unless something is done it will spread until the community hits disaster, and the sin-offering is thus understood as disinfecting or mopping up the dangerous spot. All the images of sprinkling blood and washing with blood that seem very strange to us are part of this view of sin, as a destructive power that needs to be swept out of the community. So in the ritual for the Day of Atonement sin could be dealt with not only by cleansing it away in sacrifice but also by chasing it away, that is, by loading it on to the scapegoat and sending it out into the wilderness (Lev. 16:6–10). Some sin, however, was so deep and deadly in the eyes of Israel that it could only be removed from the community by removing the sinner himself; only his death could get rid of the contagion. It was as if the 'disinfectant' of sacrifice was not strong enough to blot out serious sin that was done deliberately, 'with a high hand' (Num. 15:27–31). The New Testament proclaims that the sacrifice of Christ is greater than animal sacrifice because it deals with all

72

sin without exception, but this very limitation in the Old Testament shows once again the basic meaning of atonement as expiation. Whether by sacrifice, scapegoat or capital punishment in extreme cases, sin had to be removed.

In our own thinking about atonement today we must, of course, be aware that speaking of sin as a 'disease' or 'uncleanness' is only an image. In ancient Israel a confusion could unfortunately sometimes arise in people's minds between moral and physical diseases; a striking result of this literalism could be the abhorrence of leprosy, for example, which Jesus had to challenge with his healing touch.[28] But the value of the notion of sin as a kind of uncleanness is that it makes clear that God's action is called for to cope with it. The basic idea cannot be that God's justice is being propitiated by punishing an animal as a substitute sinner, and this is underlined further by two facts about the sacrificial victim itself. In the first place there was an alternative to using an animal for the sin-offerings; a cup of grain could also be offered by a poor person. Any idea of a transferred penalty would be absurd here, but the pouring out of the cereal, like the pouring out of blood, could be conceived as fresh life used by God to wipe out the taint of sin. In the second place the animal provided for a sin-offering had to be pure and without blemish, perhaps in order for the blood to be potent enough to cleanse sin. So there could have been no idea of transferring sin from the sinner to the lamb, goat or bull which was to be an offering, since it would then no longer be in a state of purity. There is certainly a transfer of sins envisaged in the ritual of the scapegoat, effected through the laying of hands upon the goat's head, but the scapegoat was not a sacrifice offered to God and cannot therefore be understood to be the object of God's punishment. Rather, it was sent into the wilderness 'for Azazel', a mysterious phrase that either means the goat was to be 'for the precipice', plunging into annihilation, or to be 'for the desert demons' as their prey.[29] In either case sin was well and truly carried away.

Although none of the New Testament writers identifies Christ with the scapegoat, this picture was taken up by some of the early Christian Fathers as they tried to understand how his sacrifice would have a decisive effect upon human life.[30] However, the aspect that they seized upon was not so much the carrying away of sin,

Bonhoeffer

PAST EVENT AND PRESENT SALVATION

as the making of an offering to evil powers in order to avert the threat they posed. The religions of the ancient world knew of several kinds of 'aversion' sacrifices, intended to placate malignant forces, and familiarity with these customs encouraged the idea that Christ's death had paid a ransom to the devil. The ritual in which the goat was driven out 'for Azazel' was readily understood as an aversion sacrifice, and so applied to Christ in that way. However, since the Christian Fathers could not explain how an offering could deflect the devil's actions, the aversion idea itself faded into the more general and much stronger theme of victory over the devil and cosmic powers. Today when we speak of someone's being 'made a scapegoat' this is not really a parallel to the ancient ritual of aversion. Rather it evokes the way that people try to escape their own fears and failures by *projecting* them on to someone else, a situation which is actually closer to the aspect of 'sending away sin' in the ancient Hebrew ritual. A person in a community can become the focus of other people's sense of guilt and resentment. For example, Arthur Miller's play *The Crucible*, about Salem witch-trials in the seventeenth century, makes clear that in condemning women as witches people were unloading their own inner sense of guilt upon them. We might then say that Christ himself willingly became such a target, to draw out people's sin upon himself; we recall that they said of him, 'he has a demon' (Mark 3:30).

The modern use of the scapegoat image thus expresses the need for expiation which people feel, although it also describes an unhealthy way of trying to get it. The scapegoat ritual in ancient Israel was not a sin-offering, and was not strictly a sacrifice at all, but like the sin-offering it witnesses to God's own action to expiate sin, which the sacrificial system could affirm but did not really explain. The Old Testament ritual of the sin-offering does, however, tell us that sin is a deeply serious matter, and cannot just be ignored or lightly covered up; 'covering' a sin by the mercy of God is not a matter of sweeping it under the carpet. In the phrase of Dietrich Bonhoeffer, there is no 'cheap grace', and sacrifice makes this clear. It is a costly act for the worshipper, who must choose the best animal from his flocks to present to God for him to use. Perhaps the laying of hands on the head of the sacrificial victim (as distinct from the similar ritual with the scapegoat) is a sign of this cost, saying 'this animal is mine; I give it to you'.[31] Even more costly is

74

the need for sacrifice to be accompanied by the sacrifice of a broken heart, or true repentance for sin. 'Purge me with hyssop, and I shall be clean . . . create in me a clean heart, O God' (Ps. 51:7,10). This is not just a prophetic insight; it is written into the liturgy of the Temple, into priestly religion. In Exodus 19:14 we find that forgiveness of sin must not be automatically assumed from making a sacrifice; the priest has to pronounce the word of forgiveness, announcing to the worshippers that this *is* indeed a sin-offering.

There are also hints in the Old Testament that the sacrificial ritual is a costly matter for God. The utterance ascribed to God in Leviticus 17:11 links the assertion that the 'life of the animal is in the blood' with the words 'I have given it for you'. Life belongs to God; this is the point of forbidding the life-blood to be eaten in the meat. So already there is the idea that God himself is giving the life that is being spilt, a seed that comes to full flower in the New Testament when God is said to give his own son as 'the lamb of God'. Expiation means cost for God as well as man in dealing with sin which is an enemy to life. Several early Christian Fathers were rightly uneasy about the notion that sacrifice *propitiated* God, but it was unfortunate that their reason was a philosophical prejudice against the idea that God could suffer change in any way.[32] While they were surely right to find unworthy the idea that God's hostile attitude to us could be mollified by being offered a sacrifice, their Platonist presuppositions about deity also led them to deny that God could suffer any hurt. But the sacrificial act of expiation recognises that wiping away sin is a costly matter for all involved, including the divine partner.

Sacrifice as an act of power

By doing a piece of historical research upon the terms 'sin-offering' and 'atonement', and by entering sympathetically into the thought-world which produced them, we are able to get to the experience that underlay the picture of the sacrifice of Christ. It was an experience of 'expiation', a wiping out of sin and the guilt it created. The early Christians found that the death of Christ had a powerful effect upon the problem of their disturbed relationships with God and each other, and that this effect was decisive. So they naturally said,

'It's like a sacrifice, a final one.' But how can the image of sacrifice help *our* understanding of salvation in Christ? What sense does an 'expiating' of sin by sacrifice make to us now? The Old Testament image of purifying evokes an experience, but cannot explain a process. Sin, as an offence against God and fellow human-beings, is not literally a piece of dirt or even a disease from which the body can be cleansed. Nor can we think of life as a kind of 'stuff' identified with blood, so that the shedding of blood could transfuse new life into the body of the community. We are left asking how a single event could actually destroy sin in our lives here and now.

We have already noticed that the Fathers of the Church raised this question, and answered it by moving away from ideas of expiation altogether, towards concepts of either propitiation or aversion. Neither of these, however, can explain the impact of the sacrifice of Christ upon the actual state of sin in human lives. Already in the very early days of the Christian faith it seems there was some ambiguity about the effect of the picture of sacrifice. In a study of early ideas of atonement Martin Hengel has suggested that two forms of phraseology were current in the Palestinian church to express the vicarious nature of the death of Christ.[33] Jewish Christians would probably speak of Christ's being 'given up' for many, while Greek Christians would speak of Christ's 'dying for' many. The first form of words carries associations of the sacrificial ritual of the Temple, and is most notably preserved in Mark 10:45; the phrase 'to give his life as a ransom for many' echoes the fate of the Servant of God portrayed in Isaiah 53:12, whose suffering is described as an expiating sacrifice. The second form of words would be familiar to Gentiles who were used to thinking of a hero's death for the sake of homeland or for the cause of truth. So Paul records the tradition he had received in the form that 'Christ died for our sins' (1 Cor. 15:3), and direct references to sacrifice in his letters are not frequent.[34] Hengel's suggestion is that there was a growing preference for the statement that Christ 'died for our sins' rather than that he was 'given up for us', because the 'surrender formula' was too closely connected with the Temple cult of animal sacrifice.

If Hengel is right in his analysis of the forms of text, then we have an early witness to the shifting value of the image of sacrifice. Positively, it was available to interpret the death of Christ; since a covenant would be sealed by a blood-sacrifice, this death could

76

be understood as a new covenant, establishing a new relationship between God and humankind. The finality and universality of the event ('once for all') could moreover be asserted by contrasting this sacrifice with the repetition and exclusiveness of Temple worship. But this very break with the Temple and critique of the existing system meant that the image was undermined; the idea of a final expiating sacrifice is almost auto-destructive. It stretches language to the breaking point, filling the old skins of ritual words with a new wine that cannot be safely contained within them.

In our modern age the objective side of sacrifice is even less comprehensible. In his novel *Riders in the Chariot*, Patrick White voices a criticism of the idea of a universal sacrifice of expiation. One of his characters, Himmelfarb, is a Jew who has escaped death in Hitler's gas chambers but is now persecuted by his fellow-workers in a bicycle-lamp factory in a small Australian town. They stage a mock-crucifixion of Himmelfarb, beginning as a rough joke but becoming more vicious as the victim becomes the target of all the resentments and inner fears of the bystanders. A young man who spits at him is remembering, for example, how his mother died painfully of cancer. Himmelfarb is rescued from his ordeal, though he later dies as a result of his injuries, and the narrator's comment upon the scene is: 'Very quietly Himmelfarb left the factory in which it had not been accorded to him to expiate the sins of the world.'[35] The Jew had wanted to make an offering of love for all people, but his sacrifice was only a private one, having an effect upon only the very few who were close to him and sympathised with him; the women at the cross in his passion story are a simple labouring woman who takes in washing and a half-crazed spinster with a feeling for nature. Behind Himmelfarb's story, the author is being critical about the Christian story that another Jew made a universal atonement through love.

In meeting the challenge of the relevance of the cross of Jesus to all of broken human life, it seems that for us today the idea of a sacrifice will most readily illuminate *our response* to God in the present. The balance has swung from the objective to the subjective power of the image. We can certainly speak of 'making the sacrifice of Christ our own', and the dimensions of sacrifice that come most readily to mind are gift-offering and communion-offering, both of which highlight the element of response. As gift, we offer our lives to God as a sacrifice of praise and thanksgiving, in tune with the self-offering of Christ. Thanksgiving must be central to a healed life, and this is focused in the moment of the Eucharist, which precisely means 'thanksgiving'. Moreover we are responding not only to one past act, but to the way that God goes on offering himself into human lives, constantly entering the pain and predicament of human experience. He calls us into a partnership of sacrifice, into a friendship which makes all life festivity, without ignoring its pain and sorrow. Such an experience of mutuality ·is well expressed by the third dimension of sacrifice in the Old Testament ritual that I have so far only mentioned in passing – the 'communion offering' or 'peace offering'.[36]

The 'communion offering' was not completely burnt upon the altar as was the gift-offering; while the fat and blood were consumed in fire, the lean meat was eaten by the worshippers and could be the occasion for great festivity. This common meal, eaten in the presence of God (Exod. 24:11), represented the special bond of peace between God and his people. It could, aptly, also be a means of providing social welfare, since on some occasions the person offering the sacrificial animal was commanded to share the meat with the poor, the homeless, the foreigner and the slave (Deut. 16:1–12). It seems that the Christian Eucharist from earliest days was understood similarly to be a communion-sacrifice, or fellowship meal with God. The followers of Jesus eat and drink in the presence of their risen Lord, and as the bond of the new covenant, the Eucharist focuses the nature of all of life as a costly but joyful fellowship with God and other people. The dimensions of gift and communion in sacrifice are thus readily understandable to the modern mind, and both are summed up in the secular eucharist of a party or celebration meal. In Virginia Woolf's novel *Mrs Dalloway*, the heroine is gently mocked by her family and friends for the care she expends upon preparing and giving parties, but she regards them as 'her offering to life', bringing together into one moment of wholeness the lives of people who are otherwise scattered and isolated throughout London.[37] 'Love bade me welcome: yet my soul drew back,' says George Herbert in his poem, directing our thoughts to the Eucharist as an invitation to guests.[38] While the poet protests that 'I cannot look on thee', Love gently insists upon serving:

> You must sit down, sayes Love, and taste my meat:
> So I did sit and eat.

Yet if the balance has tipped towards the subjective side of sacrifice with ideas of gift and communion, it is exactly from this perspective that its 'expiatory' or objective dimension can still be meaningful for us. We must admit that the image of 'expiation' does not in itself explain how one event can so decisively destroy sin in our lives, but it does point us towards the cross as a final event, with power to change the human situation ever afterwards. Though we shall need to turn to other images of atonement to understand this more fully, we can at least say that the sacrifice of Christ *enables* and *creates* our gift-offerings and communion-offerings. Since the offering of ourselves to God and to others is the denial of sin, the overcoming of an attitude of self-centredness and rebellion against God, then we can call the offering of Christ which produces this effect a 'sin-offering'. In this sense the sacrificial death of Christ expiates sin; it expiates sin by changing sinners.

Though this view of expiation may seem a modern one, it was propounded by Origen in the second century AD, and portrayed by the Hebrew poet who wrote the Song of the Suffering Servant (Isa. 52:13–53:12) in the sixth century BC. In his more theoretical account, Origen employs the curious phrases that Christ 'propitiated the sinner' or 'propitiated sin' or 'propitiated men to God'. Though it would have been clearer for Origen to have avoided the word 'propitiate' altogether, since he is not using it in the usual sense of appeasing God's anger, the main thrust of his meaning comes across. As Frances Young helpfully paraphrases it, 'to propitiate is to change the sinner, to produce a situation in which God can accept him back and forgive him'.[39] Origen explains that a just God can accept the sinner because when a man truly repents he is no longer evil; 'he is turning to good and is good and deserves good'.[40] Thus, if the cross of Christ has power to turn the sinner towards good, we may truly say that it 'wipes away' sin. We shall need to explore other, more personal, images of atonement to explain *how* it accomplishes this transformation of the sinner. But the point of the image of an expiating sacrifice is that it insists we think in this way.

In fact the Song of the Suffering Servant *shows* us the power of a sacrifice to transform other human lives when it is made in a person rather than in animals, fruit or cereal. The poet presents the mysterious figure of God's ideal servant, whose horrific suffering is described as a 'sacrifice for sin' (*asham*, or guilt-offering). A traditional Christian understanding of this passage, appealing to phrases like 'he bore the sin of many' and 'the Lord has laid on him the iniquity of us all', has been that the servant propitiates the righteous anger of God by receiving the punishment due to others. Though a propitiatory note does creep into the later prayers of the Maccabean martyrs to 'let our punishment be a satisfaction on their behalf',[41] this particular poem of a righteous sufferer must be taken on its own terms. If we enter imaginatively into the scene which the song portrays we find a drama of expiation, in which the suffering of the servant brings other people to a realisation of their own state, and to a healing repentance. The speakers in the poem are a group of witnesses to the rejection and grief of the servant, perhaps foreign kings who have been watching the sufferings of Israel in her exile. They speak of a moment of revelation, a 'discovery of the new thing of which they had never dreamt':[42]

> Surely he has borne our griefs,
> And carried our sorrows;
> yet we esteemed him stricken,
> smitten by God and afflicted.
> But he was wounded for our transgressions,
> he was bruised for our iniquities;
> upon him was the chastisement that made us whole,
> and with his stripes we are healed.
>
> (Isa. 53:4–5)

This is a confession of a changed attitude. They had been despising the servant, dismissing him with a self-righteous contempt as one who has received the due reward for wickedness. But then they suddenly realised the truth: *they* were the ones who were straying from God ('all we like sheep have gone astray', v. 6), and his suffering has been for their sake, to turn them back. The servant has been laden with chastisement in the sense that he has been identified with the sin of others and the punishment which is its natural consequence. This participation of the innocent in the fate

80

of the guilty has power to atone, to cleanse the sins of the onlookers. As we enter into the experience of the speakers, who have been brought to confess their guilt and receive healing, we feel the implications: God has burdened the servant with suffering in order to create a change in their perception of themselves, to make them aware of their perilous condition before God.

Although we need not here pursue in detail the vexed question about the identity of the servant, we notice that there are several layers of meaning. At the very least, the prophet is encouraging Israel in her exile to *become* the servant, to respond to God in faith and to allow God to use her sufferings, and her promised return home, as 'a witness to the nations' (Isa. 43:10, 49:6). Yet the servant portrayed is an ideal one, who is not suffering for his own sins as Israel was. So perhaps the author is also saying: 'Suppose there were a person who was completely innocent, and trusted in God in the midst of terrible suffering – would not that be a witness that would create response to God in others?' By identifying the Suffering Servant with Christ, Christian faith proclaims that this hope has come true in him. His death, 'numbered among the transgressors', creates a spirit of repentance and, we may say, of gift-offering in others. In accord with this we can now re-use the language of expiating blood as found in the key text of Leviticus 17:11. We cannot think of shed blood as a pouring of new life into the tainted life of the community, like a transfusion of some dynamic 'life-stuff', but we *can* speak of a new situation which the death of Jesus creates. After his sacrifice nothing can be the same again; life has been changed, objectively, because the human race must henceforth reckon with the promises and demands of Christ. So the shed blood of Christ does renew life; it brings something new, once and for all, into the human community. We are now all witnesses to the Suffering Servant.

The court poet and fashionable rake of the Restoration period, John Wilmot, certainly felt the effect of the Servant Song, and his reaction is an important testimony of a poet that needs to be set beside the deliberations of theologians. At the end of a career devoted to finding pleasure and to brilliantly satirical attacks on the weaknesses of others, he experienced a genuine moment of religious illumination as someone was reading the words 'Hee hath

81

no form or comelinesse, and when we shall see him there is no beauty that we shall desire him'. According to his own description:

> As he heard it read, he felt an inward Force upon him, which did so enlighten his Mind, and convince him, that he could resist it no longer. For the words had an authority which did shoot like Raies or Beams in his Mind; so that he was not only convinced by the Reasonings he had about it, which satisfied his understanding, but by a power which did so effectually constrain him, that he did ever after as firmly believe in his Saviour, as if he had seen him in the clouds.[43]

In the days left to him before his death he wrote a new satire that portrays Virtue in the form of the Suffering Servant, homeless, naked and rejected, but with a hidden power to strike the onlooker with the light of truth:

> Therefore in Garments poor, it still appears,
> And sometimes (naked) it no garment wears. . . .
> But Clouded oft, it like the lightning plays,
> Loosing as soon as seen, it's pointed Rays.[44]

The Song of the Suffering Servant makes us feel the drama of expiation, but it does not explain the process by which the sacrifice of the servant transforms the onlooker. Indeed the application of sacrificial terms to a person who is despised and rejected bursts open the categories of sacrifice altogether. As Claus Westermann notes, it 'involves a radical desacralisation of sacrifice'.[45] While the expiatory victim was meant to be a sacred object set apart from ordinary use, pure and unblemished in appearance, this victim is disfigured by suffering and 'makes his grave with the wicked'. Similarly the image of expiatory sacrifice can be applied to the person of Jesus just because of his death in forsakeness and shame; but at the same time the very circumstances of the death question the common understanding of sacrifice. Other images will therefore be needed to explain why the death of Jesus should be an event of unique power, purifying human lives here and now, but the image of sacrifice sets out the path for our exploring.

5

The demands of justice

Sermons can be heard at passiontide and on Good Friday which set out to explain the meaning of the cross of Jesus, but which make little reference to the human circumstances which brought about his death. The impression is sometimes given that the death could have happened anywhere, in any way, even on any planet. All that seems to be needed in some accounts is a bare death, in order to provide a divine solution to the problem of human sin. Some preaching thus reduces the event of the cross to a factor in an equation, formulated by a divine mathematician; a death is needed to balance the cosmic sum, and a death is provided.

But we cannot avoid reference to the political and social setting of the execution of Jesus when we think about the meaning of the atonement from the viewpoint of the demands of divine justice upon human life. It is in the image of the law court that the actual historical event of the cross seems to stand most close to the interpretation which faith has given to it. In the event, Jesus was tried, sentenced and executed as a criminal by both Jewish and Roman law. If we follow the apostle Paul in the preaching of faith, then we proclaim that we have been 'justified by God's grace as a gift' through the death of Jesus (Rom. 3:24); that is, we have been acquitted in God's own law court where we stand on trial. As Paul portrays the scene, God has 'cancelled the bond which stood against us with its legal demands: this he set aside, nailing it to the cross' (Col. 2:14). Somehow, because Jesus Christ was condemned as a criminal in a human law court, we have been declared to be innocent in God's sight. But in that 'somehow' there is vast room not only for mystery but also for misunderstanding.

The picture of the law court seems to connect so closely to the historical event on Golgotha, and yet this very image can be used in a way that destroys genuine continuity between the event of the cross and the meaning which we give to it. When the death of Jesus is presented as a legal device for satisfying a divine justice which has been affronted by human sin, this can easily reduce the doctrine of atonement to a mere formula. If the social and political circumstances of the execution of Jesus are then mentioned at all, it is often along the lines that he was given an irregular trial, and was the victim of a frame-up. But, as I have already argued (pp. 37–9), although faith can never be proved by historical enquiry, it can be illuminated and shaped by it. So the place of the law within the society of the time, and people's expectations abut the nature of justice, can set some boundaries for a Christian understanding of the cross. It seems, for instance, that the apostle Paul was influenced in developing his ideas of atonement by the difficult fact that Christ had suffered the kind of death which was shameful according to the Jewish penal system: 'it is written, cursed be everyone who hangs upon a tree' (Gal. 3:13).

The innocence of Jesus

In the earliest Christian witness, while the death of the promised Messiah obviously presented some difficulty to faith and understanding, the meaning of his resurrection seemed quite clear. It meant that God had declared Jesus to be innocent; he had approved of him and vindicated him. The one whom men had condemned as a criminal was now revealed as the Lord of the universe, as early Christian preaching proclaimed: 'Let all the house of Israel . . . know assuredly that God has made him both Lord and Christ, this Jesus whom you crucified' (Acts 2:36). In his gospel Luke has the Roman centurion on duty at the crucifixion assert that 'Certainly, this man was innocent' (23:47). But in what sense was Jesus innocent? We must not hasten quickly to the conclusion that his trial had been a travesty of justice, or that quite the wrong verdict had been passed upon the charge brought.

It does not really matter in the end whether there were technical irregularities in the way the various parts of the trial of Jesus were conducted, before the Jewish Sanhedrin and in the Roman court of Pilate. There was evidence to convict Jesus on the main charge brought under the Jewish law, that of blasphemy. He was probably accused not of committing blasphemy against God directly, but indirectly, through setting himself above the law which God was believed to have given through Moses. As I have already argued,[1] it is reasonable to conclude from the testimony of the gospels that Jesus had indeed presumed to question a way of life based on an unchangeable religious law, since he had offered the forgiveness of God freely, irrespective of success in keeping to legal codes of behaviour. However, since Jesus suffered a Roman form of execution, he must also have been condemned under a political charge of sedition, though the Roman authorities no doubt found it convenient to have him condemned first by the Jewish court on its own religious grounds. That way there would have been less chance of popular protest against the action of the occupying power. Again we must admit that there was substance in the political charge, in that Jesus was certainly disturbing the peace and troubling the status quo through his ministry, though there is no evidence that he was a Zealot or was engaged in armed rebellion.[2]

When the gospel writers assert the innocence of Jesus and find this confirmed by his resurrection, they are therefore claiming something much more profound than a mistaken verdict. They are asserting that he was right in his conflict with the very institutions of law. He was right to question the assumptions of the legal system that accused and condemned him. With regard to the Jewish law, which aimed to govern every aspect of life from the perspective of a relationship between God and his people, Jesus was right to see that the terms of this relationship could never finally be fixed in a code of rules. Useful though law was as a guideline to the purpose of God for healthy human life, it could never claim absolute authority in itself. As far as the secular law of Rome was concerned, Jesus also makes the will of God the final claim upon the citizen. Even the achievement of Roman law and order, the Pax Romana which was Rome's gift to the world, could not claim an absolute value if peace and quiet had to be disturbed by a call to national repentance.

According to the early Christian witness, Jesus was right in finding that the lifestyle which God demands will challenge the absolute demands of law, whether religious or secular. But this leads on to another sense in which Jesus is innocent; he actually lived the life which expressed the purpose of God. Those who crucified him for a breach of the law were in fact the blasphemers and rebels against the true aim of God for human life, which is more fundamental than any law. Thus they represent the whole of humankind, which has failed to fulfil the purpose of God for his creatures. The gospel writers make this representative guilt clear when they portray the Jewish authorities as bringing false witnesses against Jesus in his trial, though the exact nature of the lie is not clear. Pilate shows his guilt in a different way, through his indecision when faced with responsibility. We may think that the evangelists, in portraying Pilate as washing his hands of Jesus, are rather too anxious to show that the Roman state considered Christ to be no danger to it. After all, Jesus *was* a disturbing element, and so were his followers in the early church. But they are rightly concerned to say that Christ and Christians are no enemies to a healthy order which people need to live in peace and security.

Thus Christ is innocent, in so far as he is right to challenge the absolute claims of law in the name of a deeper obedience to the will of God. Given this meaning of 'innocence', it is hardly surprising that a prominent New Testament picture of atonement uses legal language only to blow the legal system wide open. When the apostle Paul declares that 'we are justified by God's grace', he portrays us as guilty criminals on trial in God's law court. We, no less than those who accused Christ, are deviants from God's purpose for humankind, and yet the divine Judge acquits us. This amazing behaviour on the part of God is traced by Paul to the effect of the death of Christ: 'Since all have sinned and fall short of the glory of God, they are justified by his grace as a gift, through the redemption which is in Christ Jesus, whom God put forward as an expiation by his blood, to be received by faith' (Rom. 3:23–25).

If God were acting by the strict letter of the law then he must condemn us, but he justifies us (the Greek verb is *dikaioō*) – that is, 'puts us in the right' with himself. This justification of the unjust is, as one New Testament scholar puts it, 'contrary to all the rules of human justice' and 'in plain contradiction' of conventional legality.[3] But at the same time the legal picture does have force in illuminating the *nature* of this scandalous mercy; legal language is actually being used to defeat a way of life based on mere legalism. To see how the metaphor works in this complex way, it is essential to recognise that it is not borrowed from a Roman law court, but from a Hebrew one where all procedure was civil. There was no public prosecutor for any case, and the scene is thus of two litigants going to court, one accused of a crime by the other. The judge puts the accused either in the right ('justifies him') or in the wrong ('condemns him'), with the accuser also liable to being put in the wrong if his witness was false.[4] Now this Hebrew setting means that 'justification', while a legal term, is at root a matter of relationships. Hebrew law was concerned with the health of the covenant community, and so the appellant who was justified was actually being received back into fellowship with the community by the personal will of God; the one condemned was being shut out, at least as long as his punishment lasted.

All this means that we can paraphrase the legal statement that God 'justifies us' in the more personal terms that God 'accepts us' into relationship with himself, and since he accepts the unjust it makes 'justification' virtually equivalent to forgiveness. God treats us as righteous; but this neither means that he instantly transplants perfect moral qualities into us nor that he simply *pretends* we are righteous by a kind of legal fiction. For God to make us righteous means that he puts us in a 'right relationship' with himself, in full awareness of our guilt and wrongdoing. This verdict is not only legal but 'eschatological' (belonging to the final events); the judgement which ought to be passed upon our lives on the last day of human history has already been anticipated here and now, in our favour (Gal. 5:5). Paul perceives that we cannot merit this situation by any good works of our own, and so this righteousness (*dikaiosune*) is not our own at all, but is 'the righteousness of God' – established by him and to be received in faith (Rom. 1:17). He accepts us into the fellowship of his own righteous life.

The Hebrew context provides a further dimension to this picture. The Hebrew judge was not appointed simply to apply the law in an abstract manner; he was expected to intervene actively to 'vindicate' the poor and oppressed, to *give* them justice in the face of their enemies.[5] So to say that God 'justifies us' in atonement is to say that he acts to save us from the evil powers that oppress our lives and accuse us; he does this as a good and 'righteous' Judge who is full of compassion for his creatures. But when we recall that we have actually brought ourselves into our perilous situation by our own sin, we can see that once again a legal metaphor is being used to depict an act of God which goes far beyond mere legal categories. When we ask *how* God can accept transgressors into fellowship with himself in this scandalous way, then Paul makes clear that it can only be through the cross of Jesus. Because Christ has died, God puts us in the right. But the revolutionary way that this legal term is being used, to break the very mould of law, means that we cannot directly extract a mechanism of atonement from the metaphor itself. Justification is the glorious, startling fact. The picture does not in itself explain *how* the cross of Christ achieves it for us.

Some Christian thinkers have certainly proposed the theory that God acquits us because he has already passed our sentence on someone else instead, namely Christ; they suppose that God *does* pass the sentence that the law demands, but carries it out on a substitute. However, we must be clear that a theory of 'transferred penalty' like this cannot be directly deduced from the metaphor of justifi-cation. Those who have held this view (notably Calvin) have built it out of various New Testament materials including Paul's assertion that 'we are justified by grace', because it seemed to them to make most sense of all the components there. We therefore have the right, and indeed the responsibility, to ask whether such a view can express the extravagant mercy of God as meaningfully for us today as it has in past ages. What is clear is that 'justification' itself simply asserts that when we are summoned into God's law court, against all the evidence and the strict demands of the law, he acquits us. Because Jesus who was 'innocent' has died, we are 'put in the right'.

The judgement of Jesus

The metaphor of justification makes a link between the historical event of the cross and the interpretation which faith gives to it: because Christ was condemned in a human law court, we are acquitted in the divine law court. But when Christian believers came to ask *how* the sentencing of Christ and his subsequent execution could have brought about our atonement, as well as using such metaphors as sacrifice and battle they drew upon a further range of language that belongs within a legal and penal context. They concluded that we are reconciled to God because Christ suffered not only under human judgement but under *divine* judgement in his death. Though we must be careful not to confuse this idea with that of justification, which is the bare statement of our acquittal, the ideas are obviously related. Paul brings them together when he asserts that: 'For our sake he made him to be sin who knew no sin, so that in him we might become the righteousness of God' (2 Cor. 5:21).

It is easy then to see how the theory developed in the Reformation period (following earlier hints, especially in Augustine)[6] that Christ had suffered a penalty as a substitute for us. If we believe that we are given the 'righteousness of God' through the death of Christ, and if it is the righteous obedience of Christ that has brought about this new situation for humankind, then with Paul we can graphically say that Christ *is* 'our righteousness' (1 Cor. 1:30) just as he is our redemption. But it is quite another step of thought altogether to propose a doctrine of salvation by legal transfer, where God agrees to impute Christ's righteousness to us in exchange for our guilt and penalty being imposed upon him. Such a conclusion is not drawn by St Paul or by other New Testament writers. It involves certain other assumptions about the demands of law and the nature of divine justice. We must then be careful to examine the logic of the 'coming of Christ under divine judgement' in its own right, before we go on to ask *why* this should be of saving effect for humankind. To that question there can be, as we shall see, answers of either a more objective or a more subjective kind.

At first glance an even closer link seems to be woven between event and faith if we say that Christ was condemned by God as well as man in his trial and death. The line of a well-known hymn, 'In my place condemned he stood' would thus have several levels of meaning. The apostle Paul seems to have made this shift of thought when faced by the puzzling fact that Christ had apparently died 'under the curse' of God by suffering a form of death which was reserved in Jewish thought for those who had made themselves outcasts from God's covenant people. He concluded that Christ, although innocent, had suffered the wrath of God against sin for our sake: Christ had come within the sphere of 'law, sin and death' (Rom. 8:3–4, cf. 6:10) and had been 'made as one with the sinfulness of men' (2 Cor. 5:21 NEB) for us. Another author, the writer of 1 Peter, refers to the historical scene of Christ before his accusers, and asserts that 'He committed no sin, he was convicted of no falsehood . . . [yet] in his own person he carried our sins to the gibbet' (1 Pet. 2:22–24). Above all Mark the evangelist, describing the event of the crucifixion, records that Jesus felt himself to be abandoned by God, making the terrible appeal 'My God, why have you forsaken me?' (Mark 15:34). It was these New Testament texts that Luther had in mind when he declared that Christ became the greatest of sinners. Though his language is extravagant, he catches something of the awful nature of this counting of Christ among transgressors: 'And all the prophets saw this, that Christ was to become the greatest thief, murderer, adulterer, robber, desecrator, blasphemer, etc., there has ever been anywhere in the world . . . in the sense that he took these sins, committed by us, upon his own body.'[7]

But there appears to be a logical problem in bringing together the historical condemnation of Christ under Jewish and Roman law with a standing under the condemnation of God. We have seen that the resurrection of Jesus must mean that God declares Jesus to be right in his conflict with the institutions of law. Even if we believe (with Paul) that the law of Moses was of divine origin, the mere fact that Jesus was sentenced under its provisions cannot mean that he became for that reason an outcast from the fellowship of God.[8] After all, by giving the law ultimate status above the personal will of God, his accusers were *misusing* what was meant to be a good gift of God. Is the apparent connection between the trial of Jesus by men and his judgement by God therefore an illusory one, stemming from a coincidence of language? There is in fact a real connection, and insisting upon the historical location of the judgement of Jesus puts us on the right path for understanding *why* the early Christian believers thought that Jesus had been judged as a sinner for us. Though Jesus is in the right about God's purpose for human life and lives it out perfectly, he is put to a shameful death by the authorities. That is, he willingly undergoes a death under the worst conditions of alienation and forsakenness, and so opens himself to sharing to the utmost degree our own human experience of death as an enemy.

By entering a situation where he dies as an outcast, Jesus is in a position to undergo a death of total estrangement. Relationships with his friends are broken – 'they all forsook him and fled' – and he is the target of intense hostility from all sections of human society – crowd, priests, soldiers, fellow victims. This need not in itself mean complete desolation, as other sufferers in human history have discovered, putting their trust in God or the cause for which they have sacrificed themselves. But it is a situation which makes it *possible* for Christ to suffer the same penalty against sin that human beings endure when they insist on making themselves the centre of the world. If we break our relationships with each other and with our Creator, then this isolation will be confirmed and made more terrible in death; we are left alone with ourselves. The millionaire who cuts himself off from all human fellowship, trusting no one and living in island suites at the top of hotel buildings, dies on an island of his own self. This kind of death, experienced as an enemy, is nothing less than God's verdict upon a way of life that is astray from his purpose. Thus in dying as an outcast, Jesus is poised to plunge into an abyss from which others have been saved; that he does fall into the deep is shown by his cry, 'My God, why have you forsaken me?' This can only mean that Jesus so completely identifies himself with sinful human beings that he shares their experience of standing under God's verdict upon distorted human life. He feels himself abandoned not only by fellow men and women, but by God himself; he stands with the Godforsaken. He stands in death where he need not be – among those who trust in themselves and suffer the consequences. Using a biblical expression, we may say that he dies under the 'wrath' of God.[9]

To say that Jesus dies under the judgement of God does not mean, therefore, that God directly *inflicts* some kind of penalty upon him. It is to speak of his complete identification with humankind, and so his experience of the consequences of human sinfulness. He plumbs the bitter depths where broken relationships run out into desolation and nothingness. He hangs on the cross at the end-point of human sin, at the focus of all human self-destruction. It is a thoroughly biblical perspective to call this exposure to the disaster which humankind brings upon itself an enduring of the 'wrath' of God. With our background of western legal tradition, when we speak of God as 'judge', we often think of him like a human judge, selecting (like the Mikado in Gilbert and Sullivan's operetta) 'the punishment to fit the crime' and imposing it upon the offender. This is judgement as penalty inflicted from outside. But although the Old Testament writers do sometimes speak of God as *imposing* a penalty on his erring people like this, we must remember that the Hebrew view of God's ultimate sovereignty in the world gives rise to an idiomatic way of speaking in which everything can be represented as directly caused by God. In fact when the prophets and psalmists think more personally about the relationship between God and his people, they speak of the divine judgement upon human beings in another way, in terms of his 'giving up' people to the natural consequences of their own sin. It is characteristic of Hebrew thought to depict God as 'hiding his face' from his disobedient people, or 'letting them go'.[10] His righteous wrath against sin is worked out by his surrendering people to the way they themselves desire to tread. They insist on running over the precipice of their own making, and God in his justice lets them go, although with deep pain of heart. Prophets like Hosea and Jeremiah especially make clear that God himself sorrows for the tragedy of his people's self-inflicted wounds,[11] and that while in justice he 'gives them up' to the consequence of their actions, he does *not* give up wooing and enticing them back to himself:

> How can I give you up, Ephraim?
> How surrender you, Israel? . . .
> My heart is changed within me
> My remorse kindles already . . .
> For I am God and not man.
>
> (Hos. 11:8–9 NEB)

Hosea identifies the Assyrian army as an instrument of the wrath of God against Israel, as does Jeremiah the army of Babylon a century later. But it is clear from their analysis of the nation's life that a rotting Israelite society, deeply divided within, morally corrupt and weakened by greed, is a natural victim for an invader. God's wrath is his active consent to the working out of their sin into its inevitable results. This is what the modern theologian Paul Tillich calls structural justice in the universe, which God's righteousness and human responsibility demands.[12] One of the Hebrew terms for 'offence' (*'awon*) is the very same word as 'punishment'; sin, as we have already seen in our study of the image of sacrifice, like a kind of patch of uncleanness, expands until disaster happens.[13] Wrongdoing carries the seeds of its own penalty within itself. It is this Old Testament insight that the apostle Paul takes up in his portrayal of the wrath of God against 'those who suppress the truth', repeating three times that 'God gave them up' to their own passions and their own futile minds (Rom. 1:24–28). We only have to ask *how* the judgement of God becomes visible here and now in the present, rather than at some future day of judgement, to realise that the 'wrath' of God can only take the form of the result of human actions. Otherwise we would have to start identifying punishments that God is supposed to inflict, presumably events such as earthquakes, famine, sickness or bankruptcy. It hardly needs a fable like Albert Camus' *The Plague* to realise that such a view promotes an unhealthy sense of human guilt and an image of a tyrant God.

Discussion about the nature of the justice of God has, however, often become confused by a false distinction between 'personal' and 'impersonal' views of divine wrath. Some, who have advocated the kind of view of divine wrath for which I have been arguing, have suggested that this is an 'impersonal' form of judgement, and therefore a more sophisticated approach than the 'personal' anger which the Old Testament God manifests against sin.[14] But the more we become aware of the mystery of personal reality, the less superior we ought to feel about the human emotions (anthropopathisms) ascribed to the God of Israel. To say that judgement is not a penalty imposed from outside human life, but a natural consequence flowing from the sin itself, is not at all to espouse an impersonal view of the wrath of God. If God is passionately involved in the life of his creation, guiding it and sustaining it from within, then he is involved in the process of natural justice. He consents in an *active* and personal way to the structure of justice in the world, and so this consent can truly be called the 'wrath' of God against sin which spoils his work. It is with the pain of disappointed love that God allows his people to go their own way to their self-imposed tragedy, but it is just that he should sustain creation in a way that supports these consequences.

In the isolation of the cross Christ thus endures the human condition of being under the judgement of God. He suffers the full consequences of human sin, not only because he is an innocent victim of the sin of others, but also because he enters with total sympathy into their own situation, reaping the bitter harvest they were inevitably sowing for themselves. The identification with sinners that was first marked in public by his baptism among the penitent of Israel, and which continued in his table-fellowship with the outcasts throughout his ministry, was sealed by his death among criminals. Moreover for Jesus to experience God's verdict must be a more dreadful matter than for any other person. Since he went beyond the mere code of moral rules to see God's intention for human life more perfectly, so he must have felt more intensely the depth of separation from God that sin produced. His whole life had been lived in nearness to his heavenly Father and so the loss of that fellowship must have been the greater tearing apart.

Nor could Jesus take a philosophic view, like Socrates in the hour of his execution having a drink and a joke with his friends, that his truths would live after him. As we have seen, the mission of Jesus was not a message but himself. When Jesus set the free forgiveness of God above any system of law, this was not an eternal truth independent of himself. It was bound up with his own person, for he understood himself to be the agent of God's forgiveness. The death of Jesus seems to be the end of his mission, which was God's own mission of restoring humankind to himself. The cry of Jesus upon the cross can rightly be retold, as Jürgen Moltmann suggests, in the form 'My God, why have you forsaken yourself?'[15] It is only through the surprising event of the resurrection that Jesus' ministry continues, and disciples are gathered. In the actual darkness of the cross the law seemed to have won in its conflict with free forgiveness.

In these ways we may begin to make sense of the claim that Jesus died not only *with* sinful humankind but *for* us. He dies the death that all die who are estranged from God and each other, but yet he dies it in a way that no one else ever has or ever could. He has undergone the same penalty as all God's rebellious creatures, and yet he has endured it in a unique way. Now the experience of the early Christian community was that this event had a saving effect; they found that it had removed the sting of death for all those who have faith in God, had reconciled the creation to God and had overcome the powers that foster human rebellion against him. The apostle Paul articulates this experience with a careful use of legal language, prompted (as we have seen) by the circumstances of the event itself. Christ came under judgement (was 'accursed') so that we can be 'justified'; he shares in our penalty and we share in his 'righteousness'. These are possible ingredients for a logical theory of atonement based on the law court, but Paul does not construct one. When Paul asks *how* this identification of Christ with sinners who stand under the wrath of God secures salvation, his legal language is brought into the service of his characteristic doctrine of atonement by 'union' with Christ.

According to Paul, God has sent his son into the arena of sin and death so that we can be united with him in a death and resurrection like his. Through faith and baptism we are 'in Christ', or 'in the body of Christ', so dying with Christ in the body of his death and rising with his body of life (Rom. 6:1–11). Thus we have passed through the ultimate penalty upon sin (death) with him, and we have emerged with him into a totally new kind of spiritual existence. Consequently we have 'died out'[16] on the accusations that the moral law levelled against us as sinners. Paul finds an illustration for this release in a further expansion of the law-court metaphor; any person is only subject to the law while he is alive, and by 'dying' with Christ we are now freed from all charges (Rom. 7:1–6).

Christ participates in the human predicament of being under judgement, and exposed to divine wrath. If we ask what this achieves for us, the Pauline answer is that it makes it possible for us to 'die in' the body of Christ, and rise to new life with him. But we are bound to go on then to ask what it can mean to say that we have died 'in Christ'. Some may be impatient with such a question, refusing to reduce all religious statements to deductive argument, and affirming a kind of union with Christ for which the word 'mystical' is indispensable. This is a strong position, but a reasonable faith will still want to probe a little into the mystery. We are really asking the question we have often posed before: how does the particular death of Christ so long ago have a crucial effect on our life before God? In answer, Christian thinkers since Paul have adopted his insight that Christ has shared deeply in the human penalty, and have built it into a more systematic theory of justice. The actual situation of Christ's death as a criminal, and the fact that experiences of condemnation and acquittal are basic to human social life, encourage us in this path. But the way we build such a model of atonement will be bound to depend upon the presuppositions we hold about the function of penalties within human society in general.

It will be generally agreed that penalties are meant to deter a criminal from his intended crime, or at least to deter others from copying him. Thus legal penalties aim to keep society safe. But people may well differ about the emphasis to be placed upon two other results that a penalty might have, namely retribution and reformation. If retribution is seen as the controlling feature in the application of penalties in society generally, then a strongly 'objective' view is likely to be taken of atonement when Christ is said to suffer under the divine penalty against human life. If the controlling idea is that of reform, then a correspondingly more 'subjective' view is likely to be taken of atonement. As in two other models of atonement, sacrifice and victory, we can detect a swing towards a more subjective account in modern times.

Atonement as paying a debt to justice: an objective emphasis

When we enquire why any penalty is imposed in human society, one possible answer that might be given is that it pays a moral 'debt' of some kind. Retribution falls upon the offender, in the sense that he must repair through his own punishment the system of justice which he has broken. Indignant justice requires satisfaction. This answer has, however, taken a rather different form in various ages. In the early medieval period an offence was understood as being committed against the honour of the overlord as embodying justice in his own person, and justice thus required that the lord's own dignity be restored. In the Reformation period the honour which had been infringed was understood as being that of justice itself, or law as a supreme principle which rulers simply dispensed. This political change involved correspondingly different ideas of the satisfaction that could be offered, or the payment that must be made. It also led to different versions of a theory of atonement, which are usually marked by the names of Anselm and Calvin.

If an offender must make restitution to the personal honour of another, then debt can be paid in two alternative ways – either by punishment or by satisfaction. If satisfaction could not be made through suitable payment of money, goods or service, then punishment must be inflicted. This was already the case in Roman private law, in disputes between fellow-citizens, though not in public or criminal law where the ideal of justice always required punishment. In the later setting of feudal society, where justice had become a matter of the rights of the great overlords, any crime at all was an infringing of their personal honour and so demanded the alternatives of either satisfaction or punishment. The scene was set for Anselm (Archbishop of Canterbury 1093–1109) to propose a theory of atonement based upon the demands of divine justice. He portrays God as our feudal Overlord, and human beings as his servant-subjects who have offended against his honour, for 'sin is nothing else than not to render to God his due'. By failing to submit our wills to his supreme will we have failed to give honour to God, and so we have 'taken away from God what is his own . . . and this is to sin'.[17] We must either pay a satisfaction to God which restores his honour or suffer the punishment of eternal death. The human predicament is that we are obliged not only to restore the honour we have withheld, but also to pay 'additional compensation' to his outraged dignity, repaying 'something pleasing, in proportion to the injury' we have done to him. Since this is impossible, it seems we must vindicate God's honour in the alternative way, through punishment. But this is the reason for the incarnation and death of the Son of God; by dying as a perfect man who did not deserve to die, Christ offered his life freely to God and so gave him honour in an infinite amount. Thus Christ pays off our debt through his merit, releasing us from the threat of punishment, since God was bound to reward him for his great gift.

Cur Deus Homo? asks Anselm: why did God become man? He answers: because only man *must* pay the debt of honour, and only God *can* pay it. Anselm rejects a view of 'penal substitution';[18] Christ is not punished in our place, but releases us *from* punishment *through* satisfaction. When, however, later on in the Reformation period, the Roman view of criminal law as a supreme principle had been re-established in society, replacing feudal law, there could be no alternative to punishment if the law were infringed. The only satisfaction that could be offered to outraged justice *was* punishment. When Calvin built a theory of atonement upon the principle of divine justice, he therefore concluded that 'the guilt, which held us liable to punishment, was transferred to the head of the Son of

God'.[19] God's law had been infringed through human sin, and so penalty must be inflicted upon offenders in orders to maintain the moral order of the universe. In the act of atonement Christ pays the debt to justice by bearing the necessary punishment instead of humankind. The Son offers himself as a substitutionary victim on whom the penalty of God the Father falls.

It should be clear from our earlier discussion that Calvin has rediscovered the insight of St Paul which Anselm missed – that Christ endured the wrath and judgement of God against human sin. However, he understands this situation in an Anselmian way, as a matter of reparation and 'compensation'.[20] With the other Reformers, Calvin was impressed by Anselm's argument that divine justice required satisfying, but he reworked it in terms of criminal law. The result was a theory of 'penal substitution' that is present neither in Paul nor Anselm. Modern works on the doctrine of atonement tend to go astray here when they refer loosely to a 'penal theory' in Paul, which Calvin has supposedly revived. Paul certainly has a view of the 'penal suffering' of Christ, since Christ is identified with the human situation of being under the divine penalty (understood as God's consent to the natural consequence of human sins). It would also not be entirely out of place to say that Paul conceives of Christ as a 'substitute' as well as a representative for humankind, since no human being need die the kind of death that Christ died. But these two factors do not in themselves amount to a theory of 'penal substitution', according to which atonement is achieved through a *transfer* of penalty.

Such a theory requires the addition of an Anselmian view of debt repayment and a Roman view of criminal law. The resulting concept of paying a debt to divine justice is then equated by Calvin with a sacrificial ritual of 'propitiating' God, which we have already seen to be a mistaken exegesis of the biblical portrayal of the sacrifice which expiates sin: 'He offered in sacrifice the flesh which he took from us, that through the expiation which he made he might destroy our guilt and appease the righteous wrath of the father.'[21]

Calvin's theory of penal substitution is compiled from biblical insights, and makes exhaustive reference to biblical texts. Like Anselm's account however, which makes much less direct appeal to scripture, it remains an *interpretation* of scriptural elements coloured by views of justice at the time, and as such it has a number of weaknesses. The primary defect, employing the technical distinction we have continually used, is that both Calvin's and Anselm's theories are too 'objective', at the expense of the 'subjective' dimension in atonement. They portray atonement as a transaction, or legal settlement, between God the Father and God the Son in which we are not involved, despite being the erring sinners concerned. To suggest that our debt to justice is paid, either by a gift of honour (Anselm) or a transferred penalty (Calvin), certainly expresses the once-for-allness of the cross of Jesus. But it does not integrate the human response to God, and the healing of human personality here and now, into the act of atonement.

Of course theories of this kind *add* our response of repentance and trust as a second stage or appendix. The subjective dimension is not entirely lacking. But it comes as a later appropriation of what has already been achieved, and misses the heart of atonement as the restoring of a relationship between persons, and as an event of reconciliation in which all estranged partners are involved. It is hard to see the relevance of human reaction to the atoning act if this is already complete, and Calvin is indeed quite consistent when he makes the link between past event and present salvation one of election. God includes human beings in the event of salvation only in the sense of choosing those who should have justifying faith (and alternatively, adjudging others 'to eternal death').[22] The logical conclusion to all this is the one which Calvin's successors drew: the atonement is limited to the elect, the ones (we might say) whose names are written into the legal contract.[23]

The over-stress upon objectivity in these theories is well illustrated by the Reformer's treatment of Paul's phrase that 'Christ is our righteousness'. As I argued earlier, and as the Reformers recognise, Paul is affirming that the death of Christ results in our 'right standing' before God. Yet this cannot exhaust the rich meaning of this highly compressed phrase. Since Paul's thought is controlled by the idea of our personal union with the body of Christ, the phrase must also hint at our sharing in Christ's own life of obedience before the Father. So atonement is the giving of a new relationship which actually transforms our being; it must happen to us here and now. To employ Paul's own language, justification (being put right) and sanctification (being made right) are inseparable dimensions of one process.[24] Luther and Calvin, however, are reacting against the medieval tradition that justification is an inner renewal, or an infusion of divine love;[25] they suspect the implication of this to be that salvation depends on our own good works which spring from a renewed life. Thus they emphasise God's free *declaring* of us to be righteous, but thereby create the impression that Christ's righteousness is 'imputed' or reckoned to sinners as a merely legal transfer, matched by the transfer of our punishment to Christ.[26] Calvin does open up a prospect of 'mystical union' with Christ, which can be called a 'fellowship in righteousness' because we are 'implanted in his body',[27] but this experience is completely separated from atonement. It is a life of increasing sanctification which *follows* justification as a second stage.

As soon as we understood the 'righteousness of Christ' as an active obedience to his Father throughout his ministry, coming to a climax in his willing submission to death, then it seems that our sharing in such a righteousness must be actually *part* of the event of atonement. But for Luther and Calvin, this 'active obedience' of Christ inspires a moral life which follows atonement: the act of atonement itself is founded only upon the 'passive obedience' of Christ, or his enduring of penalty. Anselm, of course, *had* understood the active obedience of Christ to have atoning effect, in so far as Christ gave infinite honour to the Father; but he still misses the personal and subjective dimension of the apostle Paul's thought, since he understands atonement to be a matter of satisfying divine justice, achieved through transfer of the surplus merit Christ had heaped up. As we shall see, Paul's deep insight that Christ's active obedience to God actually restores the relationship between God and humankind can only be properly worked out when we get away from ideas of merit altogether, and consider salvation as a matter of the healing, growth and shaping of personalities. Protestant theologians who followed Calvin were intrigued by the place which Christ's active obedience had within the scheme of salvation, but as long as they held to a theory of penal substitution they remained perplexed and confused about it.

The over-objectivity of theories of legal satisfaction is further demonstrated by their treatment of the problem of sin. It is usually said that a doctrine of penal substitution 'takes sin seriously', and the Reformers certainly seem more aware of the insidious power of evil than Anselm, for whom sin is simply failure to do what is required. But what the Reformers actually take seriously in their view of atonement is, like Anselm, the *debt* which human beings have incurred against God through sin. They are not grappling with sin as a power within human existence which warps and distorts personality and relationships in the present. A substitute penalty, like a gift of honour, only pays off a debt to the offended dignity of a divine law. Even if the offence is understood in more personal terms as being against the holiness of God, the satisfaction provided does not cope with the actual brokenness of human life here and now which God's holiness abhors. It is often said by advocates of penal substitution that 'God cannot tolerate sin', that his holiness is implacably opposed to it. But then we would expect, like a doctor who is hostile to disease, that God would want to root sin out of the lives it infests. Penal substitution simply achieves the wiping of a debt from the pages of a divine ledger. Anyway the parable of the Prodigal Son should make us ponder whether such a ledger exists at all. The loving father in Jesus' story is satisfied by the return of the erring son, and refuses to accept that there is any debt outstanding against him, despite the reminder of the elder brother than he has 'wasted all your substance in riotous living' (Luke 15:30).

As the elder brother wants to set a principle of retribution and compensation over the mercy of the father, so theories of legal satisfaction set a law above the character of God. The theory runs that God cannot forgive us until the punishment demanded by justice is exacted. This conceives justice as law with ultimate authority; even when the law is said to be God's own law, the theory still requires God to act in a way which is confined by legal restraints. Law has ceased to be a useful guideline to the purpose of God for his creatures, and has become a supreme principle. It does not allow God the freedom to exercise a justice of another kind, a justice which certainly requires a penalty to fall upon rebellious creatures while they are in the state of rebellion, but which is satisfied when they repent and return to him. In discussing the place of justice and judgement within atonement, a fundamental decision about perspective has to be taken: is the wrath of God a judgement inflicted from outside human life, or God's consent to the natural consequence of human sin from within? If it is the latter, as I have been arguing, then God is free to forgive those who repent.

101

There is no other blockage than their own stubborn resistance to the love of God. In Jesus' story, as long as the son remains in the far country and in the pigsty, he is under judgement, and the penalty he suffers is the disaster he has brought upon himself, dressed in rags and eating husks. But when he takes the road back to the father's house he finds that all judgement is lifted. The problem, if we apply this parable to human life in general, is how to get the son to 'come to his right mind' and remember the Father's house. Actual human sons do not just come to themselves; they have to be fetched, and this means that God must himself take a journey into the far country.

Both Anselm and the Reformers were in fact uneasy about the status they were giving to 'honour' or 'law', which seemed to make the atonement a necessity imposed upon God by a superior principle. As a God of love he desires to have fellowship with his creatures, but law apparently demands that certain conditions be satisfied first. Their answer was to equate either honour or law with the will of God himself: 'all (events) necessarily took place, because he willed them'.[28] But then the logic of the argument has been undermined. If God's free will is in fact the final factor, then he is also free to dispense with a satisfaction altogether. According to the Reformer's doctrine of penal substitution God is free enough anyway not to apply the law of retribution in a thorough manner; law should demand that the offender himself be punished, and in allowing for a substitute to take his place the strict logic of the law has already been broken. Why should God then not be free to dispense with retribution altogether? The historical location of the condemnation of Jesus in a human law court ought to shape the meaning of atonement here. In the name of religious law Jesus was crucified as a blasphemer, and yet God vindicated him by raising him from the dead. It would thus be very odd if the meaning of atonement were that God was exacting a penalty that had to be paid off before he could forgive, since this would be just the rigid view of law that Jesus was opposing in his Father's name.

The doctrine of penal substitution relies even more strongly than Anselm upon a retributive view of penalty, and in this it is heavily conditioned by its social context. Calvin assumes that when law, whether human ('positive law') or divine, is broken punishment must always be inflicted. As a matter of fact this no longer seems as self-evident to us today as it did in past ages. In our society when a law is broken punishment is not inevitably imposed. It will be appropriate at times, but other kinds of response to crime can also be suitable, such as probation, suspended sentences, conditional discharges and community service. Moreover the abolition of the death penalty in many western societies means that we no longer attempt to exact the equivalent penalty for wrongdoing that Calvin assumed was axiomatic for a doctrine of atonement as transferred penalty. Indeed every preacher ought to ask himself whether a theory of penal substitution can even be understood in a society where it is no longer possible to use such words as 'Christ suffered the death penalty for us'.

Though voices are raised from some quarters of the Christian church today protesting that these circumstances just go to show 'how far standards of law and order have slipped below Christian ones', the situation in fact reflects the mind of Jesus; he himself set aside the Old Testament law of retribution which called for a just equivalence in punishment: 'You have heard that it was said of old an eye for an eye, a tooth for a tooth. But I say to you – do not resist one who is evil.' Jesus cannot be making an inflexible rule that one should never resist violence, for that would be simply replacing one law by another. Rather he is giving a picture of what it can, in some circumstances, mean to love in the kingdom of God. There are no limits to love, and it may even be the loving thing in some situations to offer no resistance to an aggressor. On other occasions love for neighbour may demand that we resist. The point is that love lays down the limits; there is no such thing in the kingdom of God as offended honour that must be satisfied. If our love may involve setting aside a penalty, can God act any differently?

The absolute place that Calvin gives to law is understandable in the political context of his time, where the authority of law could operate as a check upon the arbitrary behaviour of earthly princes. In the end, however, the theory of penal substitution fails to unify the love of God with his wrath. This is not because its proponents have little to say about the divine love: both Luther and Calvin emphasise that love motivates God to provide the means of propitiation for humankind. Nor is it because they revive the Pauline insight that the judgement (or 'wrath') of God against sin is revealed

103

at the cross alongside his love for the sinner; after all, love that ignores justice is mere sentimentality. Rather the problem lies with the particular concept of divine wrath with which they are working, as a penalty imposed from outside to 'match' the crime. This entangles the Reformation theologians in such disputes as to whether the Father is actually angry with his Son, and what the exact nature of the death is which he inflicts upon him. In contrast, when the judgement of God is understood as his personal consent to the natural outworking of people's estrangement from God and each other, then we can think of Christ as participating in our experience of being 'accursed' without any suggestion that the Father is punishing the Son on our behalf. Further, the affirmation that 'God was in Christ' entails the belief that God himself shares in the desolation of human life, entering the realm of estrangement and hostile death. Paul Tillich sums up: 'Not substitution but free participation is the character of the divine suffering.'[29] But we still have to ask *why* such a coming of Christ under judgement should have atoning effect, if it is not a matter of paying a debt to justice, and here we need to begin with a different perspective upon the function of penalties in society.

Atonement as responding to the aims of justice: a subjective emphasis

Prominent among the reasons why human societies, or the guardians of their law, inflict penalties should be a concern to reform the offender. If penalty is to help achieve a harmonious society striving for a common good, then it must lead to penitence in the offender, to an acknowledgement of wrongdoing and to a change of will. If a penal system can achieve this, it has done all that it really needs to do. In large social groupings this aspect will always have to be mixed with other (lesser) elements such as deterrence and an upholding of the dignity of law, but within the intimate group of a family penitence will be all that is required when the parents impose discipline. What justice demands is not payment but repentance; it is finally 'satisfied' not by any penalty in itself but by the change of heart to which penalty is intended to lead. Here R. C. Moberly, in his study *Atonement and Personality*, has plumbed the depths of relationships within the family:

A child sent away for disobedience, offers shyly to come back. Is that shyness the wistful shyness of desire? or is it the awkward shyness of defiance? . . . In that wistfulness, dim, child-like, half-unconscious as it is, may be the true germ of what, in its perfected blossom, would be the outpouring of the confession of a penitent.[30]

If we take the model of the family as a paradigm for all levels of society, then we begin to see more clearly what God in his justice demands from his rebellious creatures. The Father wants nothing less than the return of his children to him; he passes his verdict against sinful human life in order to awaken a spirit of penitence within human beings. The 'wrath' of God is manifested (in the sense I have defined it above) only to evoke a wistfulness for the renewal of fellowship. There is a clue here for understanding how Jesus can stand *with* human beings in death, in all its physical and spiritual dimensions, and yet also do something *for* them which they cannot do. He offers the perfect confession of penitence to the Father, which humankind has otherwise failed to offer. This insight was first powerfully set out by J. McLeod Campbell in the mid-nineteenth century; in a striking phrase Campbell maintained that at the cross, enduring the divine verdict against human sin, Christ said 'Amen to the judgement of God'.[31] He says yes, not from the heights of heaven but from the depths of human despair. This thought was extended by P. T. Forsyth, who called the central chapter in his study on the atoning work of Christ 'The cross, the great confessional'. Forsyth underlines the fact that what must be confessed in penitence is not merely human sin, but the rightness of the divine view of it:

As with one mouth, as if the whole race confessed through Him, as with one soul, as though the whole race at last did justice to God through His soul, He lifted up His face unto God and said, 'Thou art holy in all Thy judgements, even in this judgement which turns not aside even from Me, but strikes the sinful spot if even I stand on it' . . . This is the taking of sin away . . . the absorption and conversion of judgement into confession and praise.[32]

Thus, in the irony of the divine mercy, Jesus is crucified as a law-breaker. In setting his ministry above the letter of the law he perfectly fulfils the lifestyle God intends for humankind, and just because he so completely knows the aim of God for human life he can the more fully confess human failure when he undergoes the death of estrangement. But now the usual question arises as to how that one event in the past can relate to the salvation which we experience in the present. If we were to suppose that God's justice were satisfied simply by the confession of Christ on behalf of all humankind, this would come very close to Anselm's notion of a payment of honour to God, with all the problems of excessive objectivity we have explored. Indeed a substitutionary penitence would be quite as detached from us as the substitutionary penalty proposed by Calvin. Rather, the justice of God demands, and is satisfied by, the penitence of people down through the ages as they share in the penitence of Christ. This of course is a more subjective account of atonement than paying a debt, but we can secure a firmly objective element when we perceive that the restoring of our relationship with God here and now *depends* upon that one great confession. In Chapter 4 I have argued that the image of sacrifice can help us to visualise the cross as a creative event, with power to enable continual response to God. The images of judgement and penitence make another contribution to this idea of atonement, when we consider the influence of the penitential spirit of the crucified Jesus.

Moberly in his account of atonement gives an illustration from family life (at least as he knew it in his time) which illuminates the power of one personality to create a change of attitude in another. He draws the sketch of a child who has gone 'very far wrong', and who does not really understand the situation or the reason why his father is disciplining him (which need not, Moberly hastens to add, necessarily involve any formal punishment); the child has mixed feelings of shame, rebellion and bewilderment. The problem then is how to create a change of attitude in the child, and Moberly suggests that the mother here can act as a mediator of feelings. She can enter into the experience of the erring child, identifying in profound sympathy with his confused feelings, while at the same time knowing the reality of the situation and the mind of the father in the way that the child does not. So she can feel the shame that he should, and as the child feels her own feeling, he is moved to a true repentance despite his limits of understanding. This is true mediation, not a reconciling of the father to the child, but a communication of feeling to the child that has a transforming effect:

> Do we not recognise at once that the profoundest hope for the child's real change lies in the reality with which the parents enter his grief and shame; so enter into it, on his behalf, as to win it to be in him, where in fact it was not until it was first in them, and in him only from them? Do we not recognise, in particular, the place, in his discipline and purifying, which may belong to the voluntary distress and endurance of the mother?[33]

This is no question, it is to be observed, of a penalty which the father insists on inflicting upon someone, and which the mother intervenes to bear. Nothing whatever is inflicted by the father on the mother. Indeed nothing is, strictly speaking, inflicted on any one by any one. This experience illuminates the work of Christ on the cross, as our 'mediator-mother'. The penitence of Christ, on our behalf, wins us to repentance. The confused sense of shame and truculence that might have made us turn further from God, as portrayed in the story of the childlike Adam who hid from his maker in the garden, can now be taken up into the confession of Christ. We are awakened to our responsibility, and made to face up to the real damage done by sin, which is exposed in the cross of Jesus. This analogy of mediation in the family requires, we notice, that the penitential spirit of Jesus be more than a phenomenon of past history. The experience of having our rebellious feelings transformed into a healing repentance can only be expressed by saying that the mediator is present in his community, 'thereby attracting men to himself' (Schleiermacher).[34] Faith in the resurrection of Christ involves the claim that the crucified Jesus goes on living in a manner which is more than merely in the memory of the church. The Spirit of God, moving in human hearts and minds, is now characterised by the personality of the earthly Jesus. When New Testament writers represent both Jesus and the Spirit as making intercession for us before the Father, they are not describing a legal plea on our behalf by skilled advocates; they are expressing the experience of having our human response to God taken up into a deeper and wider movement of response within the being of God himself.[35]

Moberly recognises a breakdown in his analogy of sympathetic identification, for in the case of a human family, 'the father is not the mother, and the mother is not the child'. The father certainly enters into the feelings of the mother-mediator; as one in sympathy, whatever the mother bears in grief and shame the father bears too. Yet they are not at one in the sense that Father and Son are one within the triune Godhead. Nor is the mother so totally identified with the child as Christ is with humankind. Moberly thus rightly appreciates that his illustration is only 'suggestive' of atonement. But his illustration also needs modifying in a way he fails to realise, conditioned as he is by family life of the late Victorian period. As Moberly depicts the scene, the father enters into the feelings of the child only through the mother; he feels with her, and she in turn feels with the child. According to Moberly, she thus mediates the experience of the child to the father, but many modern fathers (including myself) would resent this assumption that only the mother can empathise directly with the child. The picture is of the Victorian father as an external figure, belonging to the wider world, and the mother as belonging to the home and so nearer to the children. But surely we must say that the father enters into the situation of the child just as the mother does; it is with a more fundamental togetherness that they mediate sorrow and repentance to him.

Following through the analogy in its revised form, we can affirm that God the Father also participates directly in human estrangement. He always suffers the pains of rejected love as, in his justice, he allows his creatures to go their own way to their self-imposed tragedy, and he feels their own sense of waste and disappointment with them. One of the problems of a theory of penal substitution is that it depends for its logic upon a strong individualisation of Father and Son as independent subjects, which makes it hard to speak of the one personal reality of a God who becomes vulnerable for love's sake within his own creation. Advocates of the theory of propitiation may insist that the Father is in effect propitiating *himself* through sending the Son to die, since he is one in will and love with the Son, but the logic of both Calvin and Anselm is that the satisfaction must be offered by a man (the human nature of Christ) to God, since it is man who has failed in honour or law-keeping. Thus one cannot avoid speaking of a propitiation being offered in some way *to* the Father, and as humanity can only offer a proper satisfaction (infinite honour or infinite pain) in union with the divine Logos, the divine Son must be the one who finally makes the offering. In contrast, the idea of the participation of God in human alienation avoids the danger of separating the persons of the Godhead, while no less recognising their distinction. For if participation is to be atonement, God must identify his being with a human *son* who is open in relationship to God as father, and this identification is only possible (as I have argued in Chapter 3) if there is already something 'son-like', or a mode of sonship, within God himself.

The fact that atonement-as-participation requires God to share in human life as both Father and Son can be seen in the aspect of judgement within atonement. If God is to participate in our situation of being under his own judgement, and if this participation is going to enable us to respond with true penitence to his offer of forgiveness, then participation must take a form that awakens us to our predicament and God's reaction to it. This form can only be a relationship between a son and a father. For in the cross there was the awakening of one son of man to a clear understanding of the tragedy of human sin, and there was the response not of antagonism and self-excuse but of agreement to God's judgement upon human life. As the true Son confesses the rightness of the Father's viewpoint upon spoiled human existence, he moves us to make the same confession. The cost of confession could be nothing less for him than a sense of total forsakenness; confession on behalf of others meant a complete identification with them, and so a breaking of communion with his Father. This means a sharing in human desolation by God in the modes of both Father and Son, though from different perspectives; if for the Son this was the suffering of his own death, for the Father it was a suffering of the death of his Son.

As we survey the situation in which the true Son stood, we can see another dimension of objectivity in atonement. Though God is always offering forgiveness to human beings at the cost of entering into their situation and suffering human hostility against him, in the event of the cross of Jesus there is a unique experience of the human condition. God has never gone further, nor will he ever go further, into the far country of our estrangement and despair. This we can say because of the unique response of the Son involved. In the response he receives from this Son the forgiving Father has the deepest possible experiences of human life, in its thought, emotions and attitudes. At the same time the particular historical circumstances form a theatre where the other actors in the scene (crowd, priests, rulers, criminals) express typical human hostility to God. If we think of forgiveness as a healing journey which the forgiver makes into the experience of the offender,[36] then it is clear that God has always been entering into the human experience of death and alienation; he could not have done so for the first time at the cross. But a God who journeys like this can enter a new depth of the human predicament when a Son so intimately bound to him in obedience suffers desolation, and makes response from that abyss.

This 'new experience' for God is the truth behind the 'objectivity' of the theory of penal substitution, which declares that something has happened for God the Father as well as for human beings at the cross. Despite the approval given by Calvin to the classical doctrine that God cannot change or suffer, the idea of propitiation must imply some change in God, as several Church Fathers perceived in early years; if God is propitiated, he is satisfied where before he was not, and can now forgive us where before his justice forbade it. But the true objectivity of the cross cannot be that God undergoes a change of attitude to humankind; instead we see that he increases in experience. That God should have new experiences of the world is not, of course, a necessity thrust upon him, but is founded in his own free choice to limit himself out of love for his creatures.[37] The longer the pilgrimage of God into human life, the more decisive the effect will be upon *us*; so God faces what is new for him, not in order to change his attitude, but to change ours, as we encounter the God who has taken the journey into the far country in extravagant love for the prodigal.

Christ, the obedient Son, comes under judgement in the human law court and also before God his Father. This legal model of atonement tells us not that he endures a penalty instead of us, but that he can create a penitence within us. Such penitence is expiating, in that it wipes out sin by replacing an attitude of sinful rebellion with an attitude of home-coming. Tragically, however, the human spirit can turn even penitence into an attempt at propitiation. Such a feeling is expressed in Jean-Paul Sartre's play *The Flies*, in which Sartre retells the ancient myth of Orestes as a powerful protest against the need to atone for guilt. In Sartre's version Orestes refuses the demand of Zeus that he should repent for the murder of his mother, Queen Clytemnestra, who had earlier connived at the murder of his father. Orestes perceives that the gods want to imprison him in a life of continual remorse and mourning, and so take away his freedom as a human being. When Zeus offers salvation in exchange for the 'trifle' of a little penitence, Orestes warns his sister, 'Take care, Electra. That trifle will weigh like a mill-stone on your soul,' and resolves defiantly to accept the consequences of his own actions: 'human life begins on the far side of despair'.[38]

Sartre well understands that the religious idea of atonement calls for spiritual sacrifices of expiation, namely sorrow and penitence. But he can only understand these as a propitiation of God, leading to the loss of human freedom. Of God himself, however, we may say that his life is now 'on the far side of despair'; he has faced despair with us so that we may turn our faces to him as free people.

6

The decisive victory

'We shall overcome . . . some day.' The song which sprang from the Civil Rights Movement in the United States has been adopted as the anthem of many movements for liberation in our time. Whether sung by people struggling for political freedom, for women's rights, for racial equality or for the protection of our environment, it expresses a widespread feeling that wholeness of life can only be attained through the defeating of hostile forces. It affirms that there are oppressive powers in our world to be over-come, and though at present they seem to hold the upper hand they are doomed to pass away. The theme of victory over dark powers also takes shape in the modern literature of fantasy, in such classical forms as J. R. R. Tolkien's *Lord of the Rings*, and in more popular forms like the film *Star Wars* (with its secular benediction, 'May the force be with you'). Nor is it only the world outside us that seems like a battleground; modern psychology has made us aware of the conflicts that surge within us, especially between our conscious mind and those elements of our personality that have been forced down into the dark depths of the unconscious to emerge as ferocious threats.

It seems then immediately relevant to our experience to interpret the atoning work of Christ as a divine victory over hostile powers. In 1931 the Swedish theologian Gustav Aulen wrote his influential book *Christus Victor*, lamenting the neglect of this image of the atone-ment, drawing attention to its prominent place in the New Testa-ment and the thought of the early Church Fathers, and predicting that what he called 'the classic idea' was coming back. The last couple of decades have shown how right he was, as both in theology and practical Christian action appeal has constantly been made to the *victory* of Christ in his life, death and resurrection. Wisely Aulen believed that the Christian church needs this understanding of the work of Christ in order to 'keep steadily in view the reality of evil in the world, and [to] go to meet the evil with a battle song of triumph'.[1] We can indeed hear many echoes of this song from the earliest days of the church. The scriptures of ancient Israel already portray the saving activity of God in human history as a defeating of the dragons of chaos,[2] and the New Testament writers draw upon this colourful imagery when they proclaim the victory of the cross of Christ, through which 'the Prince of this world [was] cast out', 'the great dragon was thrown down' and 'the power of him who has death at his command' was 'broken'.[3]

The dramatic theme of the victory of Christ over evil certainly grips our imaginations. However, questions still arise, as with other images of the atonement, about the effect that one past event can have upon our experience of salvation today. In what sense *could* evil have been decisively defeated in the cross of Jesus, if its power seems undiminished today? We live in a century which has already witnessed the monstrous evil of the Nazi Holocaust, and in which the whole of humankind is threatened with a nuclear holocaust. In the face of such rampant evil in societies and individuals, what victory could have been objectively achieved in the death of Christ? Aulen suggests that we should think of a 'turning point' having been reached in a war which is not yet over,[4] but we must still enquire in what sense the tide of battle could have turned, given the evidence of persistent evil. Again, if any defeat *was* objectively inflicted upon evil at a single point in the past, what link can there be between *that* victory and the overcoming of sin and evil in our own lives in the present? In the subjective dimension of salvation we may affirm that the Spirit of God calls and enables us to confront evil here and now, but in what sense can this battle actually depend upon the victory of Christ? We can answer these questions, I suggest, only when we have identified more clearly who these enemies are that we claim to have been overthrown, and so it is with naming the tyrants that we begin.

Identifying the tyrants

Although the enemy whom Christ overcomes has simply been identified as the devil or 'Satan' in much of Christian tradition, the New
Testament actually portrays a wide diversity of forces that threaten
to destroy human life and whose power has been broken by the
cross of Christ. The oppressors fall into three main groups: first the
sinister triumvirate of sin, law and death, second the ambiguous
figure of 'Satan', and finally the host of 'principalities and powers'.
'Demons' are harder to classify, but there is a sense in which (as
we shall see) they can be associated with all three groups. In fact
all these enemies interact with each other and foster each other's
attack upon the wholeness of human life.

This conflict between darkness and light, in all its varied forms,
must not of course be read as an eternal one, as if the very nature
of the universe were that of a struggle between God and a principle
of evil. In the Christian perspective there is no absolute 'dualism'
of two equally balanced powers locked in everlasting and mortal
conflict. The forces of evil have no power in their own right, but
live like parasites upon what is good. That is, they are powers in
rebellion against God and are perversions of what is God's real
purpose in creation. If we can apply the word 'dualism' to this
picture then it is a highly modified one, in which the cosmos is a
theatre of revolt. We shall find this insight into the nature of evil
to be fundamental to the answering of the questions I have raised
above. But at the same time, the fact that atonement can be understood as God's overcoming of powers that are *opposed* to him makes
clear that God himself is the agent in salvation. Models of atonement where God is placated by a human offering interrupt the
action of God himself in love and compassion for humankind, even
if the offering is made by Christ in his humanity; by contrast the
image of victory makes clear that atonement is initiated and carried
through by God himself in Christ.

Sin, law and death

In the thought of the apostle Paul the chief enemies who confront
human beings are sin, law and death; each is a perversion of something good, and they are linked together to hold humankind in a
severe bondage from which Christ has now released us. 'Sin' as

disobedience towards God and rejection of his intentions for human life is a distortion of the freedom which God has granted to his creatures. Although it is therefore a human attitude towards God, a wilful breaking of relationship, Paul speaks of sin as if it has a kind of objective existence, 'reigning' in our bodies, making us slaves and finally 'killing' true life.[5] By personifying it in this way, almost as if sin itself were a kind of 'demon', Paul is naming a dimension in his experience and alerting us to the reality of sin.

Earlier I outlined the way in which our freedom, in tension with our limits as human beings, makes us anxious.[6] In an attempt to quell this anxiety, we place our security in things within the world that are less than God. We make things that are 'less than ultimate' our 'ultimate concern' (using the helpful terms of Paul Tillich), and thus we fashion idols out of our possessions, our careers, our spare-time interests, our political allegiances and finally ourselves. Sin is a failure to trust God in the midst of our anxiety, and its nature is idolatry. As the apostle Paul concludes in his exposure of human sin, 'They exchanged the truth about God for a lie and worshipped and served the creature rather than the Creator.'[7] The result is that the good things of the world that ought to be our tools become our masters: if we *must* have something because it has become our final concern, then it has enslaved us. Thus idols acquire a power over us that can only be called demonic. As John Macquarrie sums the matter up, 'The idol, in so far as it has become the focus of a distorted existential concern, reacts by further distorting, enslaving and finally destroying the being of the person who has given it allegiance.'[8] While this is a modern way of analysing the situation, it is built upon the ancient experience of idolatry, and helpfully interprets the way that Paul speaks of sin as an objective power.

Paul links sin with the bondage of human life to the law. He believes that the rules for right living which Israel received through Moses and other religious leaders did in fact have their origins in revelation from God; in this sense the law is 'holy and just and good'.[9] But with the law another good thing has become perverted. What was meant to point, in a shadowy and provisional way, to God's will for human life, had been made into an end in itself. Paul considers the law as a kind of emergency measure, provided by God to deal with the crisis of human sinning.[10] In one sense then, the law as an enemy to human life was sanctioned by God; in its commands and warnings it proclaimed God's hostility to a life lived under the power of sin. It exposed wrong-doing. But it had also become an enemy in quite another sense. No legal regulations can properly express God's character and his purpose for his creation, which are fully revealed not in a written code but in the life of a person – Jesus Christ. What matters, according to Paul, is to obey 'what the law *aims* at', so that the law may be regarded as a mere 'tutor', preparing us to live in tune with the life of Christ who is 'the end of the law'.[11] But the law had been treated as an absolute and had thus become a tyrant. People looked to the keeping of the law for their security, and so we may say that even the law of Moses had become an idol, with demonic power.

Thus as soon as the law, spiritual though it was, came into the human realm it was distorted by sin. Conversely Paul perceives the supreme irony that the religious law actually becomes an incentive for sinning. 'In the absence of law, sin is a dead thing.' He points out that it is only when the law forbids us to do certain things, such as coveting, that the desire is aroused within us to do them! So 'sin found its opportunity in the commandment'.[12] Significantly, Paul calls the whole Old Testament, including its legal parts, 'the oracles of God', and finds the basic nature of God's address to his people to be that of promise.[13] Writings with this character point towards a future in which God will fulfil his promises, in ways that may be quite unexpected. But humankind cannot read law in that perspective; people cannot bear the openness and uncertainty of promise and so turn law from a 'foreshadowing' of the new life[14] into inflexible rules which bind life and actually foster sin.

Human life today is still bound by legalism. Faced by the uncertainties of life, we take sets of rules that have a perfectly proper place as guidelines and turn them into absolute masters. Some may extract rules from the scriptures of the Old and New Testaments, usually making a selection that suits their own view of life, and treat these as the touchstone of the spiritual life; for others the regulations may be a union rule-book, or the constitution of a club or society. Others treat the laws of the state as infallible precepts that must be obeyed whatever the circumstances; protest and campaigns for reform are always branded as disloyal or unpatriotic.

The apostle Paul perceives that the unholy alliance between sin and law leads to the dominion of the third tyrant – death. 'The

commandment which should have led to life proved in my experience to lead to death.'[15] Once again a good thing – the natural
boundary to human life – has been distorted by sin into 'the last
enemy'.[16] As we have already seen in Chapter 5, death can only
confirm the nature of a life in which relationships have been broken,
and so it brings an utter alienation to those who have alienated
themselves. Within the Christian understanding of resurrection from
the dead, God overcomes the nothingness of death with a new act
of creation. In contrast to the Greek view of immortality, we have
no guarantee in ourselves of defeating death, no built-in survival
capsule of an immortal soul. We are summoned to hope in God for
something new in the face of death. If we trust in ourselves, death
is thus bound to appear to us like a threat lurking on the horizon
of life. So the writer of the letter to the Hebrews speaks of Jesus as
liberating through his death 'those who, through fear of death, had
all their lifetime been in servitude'.[17]

Of course people do not usually live in fear of death in the sense
that a fear of *dying* haunts their days; this is only true of people who
have a psychosis. Even those who know they do not have long to
live need not fear the process of dying; hospices have been founded,
often by the Christian church, to relieve the terminally ill of
unnecessary pain and anxiety, and to provide an environment in
which they and those who love them can accept the natural fact of
death. It is often said that death has taken over from sex as the
taboo subject of our day, but there are signs that this observation
is getting out of date. Nevertheless this ancient text about slavery
to 'fear of death' still has a truth; the more that we face up to the
fact of death, the more this horizon shapes and dictates the way we
live and the choices we make. Oppressive governments can use the
fear of death as a weapon to gain submission from their subjects.
In more everyday terms it is hard to live freely, to make generous
decisions about the spending of our time and energy, when the end-
point of death keeps reminding us that time is running out. We
tend to calculate how much time we can afford to offer to others,
and cannot adopt the spendthrift nature of self-giving love. So if we
allow ourselves to be dominated by 'idols' we shall find that the
lurking fact of death increases our slavery to them. A person who
puts his career before the relationships of his family will find that

reckoning how much time he has before he dies will only drive him into a more frantic slavery to work.

Moreover if we put our final values in the works of our hands, death becomes the enemy which makes a mockery of our achievement. In the story of the first man and woman in Genesis 3 the narrator does not actually say that physical death was the result of their fall from obedience; what is inflicted upon them is the power of death to blight and spoil life, to destroy the results of work and to disturb relationships: 'You shall gain your bread by the sweat of your brow until you return to the ground.' Again something that is a gift of God in itself – 'Dear Sister Death' as Francis of Assisi greeted it in dying – has become distorted by human sin. Through hope in God it can be received again as the framework in which God himself places life.

Satan

In Christian tradition, the figure of Satan has come to represent the sum total of all evil. It may seem surprising then to discover that where Satan first appears in the scriptures of ancient Israel, he has a recognised and legitimate place in God's service. The 'Satan' or 'Adversary' appears in God's heavenly court as the public prosecutor, accusing sinners before the bar of divine justice. As one who advocates strict compliance to the law of God, we find him outlining a rather shaky case against Job and a stronger case against the High Priest Joshua.[18] Here and in the later writings of the Jewish rabbis he is portrayed as the instrument of God's wrath against sin. Yet this same Satan appears in the New Testament as another kind of 'Adversary', as the devil who is the enemy not only of man but of God. According to the gospel accounts, when the kingdom of God breaks in through the teaching, healing and exorcisms of Jesus, it provokes a direct conflict with the kingdom of Satan. Some New Testament texts still show remnants of the Satan's former legitimate function, but for the most part he has now become a malicious destroyer.

This seems, in the apt phrase of G. B. Caird, to be 'a remarkable Rake's Progress', or the spoiling of yet another good thing. There is however a coherent link between the two characters of Satan – his rigid insistence upon the letter of the law. As we have already seen, the law is not the ultimate expression of the will of God, and

118

so it is the tragedy of Satan that 'in defending the honour of God's law, Satan becomes the enemy of God's purpose'.[19] It seems that by New Testament times both Jewish and Christian thinkers felt that the objective reality of evil could only be properly expressed by personifying it, and the figure of the Satan was available. He had already been acquiring an ambiguous reputation through his over-zealous concern for the law; the stories of his testing of Job, and his provoking of David into the presumptuous sin of conducting a census, show him sliding from the role of prosecutor to *agent provocateur*. To secure a conviction he is ready to incite the committing of a crime. His proper function of testing and 'sifting' human characters has slipped into a malicious tempting. So Jesus teaches his disciples to pray: 'do not put us to the test, but deliver us from the Evil One'.

The developing view of Satan as a fallen angel was probably both a way of expressing the degradation in Satan's character, and an actual influence *upon* the shift in his reputation. In the New Testament, however, the fall of Satan from heaven is not located in some primeval event before the creation of the world, as it came to be in later Jewish and Christian stories; it happens with the ministry of Jesus, and particularly in his victory over evil at the cross.[20] There is no more place for an accuser of sinners in heaven when they have been reconciled by God's act of grace. When we come to reflect more exactly on the sense in which Christ can be said to have conquered evil and its representative in the act of atonement, we shall need to reflect carefully on the dual character of Satan.

Meanwhile what we are to make, in our modern world, of this ambiguous figure of the Satan? In ancient Israel he fitted, in his legitimate role, into the company of the 'sons of God' or angelic inhabitants of God's court. We shall be returning to these cosmic agents when we consider the 'principalities and powers' to which Paul refers. Intolerable strains develop, however, when the Satan is understood literally to be 'a totally evil person' (the devil) since this contradicts the very meaning of personality. We use the word 'person' to speak of beings who make others personal, since we are always persons in relationship with each other. Even the most wicked human being cannot be one hundred per cent evil, which is why there is hope of repentance and renewal even for the guard of a concentration camp. Above all, we affirm that God is personal because he creates persons and deepens their personal relationships. It is not possible to apply the term 'person' to an entity which is absolutely evil and thus capable only of depersonalising. Moreover a concentration of evil into one single being tends to distract attention from the radical evils that need to be recognised and resisted in our society We blame the wiles of the devil, and miss the way that economic **and** political organisations deprive people of civil rights, exploit their labour for the sake of small privileged groups, and squander the resources of the earth to supply the material of warfare.

What is surely essential is to recognise the spiritual reality to which the name 'Satan' witnesses. The personification has an indispensable value in calling attention to a reality we would otherwise miss. Here we must recognise both sides of his character, as well as the shift between them that a spirit of legalism produces. As Walter Wink provocatively suggests in his study of 'The Powers',[21] we can still catch echoes of the Satan who is in divine service when we hear a 'sifting voice' within us, presenting alternatives and so forcing us to discover things about ourselves and our motives. In this way the Satan who encounters Jesus in the desert makes him face the expectations which the crowd will have of him, as miracle-worker and a leader using worldly tools of power;[22] the Satan brings to consciousness possibilities that may be good enough in themselves, but which we must recognise are not the will of God here and now. This kind of testing can perform, though perhaps unwittingly, a divine office, but it slides easily into a tempting which slanders and destroys. In the story of the temptation of Jesus we hear a voice of malevolence, and when Peter later becomes the Satan for Christ, urging him to avoid the cross, he earns the sharp rebuke 'Away with you, Satan'. In our own experience there is a voice within us that makes us face our weaknesses and failings, not to cope with them but in order to break us; it harps upon our flaws in order to persuade us that we are worthless. It uses the yardstick of the law to beat us into despair. It is on this aspect of the Satan that Jesus comments, when he calls him 'the father of lies',[23] for nothing can in fact separate us from the divine love which accepts us and values us as we are.[24]

So the useful testing voice modulates into a voice that wants to destroy. We have arrived at the second dimension of the character of Satan – an experience of the utter darkness of evil. To speak of a 'Satan' is to witness to the fact that the evil we confront is more than the sinning of any one human individual, or even any one group of individuals. Evil cannot be reduced to the private sins we commit. 'The Satan' recalls our experience of being from time to time enveloped in what seems like a totally negative field of force, or stumbling into a quicksand which sucks us down into the depths. In thinking about the objective reality of the devil we are not forced to choose between regarding him either as a single being with independent existence or as a symbol of the evil choices of human individuals. There is a mysterious area that lies between these two rational options which the name and personification 'Satan' evokes. It may be that we do not yet have the conceptual tools to analyse this experience of universal evil, though helpful insights are provided by ideas of a 'collective unconscious' described by the psychologist Karl Jung, and the 'corporate personality' of a community described by the Old Testament scholar H. Wheeler Robinson.[25] Drawing upon these ideas, Walter Wink defines Satan as:

> the world's corporate personality, the symbolic repository of the entire complex of evil existing in the present order . . . the collective shadow, the sum total of all the individual darkness, evil, unredeemed anger, and fear of the whole race, and all the echoes and reverberations still vibrating down through time from those who have chosen evil before us.[26]

Satan is a reality of experience, and is no less real if we decline to follow the world view of the first century in regarding him as a single spiritual being without a body. The 'personal' features in his assault upon us (the experience, for instance, of being confronted by an evil which seems to employ an intelligent strategy and possesses a purposeful ill-will) are accounted for by the network of interpersonal relationships between human beings which is deeply hidden beneath the surface of conscious life and which often eludes our notice and understanding The sum total of human evil is more than a mere mathematical sum; something new and mysterious is brought into being by the way that we react upon one another. It is significant that the 'demons' which appear in the gospel narratives and which Jesus confronts are subordinated to the figure of Satan: the local manifestations of evil are taken up into the great conflict between Christ and Satan, the 'strong man' whom Jesus has come to bind.[27] From about the middle of the second century the church lost interest in the victory of Christ over demons, and focused the whole struggle with evil in the figure of the devil.

The principalities and powers

While the apostle Paul has little to say about Satan, he makes more extensive appeal to the angelic 'powers' which, from the outlook of his Jewish heritage, he believes to lie behind the visible fabric of the world. Ancient Israel had coped with the challenge of the 'gods' worshipped among other nations by down-grading them to inferior powers acting under the supreme sovereignty of Yahweh, the God of Israel. They were identified as angels, 'sons of God' or members of Yahweh's heavenly council, who had been given the task of guarding and ruling the nations on Yahweh's behalf. This belief is set out in a poem preserved in the Book of Deuteronomy, which also affirms that Israel had the privileged position of being ruled directly by Yahweh himself, rather than by a mere angel:

> When the Most High parcelled out the nations,
> when he dispersed all mankind,
> he laid down the boundaries of every people
> according to the number of the sons of God;
> but the Lord's share was his own people,
> Jacob was his allotted portion.
>
> (Deut. 32:8–9 NEB)

According to the religious thinkers of ancient Israel these angels had been led astray and corrupted by the worship offered to them. In a clear way the nature of human sin manifested itself as idolatry, as what was less than God was exalted into the ultimate place: 'the gods of the nations are idols every one'.[28] Furthermore not only had they consented to be regarded as gods but they had connived at injustice in the earthly kingdoms for which they were responsible.[29] When Paul speaks of the 'powers in high places' and 'the rulers of this age'[30] he thus has in mind *both* the spiritual powers in the cosmos, *and* their visible face in the organisation of the state. The angelic powers, while partly still administering the rule of God,

122

were at the same time in rebellion against him and had become (we might say) 'demonic'. Likewise, in Paul's view, the earthly authorities of the state could exercise the legitimate function, given them by God, to keep order and peace in society;[31] but like their angelic counterparts they could also become perverted and distorted, regarding themselves and their survival with the ultimate value that belongs only to God. This ambiguous status is reflected in Paul's two-sided description of the Roman state in one letter, regarding it as both 'the restraining power' and 'the mystery of lawlessness'.[32] The Pax Romana, with all the benefits it brought to the ancient world, could become a reign of terror as it consolidated its power by oppression in the hands of an emperor like Caligula.

There is an obvious parallel between the corruption of the law and that of the powers, both becoming demonic as they are treated as idols. In fact Paul seems to have envisaged the religious law as actually having its *own* guardian powers. Drawing on the Jewish tradition that the law had been mediated to Moses by angels,[33] he sees both Jews and Gentiles as 'enslaved to the elemental spirits of the world', the Jews under bondage to the curse of religious legalism and the Gentiles bound under laws of the pagan state which were sanctioned by rebellious powers. Sin could work on the powers ordained by God and transform them into the world rulers of darkness: 'So it had come about that Israel and Rome, the highest religion and the best government that the world had seen, had conspired to crucify the Lord of Glory' (G. B. Caird).[34] Through that same cross, however, Christ has conquered the rebellious powers of the nations and the law:

> He has cancelled the bond which pledged us to the decrees of the law. It stood against us, but he has set it aside, nailing it to the cross. On that cross he discarded the cosmic powers and authorities like a garment; he made a public spectacle of them and led them as captives in his triumphal procession. (Col. 2:14–15)[35]

Though their hold over human beings is broken (*how*, we must explore shortly) they are still in rebellion; their immediate liege lord is Christ as the representative of the Father. He is Lord of the powers not only through the cross but because the divine purpose in creation itself is summed up in the person of Christ. He is the

123

'wisdom of God', the pattern of sonship for which all personalities have been made. Just before the above passage, an early hymn is quoted proclaiming that 'in [Christ] all things were created, in heaven and on earth, visible and invisible, whether thrones or dominions or principalities or authorities'.[36] This identifies a further kind of power, angels who stand behind the fabric of the whole world of created nature,[37] and which are also in rebellion against God's purpose at present. Picking up the Old Testament insight that there are parts of nature which are still chaotic, wilderness elements which have not yet been brought under the divine dominion, Paul affirms elsewhere that the whole fabric of the universe groans at present in futility. But it *will* be redeemed when human sons are finally perfected in the pattern of Christ, and can exercise their true function of administering creation and so 'ruling the angels'.[38] The gospel narratives portray one Son of Man already doing so, as Jesus rebukes the wind and waves and walks upon the water.

What shall we make of this talk of the powers today? How can we name them in our modern world? We can recognise the earthly face of the principalities and powers in all systems and institutions that lay a claim to ultimate authority and demand absolute devotion. The powers can be found in any structures and organisations before which the individual feels powerless, and which aim to squeeze people into a mould of conformity for the sake of their own security and survival. The best systems can become demonic, whether economic, political or ecclesiastical; bureaucracies can add a spirit of legalism to their particular demonic tendencies. One example of a power that had become idolatrous was well exposed by the 'Open File' column of the *Guardian* newspaper (31 October 1973). The reporter had obtained a copy of an internal memorandum circulated to all administrators and receptionists in the offices of the London Borough of Lambeth who might receive enquiries about their services from handicapped people. The memorandum revealed that the Senior Administrative Officer had invented a mythical person called Hilary Green who was supposed to be handling inquiries, and it advised as follows: 'Please note that this mythical officer can be Mr, Mrs or Miss according to the reader's mental reaction . . . any office of this directorate may claim close acquaintance with the said Mr/Mrs/Miss Hilary and take action appropriate to the inquiry.' The invention of 'Hilary Green' was no doubt done with the best of intentions, not only to improve efficiency but to make enquirers feel that they were being dealt with by a person and not simply by a system. We are reminded that the powers exercise what is, in origin, a God-given authority. The result in this case, however, was actually to depersonalise the whole relationship between the helping service and the one needing help; a myth cannot make personal relations and cannot take responsibility. The reporter broke the idol by giving the name and telephone number of a real person – the Senior Officer himself.

I have surveyed the 'tyrants' which confront humankind in some detail, because we cannot begin to ask what it means for Christ to have conquered the hostile powers without identifying them. The New Testament categories draw our attention to the diversity of these demonic forces, while at the same time we have found lines of intersection between them. The nature of sin is idolatry, and both religious legalism and structural 'powers' can become idols. The ambiguous figure of 'the Satan' is closely associated with the tendency of law to become demonic as well as summing up the whole darkness of human sin; finally death draws its power to distort life from idolatry in all its forms. Human sin even seems to affect the 'powers' within nature, which we might in modern terms identify as the first principles and regular patterns of the natural order – what are often (not quite accurately) called 'laws of nature' or, more poetically, 'Mother Earth'. It is not only that sin has prevented human beings from cooperating with the powers of the universe, so that 'futility' has resulted instead of an environment of harmony and we do not yet see 'everything under [human] feet'.[39] We have also made the natural powers into tyrants. For example, by investigating nuclear mysteries without a proper moral sense, we have become enslaved to the genie of nuclear destruction.

The cost of victory

The Christian story of redemption affirms that Christ has decisively conquered all the hostile powers that trap and spoil human life, but that it has only happened through the great cost of suffering. The hero has been beaten down by the powers; he has descended into

125

the utter depths of weakness. He is not like the hero of *Siegfried*, Wagner's portrait of the Superman of the new era; in this portrayal only 'the one who has never known fear' can forge the shattered pieces of the magic sword and kill the dragon. That is one kind of hero, and distorted images of his successors stride across the television screens of children's programmes today. A whole crew of Supermen and Superwomen (Batman, Wonder Woman, He-Man, The Incredible Hulk and so on) are mere shadows of the 'Overman' portrayed by the philosopher Nietzsche who inspired Wagner, but they have at least a faint family likeness. They assert the potential of humankind to go beyond its limits, and they do not take human weakness seriously.[40]

In contrast the hero of the Christian story trembles with human fear and anxiety in the dark garden of betrayal. 'Beset with weakness . . . he offered up prayers with loud cries and tears to God who was able to deliver him from the grave.'[41] Afraid of the onset of death he asks, weeping, whether there might not be some other way to bring in the kingdom of God. The gospel writers give us the words of his prayer, 'Father, if it be your will take this cup away from me.'[42] He is asking that his mission should triumph, that his message about the forgiving and accepting God should be vindicated and that his critics should be shown to be wrong, by *some other means* than the pathway of death. Yet in obedience ('not what I will but what you will') he treads that path, and is finally not overwhelmed, winning victory out of the very teeth of defeat.

The pattern is of a victory through weakness, and so a victory wrenched in a surprising manner from the very jaws of evil. Christian belief in the resurrection of Jesus fits into this scheme of an unexpected vindication of the hero. 'Resurrection' certainly points to victory over death, and the linked theme of 'ascension' points to the exaltation of Christ to a cosmic lordship. Yet these are not events which can be rationally proved; they cannot even be described without the aid of evocative images. This is because, as I have already suggested, they challenge all our preconceptions about 'how the world is'; belief in the resurrection is belief that God has done something so new and unexpected in the midst of our history that none of our tools of scientific and historical enquiry can grasp it.[43] God has vindicated Jesus, but in a surprising way; he had not saved him *from* the cross but *through* it. So great is the humility of God that he has, as Luther affirmed, 'hidden himself' deeply within human life, exposing himself to all its hazards. The victory over evil is at the same time a sacrifice, as God puts his very self into the fray. In love God has made himself vulnerable, hiding his glory in the shame of the cross, participating in the estrangement of human life. God thus reveals himself in the veiled form of lowliness. But even in the resurrection the glory of God is hidden; through the raising of Jesus God protests against a human life which is marked by suffering and threatened by the shadow of death, but he does so in a way that does not force response upon human beings. The glory of God is hidden in the ambiguities of history. The *parousia*, or the 'appearing' of the glory of God is yet to come when all things are reconciled.

The pattern of a surprising victory won from the jaws of defeat by a hidden God can be recognised in what may at first seem a grotesque theme, which enjoyed widespread popularity in early times. The devil is said to have been deceived into thinking Christ was an easy prey, because his divinity was hidden under his human nature. Thinking he has gained the best piece of humanity into his power, the devil does not notice until too late the danger he is facing. In the colourful account of Gregory of Nyssa, the devil would never have put himself at hazard by confronting 'a God unveiled in heavenly glory'; thus the human flesh of Christ was offered as a bait to Satan, with the fish-hook of his divinity concealed beneath it. Satan, like a 'greedy fish', swallows the hook of the Godhead with the bait, with the result that his darkness is quenched by absorbing the light of Christ: 'through life passing into death, and the light arising in the darkness, that which is opposed to life and light might be brought to nothing'.[44] Much later, Luther delighted in using the same dramatic picture, exploiting the scriptural text 'I am a worm, and no man' (Ps. 22:6); Satan finds Christ in the world as a fish finds a worm, but it has been hung on the line by the crafty fisherman (God): 'For Christ sticks in his gills, and he must spew him out again, as the whale the prophet Jonah; and even as he chews him, the devil chokes himself and is slain, and is taken captive by death.'[45]

Similarly Augustine and Gregory the Great portray Christ as the bait in a mouse-trap, and Gregory of Nyssa (again) compares the hiding of Christ's divinity to the concealing of drugs in food. In the same tradition (but with greater dignity) are presentations of the harrowing of hell in the medieval mystery plays, based on a scene in the apocryphal gospel of Nicodemus. There Satan is depicted as waiting eagerly in hell for the arrival of the famous Jesus of Nazareth, since he thinks 'he is (only) a man'. But when he hears a voice like thunder crying 'Lift up your gates, O rulers, and the King of Glory shall come in' he knows that he has overreached himself. His prison house will be broken open, he will be bound and his righteous captives released. Hell itself speaks to rub in the lesson that 'You wished to kill the king of glory, but have killed yourself.'[46]

Though most of these images appear preposterous to the modern mind, they do evoke the sense of a triumph won unexpectedly at the very moment of defeat, and so the costly self-offering of God which is involved. God does not proceed by a brute show of external force, but puts himself into the process; the redeemer goes right into the jaws of death. Similar in effect, though very different in origin, is the appeal of the Christian Fathers to the ritual of the scapegoat from the ancient Day of Atonement in Israel. The sins of the people are laid symbolically upon the goat which is sent into the wilderness 'for Azazel'.[47] The wilderness represents the forces of chaos that are opposed to God's will, the powers of 'nature' that (as we have just seen) have become distorted and elude God's control at present. Evil is returned to the place where it belongs, with the demonic powers. Such an offering was probably originally thought of as averting and placating hostile evil forces (Azazel), but when taken up into a Christian understanding of atonement it took on much more the aspect of victory over them. As Origen expresses it, Christ our scapegoat 'leads off' the spiritual hosts of wickedness into the desert.[48] They think they have mocked and destroyed him by expelling him from the city of humankind, but they have themselves been led by the nose.

There is a pleasing irony in the theme of 'the deceiver deceived' or 'tricking the trickster'. But we are bound to ask *in what sense* we can share in the particular victory of Christ. If we recall our review of the tyrants that oppress humankind, we must surely affirm that God is always, through his Spirit, coming into conflict with these enemies at great cost to himself, and enabling us to cooperate with him in his victories on behalf of life. The questions which arise (as with all images of atonement) are why the specific victory of Christ in the past should be decisive, and how it actually involves us. How, then, does this victory make all other victories possible? In speaking of a once-for-all victory we are affirming that the control of evil over human life has been fundamentally weakened through the cross, but what sense can we make of this?

Breaking the reign of Satan: an objective emphasis

As presented by the early Christian Fathers, the decisive nature of the victory of Christ was his defeat of Satan. The victory was drawn in terms of a battle between two cosmic figures – the champion of God and the champion of the legions of darkness. This was the picture that impressed itself upon the early Christian mind and gripped the imagination of people who were anxious that they might be the playthings of astral powers and other supernatural forces. Yet there are problems with this emphasis upon the conquest of the devil. There is, as we have seen, a much wider range of hostile powers that oppress us, and there are real difficulties in identifying the devil as a discarnate 'person' who can be literally attacked. Moreover if he were an individual being who could be overcome in single combat, why is there no real evidence of the weakening of the objective power of evil in the world? Even more fundamentally, however, the idea of a conflict with Satan or with demons at the cross seems to be (as Paul Tillich puts it) a drama which 'happens above our heads'.[49] Salvation, if it is to be the healing of personalities, must involve *our* response, and yet we stand on the sidelines in this cosmic trial of strength. In the technical terms we have been using, the older form of the *Christian Victor* model is too objective, seeming to be a private affair between God and his rebellious subject the devil.

Moreover it is difficult to see how a victory over Satan can be relevant to the enemies that are abroad in our personal experience. It does not adequately touch the problem of our sin, which is *our* rebellion against God, a terrible disruption in life caused by our lack of trust. Salvation must heal this brokenness in our lives which – as we have seen – was so clear to the apostle Paul. He identifies the main enemies of human life as sin, law and death; that is, he is concerned with what we would now call 'existential' threats, those

arising within our own existence. The most vivid account of a
battle in Paul's writings is the anguished struggle in his experience
between the old self ('in Adam') and his new self ('in Christ'): 'I
do not do the good I want, but the evil I do not want is what I
do.'[50] This is the death from which he cries to be delivered, from
the fatal conflict between his old impulses to turn from God and
his new impulses to live in fellowship with God. Further, when Paul
refers to the 'powers' he is thinking not only of cosmic forces, but
their manifestation in the oppressive powers of the state and legal
religion of which he feels the weight in his own experience. In the
ministry of Jesus himself sin is the prime enemy to be overcome.
The gospel writers understand Christ's victory over demons as a
hallmark of the wider coming of the kingdom, rather than as the
key matter in itself. By offering God's forgiveness of sins and acceptance to all, including the outcasts in society, Jesus releases from
oppression. He deals with the inner enemies of sin and guilt, and
with the outer enemies of a sinful social structure, releasing people
from the stereotypes in which they had been imprisoned. By offering
acceptance into his company, and thus into the coming kingdom,
Jesus breaks the type-casting of 'only a woman', 'only a child', 'a
sinner', 'a law-breaker' or 'the poor'.

Thus it is upon personal and social sin embedded in the structures
of our lives that the victory of Christ must have its impact. An
overcoming of the devil seems detached from the real battleground;
it is a transaction that takes place outside us. Christian thinkers
have felt this oddness about the picture, and have tried in various
ways to bring human beings and their actual sin back on to the
scene. This is an important motivation behind the curious theme
of 'tricking the devil' that we have already surveyed. According to
many of the early Christian Fathers, the devil is offered a 'ransom'
– the payment of Christ's death – and overreaches himself by
accepting it. He finds he has bitten off more than he can chew. The
ransom is not presented as a strictly legal arrangement but an act
of 'fair play' on God's part, since it is recognised that the devil has
rights over human souls. God, as Irenaeus says, acts 'reasonably';
he 'behaved with justice . . . and he redeemed that which was his
own, not by violence but by persuasion'.[51] Most of the Fathers held
that, while the devil was a usurper who had wrongly captured
humankind, he nevertheless had a right to possess human souls

130

since they had sinned and broken God's law. The devil was induced to yield his victims by being paid the proper price for them: as Origen explains it, 'the slain lamb of God . . . submitted to death, purchasing us back by his own blood from the devil who had got us in his power'.[52] Some Fathers explained that he was justly deceived, since he had exceeded his rights by seizing Christ who was sinless.

Thus the whole complex of ideas – the devil's rights, the ransom and the deception – hangs together and is a way of bringing human sin back on to the scene. The devil is conquered through the ransom, which is paid because of human guilt. The Fathers, reading the gospel text that Christ gave his life as a 'ransom for many' (Mark 10:45), asked to whom the ransom had been paid. Since the term 'ransom' means the price offered to set a slave free, it could hardly have been paid to God who was the one who was doing the emancipating, and so they concluded it had been paid to the devil. The question was, of course, misdirected in the first place; as in the Old Testament assertion that God had 'redeemed' his people from slavery in Egypt, the stress is upon the cost and sacrifice involved in the act of liberation, not upon a commercial transaction. What matters is not *to* whom the price is paid, but *by* whom; the Old Testament narratives make clear (sometimes with a wry humour) that the redemption of Israel from Egypt was a costly matter for God, in that he involved himself with a complaining and trouble-some people, and suffered constant frustrations of his purpose.[53] The Fathers were, however, inclined to think of paying a ransom to Satan because of their presupposition of the devil's rights, and *that* was an implicit recognition of the problem of human sin and God's judgement upon it.

This way of placing human sin in the picture is not, however, satisfactory. Apart from the vexed question of whether the devil could actually have rights, which later theologians such as Anselm and Abelard vehemently denied (and which Gregory of Nazianzus contested at the time), it treats sin as a kind of impersonal debt rather than an active power in human existence here and now. Athanasius, by contrast, seems to echo Paul when he speaks not of the rights of the devil, but the lawful dominion of death which follows naturally upon sin.[54]

A second attempt to get human sin on to the stage of a battle

with the devil is found in Luther, and is strongly advocated by
Gustav Aulen in his study of *Christus Victor*. This leans upon the
ambiguity of the figure of the Satan, recalling his legitimate role as
advocate of God's law and executant of his judgement, as well being
the prince of darkness.[55] The victory over Satan is thus understood
as God's removal of his own wrath against sin. Triumph over the
devil is the quenching of divine wrath. Aulen urges that this 'double-
sidedness' of the victory is essential to atonement.[56] In so far as the
devil is the enemy of the good, God reconciles the world by defeating
him; but in so far as the devil is God's own prosecutor, God is
reconciled by removing his own hostility against sinners. God not
only changes the situation of the world, but his own attitude to the
world is fundamentally changed.

Aulen points out that all models of atonement try to integrate
God's love with his righteous wrath against sin. But while legal
theories resolve the tension in a rational way, satisfying God's justice
by a payment of some kind, the 'classic' view resolves it in a
dramatic way.[57] Luther affirms that Christ undergoes the punishment that God inflicts upon human sin, but this is not any kind of
legal transaction; through this event God's love overcomes his
wrath. In an act of love which breaks through wrath, Christ goes
in under the judgement of God, and 'God fights for me'.[58] It is a
battle of God against God. Luther constantly affirms that the work
of God bursts all the bounds of reason and law: the atonement is
being 'made safe and free from the law, from sin, death, the power
of the devil, hell . . . the wrath of God'.[59]

But how is the wrath of God overcome in the cross of Jesus?
Aulen refuses to answer this question, repeating that the 'idea' or
motif of *Christus Victor* is not a theory. It is less a doctrine than a
drama. Yet to tell a story of God's fighting the devil as the representative of his own wrath is actually no more metaphorical than
other models of atonement, and it *does* present a theory, as Luther's
treatment of it makes clear. The theory is that there is a struggle
in God between his wrath and his love, and his love is stronger:
'the curse, which is the divine wrath against the whole world . . .
clashes with the blessing and wants to damn it and annihilate it.
But it cannot.'[60] This is the 'how', and it is a theory that raises
inescapable and uncomfortable questions about the character of
God. Moreover in running together the two versions of Satan, Aulen

neglects the fact that as an over-zealous guardian of the law Satan is not fulfilling the original and final will of God. As we have seen, to treat law as absolute rather than as secondary and a merely provisional step, is to be an enemy to God's true purpose of grace. We cannot then appeal to the tradition of the Satan in order to sanction a view of atonement in which God wins a victory over his own wrath.

There is no conflict in God. In his love God passionately desires to bring all humankind into fellowship with himself. In his justice God underwrites the consequences of sin, though (as the Old Testament prophets make clear) he does so with an agony in his heart.[61] When sin is wiped out, then judgement is lifted and the accusing voice of law is silenced. Irenaeus is surely right to locate the taking away of God's enmity against mankind in the *moment* of Satan's defeat,[62] but we need not follow Aulen in supposing that God conquers his judgement *as* Satan. Rather we may say that Christ enters the human situation of being under divine judgement in order to be in a position to confront sin and slay it. The heart of the matter is the killing of sin, and we have seen that the 'Satan' is an apt (and perhaps indispensable) way of speaking about the reality and the mystery of creaturely sin in its totality. The defeat of 'Satan' is thus going to mean a removal of wrath and a new relationship between God and the world, but I believe it is misleading to call this (as Aulen does) the 'reconciling of God'. God, who does not need to be reconciled, reconciles the world to himself by acting to conquer sin and the non-being that it generates.

The modern theologian Karl Barth works out this idea in a dramatic way, portraying Christ as coming into conflict with the nothingness that human beings have brought upon themselves. He affirms, with Paul and Luther, that Christ in becoming a human son comes under the shadow of divine judgement against human sin. This is the passion story in which 'the Judge himself was the judged'. He treads the dark path to meet the death that sinners have inflicted upon themselves, and to which God consents, in so far as 'my turning from God is followed by God's annihilating turning from me'.[63] The sting of this death is the 'nothingness' whose power and aggressive vitality sinners themselves have fostered and 'towards which they relentlessly hasten'.[64] 'Nothingness' is the great adversary of both God and humanity, and is a way of speaking of the destructive forces that emerge from the broken relationships between Creator and created and which attempt to bring life down to nothing.[65] Barth, then, rejects any idea that Christ atones for our sin by bearing a punishment in our place. Rather by identifying himself with humankind in a representative way as 'the one great sinner', Christ 'caused sin to be taken and killed on the cross in his own person'. The nothingness that lurks in death takes its rightful prey by engulfing the sinner, and sin together with him. Thus God employs his enemy of nothingness or 'eternal death' in his own service, wiping out the sin which is the obstacle between humankind and himself; 'this worst becomes an instrument in the hand of the merciful and omnipotent God for the creation of the best'.[66]

There are unmistakable overtones in this drama of the now familiar story of 'tricking the devil'. In an ingenious move, God employs the punishment for sin as a mean of abolishing sin and thereby emptying nothingness of its power. Christ in his resurrection overcomes death and destroys the nothingness, which has no power left now that sin has been eliminated. In slaying sin, nothingness has unwittingly disarmed itself. In telling the story in this dramatic way, Barth has rightly uncovered the heart of the atonement as the killing of sin, but it must be said that he has not really succeeded in relating an event in the past to our present. It is as hard to see how 'sin' as a whole has been once and for all killed on the cross as it would be to see how a literal Satan had been destroyed. Barth slips, by a sleight of theological hand, from the idea that death has cancelled out a *sinner* (Christ, representatively) to the cancelling out of *sin* altogether. How can our sin be killed in another person? Sin must be dealt with here and now, since it is a matter of our response and attitude to God.

Moreover the threat of nothingness ought no longer to be present if 'sin' itself has really been so comprehensively dealt with in one past event that nothingness has been brought to nothing. Barth argues that, after the cross, God allows nothingness to appear real to our blinded eyes, as a reminder of what evil used to be like.[67] But while it is true that evil is strictly 'nothing', in that it has no reality of its own but is always parasitic upon what is good, it hardly corresponds with experience to suggest there is anything illusory about it. It seems that the decisiveness of the past event of the cross can be no more convincingly explained as the slaying of sin than as the dealing of a fatal blow to Satan. Both express a truth, and are a story that must be told. But they do not *explain* the decisive effect of the cross upon the present.

The transforming victory: a subjective stress

The alternative way of understanding the finality of Christ's victory over the powers is to see it as an event that creates and enables a victory in our lives here and now. In the words of G. B. Caird, 'the transforming of sinners into righteous men is the final defeat of the power'.[68] Through his Spirit God is always coming to us, offering victory against all the hostile forces that spoil life, holding out the possibility of victory through his gracious presence in our world. The problem is human cooperation with the divine purpose. God wants us to respond and work with him in the conquest, but how can our wills be moved to harmony with his? How can we know what the scope of the conquest is? The victory of Christ at the cross empowers us to enter upon God's victory in the present.

This kind of victory fits in very well with the emphasis upon sin as 'idolatry' in a good deal of modern theological thinking. In naming the powers, we found the consistent theme that something which was less than God (though often good in itself) had been given final value, and so had acquired a demonic hold over us. As we read the gospel accounts, we find that Christ has, for the first time in human history, broken all the idols that confront human-kind. We make idols because, in our anxiety, we fail to trust in God and instead we seek our security elsewhere. Jesus smashes the idols through his unfaltering obedience to the Father and trust in him. He refuses to be conformed to the idol of religious law; faced with authorities who assumed that God's purpose for life had found total and final expression in written codes of ethics, Jesus offers free forgiveness to those who desire to enter the kingdom. Faced by oppressive political authorities, he does not make an idol of a quiet life; he continues to disturb the fabric of the status quo by announc-ing the kingdom and calling for a repentance that would be bound to shake up the present order. He also confronts the powers by breaking the roles that have been thrust upon the outcasts and

135

rejects of society. He breaks the idol of sin itself through unremitting obedience to the Father and finally breaks the idol of self by offering himself to death. In the midst of utter anxiety, focused in the prayer of Gethsemane, Christ does not seek to overcome anxiety through any security except trust in the Father. One's own self is the last idol, and to give oneself unreservedly is to have vanquished the last demon. So the sacrifice of Christ is his victory, and since God gives himself in this event it is also the victory of God himself.

But in what sense does the definitive act of Jesus in breaking the idols enable us to break our idols here and now? There is no atoning act of God if it is simply a matter of our *imitating* the work of Christ; our wills are too frail and our habits too perverse for us simply to be able to copy Christ. Here John Macquarrie helpfully points to two ways in which the victory of Christ actually *creates* victory in us. In the first place there is the power of revelation. The act of Christ is one of those moments in human history that 'open up new possibilities of existence'.[69] Something genuinely new has been achieved in them, and they can be called 'eschatological' in that they are open to being repeated in the future. Once a new possibility has been disclosed, other people can make it their own, repeating it and reliving the experience. Take for example (Macquarrie does not) the human achievement involved in climbing Mount Everest for the first time; as soon as this has been done, what was once thought to be an impossible conquest of the hostile elements can be repeated, and the new horizons of experience it opens out can be opened for others. So we can (in the words of Rudolph Bultmann) 'make the cross of Christ our own'.[70] The author of the letter to the Hebrews has this kind of picture in mind when he speaks of Jesus as the 'pioneer' of our salvation;[71] through his obedience, learned through suffering, he enters for the first time right into the inner presence of God, and can take us *with* him.

Macquarrie rightly points out that this idea is more than an 'imitation' of Christ, because a truly eschatological event is actually one in which *God* is present to unveil his being to us. The disclosure is not just a quality of the event, but a divine revelation. Through his Holy Spirit God acts both in the original event and in its repetitions, so that 'the event is an event of grace, working in those whom it addresses and making possible their response of faith'.[72] The event is creative because God is present in it, to enable our response. I believe then that we can go a step further in describing the creative power of the past event or, to use the technical terminology, its 'objectivity'. An event in which some really new possibility is disclosed surely actually *provokes* repetition of itself; it is not only capable of repetition, but calls out to be re-enacted. This must be even more true of the event in human history where God is present to a unique depth of involvement, identifying himself totally with Jesus Christ. The objectivity of the event, then, is not only that God is present to elicit response, but that through the event he draws out repetitions of victory in the future.

We may add that the idea of victory through revelation is already anticipated in St Paul's account of triumph over the powers. In the cross Christ has made a public exhibition of them, exposing them for the tyrants and usurpers they are; the unveiling of the divine glory in the weakness of death has de-glorified the powers before which human beings tremble, showing them up as mere weak and beggarly elements.[73] Through the Holy Spirit the revelation that the rulers of this age have defeated themselves by crucifying the Lord of glory continues in human hearts.[74] This revelation is victory, because it transforms the one who receives it, altering his whole attitude to the powers. This is not only a force which overcomes individual sin in the individual human heart; later we shall explore the way that those oppressed by sin in society can make revolution by exposing the truth about their oppressors. Once again we find an echo of the 'deception' of the devil; evil overreaches itself and exposes its true character, so that all its actions thereafter can only accelerate its decline.

The other factor linking our victory with that of Christ to which Macquarrie calls attention is that of the *community* of the crucified. There is objective atonement in that the absolute self-giving of Christ has created a community in which his victory is repeated. The community of the church precedes and enables any individual appropriation of salvation, as 'an ever-expanding centre in which Christ's reconciling work continues'.[75] Evil wins victories by making us retort and pay others back, so perpetuating its power. But Christ has absorbed evil, refusing to give it out, reversing the tendency of evil to spread. Thus he has created a new situation, a new human community which can go on absorbing evil and stopping its cancerous growth.

Here, for the last time, we return to the theme of the tricking of Satan which at first sight appears so absurd, and yet expresses the profound insight that evil always bites off more than it can chew. In an ironic comment in 1 Corinthians 2:8 the apostle Paul remarks that 'the rulers of this age' (the 'powers') blundered in killing the Lord of glory. G. B. Caird suggests that what 'they did not know', according to Paul, was the nature of Christ's membership of the race of Adam. They did not realise that Christ belonged to the old community of humankind by free choice, so the general rule that all human beings are sinners did not apply to him.[76] Far from holding him, death thus became the means through which he broke free of the whole realm of sin and death, and became the head of a new community into which human beings can freely choose to transfer. A new humanity comes into being which has 'died out' on sin as Christ did, and over which the powers have lost control: 'He who has died is freed from sin. . . If we have died with Christ, we believe that we shall also live with him. For we know that Christ being raised from the dead will never die again; death no longer has dominion over him' (Rom. 6:7–9).

At the centre of this corporate life, providing moments in which we can share the movement of Christ from death to life, are the sacraments of baptism and Eucharist. In them the factors which link past event and present salvation intersect; they are symbols through which we are immersed into the life of the church as the continuing body of Christ on earth, and in which Christ's act of victory is repeated. At (or near) the beginning of the Christian life, baptism provides a place where we can die with Christ to our old life, dying 'out from under the elements of the world',[77] and rising into a new quality of life within a new community. The Eucharist thereafter provides a continual focus of the drama of redemption: the command 'this do in *remembrance* of me' promises more than an aid to memory. In ancient Israel 'remembering' the escape from slavery in Egypt at the Passover celebration meant reliving the event; the worshippers shared in the past happening because they encountered the same God in the present who had acted to deliver in the past. So in the Eucharist, the risen Christ is present to encounter his disciples and draw out a repetition of the same victory that he achieved in his death.

Now the idea that the victory of Christ enables our victory is clearly a shift from the original thrust of the *Christus Victor* motif. It is a tilting of emphasis from objective to subjective. Although Macquarrie's thought follows this change, in a rather misleading way he follows Aulen in claiming that the 'classic view' alone properly combines objective and subjective elements of atonement. They are both rather dismissive of the 'subjective' understanding of atonement developed by Abelard, who believed that the love of God revealed in the cross moves human hearts to respond to him. Aulen objects that this amounts to making atonement dependent upon human repentance, rather than upon the act of God which is so clearly presented in the theme of *Christus Victor*.[78] But we may reply that atonement is still initiated by God if he *creates* the change in human attitudes. The question is *how* hearts come to be moved. In fact the so-called 'subjective views' of atonement (at least as propounded by the major thinkers of the Christian church) have always tried to express the enabling or creative quality of the act of God in Christ. Aulen's own depiction of the struggle between Christ and Satan seems by contrast to fall firmly upon the objective side of the scale.

In his account John Macquarrie finds a strong element of objectivity in the fact that the self-giving act of God has come 'right into human history in a new and decisive manner'[79] in the victory of Christ, so empowering its repetition in our own experience. But his approach clearly falls into the subjective pattern he ostensibly criticises. Though atonement has been achieved potentially in the event of Christ, it only becomes *actual* in the present, as people make the victory of Christ their own. The objective dimensions to which he points – the creative quality of the event, promoting repetition, and the existence of the Christian community – are also features in other models we have surveyed which take traditional images and move them to the subjective side of the spectrum.

The presence of God in Christ thus calls forth not only sacrifice and penitence, but victory. This is the triumph over the powers, and its nature as a conquest of love remains to be shown in the next chapter.

7

The act of love

O, dearly, dearly has he loved,
　　And we must love him too,
And trust in his redeeming blood,
　　And try his works to do.

(C. F. Alexander)

This verse from a well-known hymn written for children conceals some very large questions about the nature of redeeming love. Although those who sing it regularly in Passion Week may not consider the force of the words 'must', 'too,' and 'try', it seems clear on reflection that the hymn-writer is urging us (at least in her final verse) to imitate the love of God displayed in the cross of Jesus. Yet we are bound to ask whether our human predicament of moral weakness does not render it futile to say that we '*must* love him too'. It is this kind of 'moral' or highly 'subjective' theory of the atonement which is usually attributed to Peter Abelard (1079–1142), and theologians have often been quick to condemn him for being similarly unrealistic about human moral impotence. In an often quoted passage from his commentary on the Epistle to the Romans he writes:

> Now it seems to us that we have been justified by the blood of Christ and reconciled to God in this way: through this unique act of grace manifested to us – in that his Son has taken upon himself our nature and persevered therein in teaching us by word and example even unto death – he has more fully bound us to himself by love; with the result that our hearts should be enkindled by such a gift of divine grace, and true charity should not now shrink from enduring anything for him.[1]

Is this passage simply a prose version of Mrs Alexander's later – and briefer – versifying? For the sense of the passage, much depends upon what Abelard means by stating that the love of God 'enkindles' love in our hearts, together with similar phrases elsewhere like 'incites' and 'inclines'. Clearly Abelard believes that the love of God revealed in the cross has the power to *move* human hearts and minds to a similar love, but the question is what kind of moving this might be. If it is no more than an emotional prompting, so that human beings contemplate the cross and then make a response to God through their own efforts, then Abelard's thought on atonement is indeed not more profound than Mrs Alexander's.

However I intend to show that Abelard is attempting, though not with complete success, to express something more objective than this; he has grasped the power of the divine love to *create* or generate love within human beings. When God 'binds himself' to us by love he takes the initiative in overcoming the defects in human nature that bind us in a circle of lovelessness. Through the life and death of Jesus he actually renews the bond of love that he implanted in creation. As a hymn writer himself, Abelard would certainly want to revise Mrs Alexander's lines to read 'O, dearly, dearly has he loved, to *make* us love him too.'

The redemptive power of love

Thus, despite the almost ritualistic dismissals of Abelard's thought by modern thinkers on the doctrine of the atonement, the basic thrust of his thought actually underlies the modern form of the three models of atonement we have already examined. While the older versions of sacrifice, victory and justice in the cross tend to be 'objective with a subjective appendix', the modern ones have swung to being 'subjective with an objective focus'. That is, they find the past event of the cross to have a creative power, *enabling* sacrifice, victory and righteousness in present experience. As we have seen, the model of sacrifice points to the potential of the cross for evoking a repetition of Christ's sacrifice in us, but does not in itself explain how this happens. We do not seem to get much beyond an imitation of Christ. The modern form of *Christus Victor* lays stress upon the effect upon future ages that a disclosure of new achievement in

141

human life can have, together with the power of a community (the church), to shape response. The model of justice, understood from a modern perspective, suggests that the objectivity of the event of the cross involves a new experience for God himself. In such ways these models make the link between the cross in history and life today.

Abelard's concentration upon the cross as an act of love adds a further dimension to its creative effect, drawing particular attention (as we shall see) to the power of a story. But more than this, his explorations into the transforming energy of love make him an important test case for the approach to atonement that I have been commending throughout. His success and his failure in describing an objective 'kindling' of love through the cross should enable us to ask our own questions about the creative power of a past event, and so the dependence of our salvation upon it. At the same time we shall find that engaging with his thought prompts further reflection upon all those elements of *imitatio Christi*, disclosure, community and divine experience, that previous models have already exposed.

Abelard was one of a new generation of theologians in the second half of the twelfth century who had developed a deep curiosity about the life of Jesus as a human being.[2] Anselm had already raised the question 'Why did God become man?' and his successors laid even more stress on the 'man' part of the query. Abelard, for instance, wants to know why Christ spent so long living on earth among men before his death.[3] He can find no adequate motivation for the particular path of salvation God had freely chosen in either of the two popular main theories – the honouring of the devil's rights or the respecting of God's honour. Moreover both these accounts seemed to him to impose a necessity upon God from outside himself, as if God had to find some way of solving a problem that faced him. If Abelard is directly attacking Anselm's views, he is not entirely fair to them; Anselm, as we have seen, also denied that God was under the constraint of any external necessity. But Abelard here makes a shrewd point that if humankind owed a debt to God's honour which had to be satisfied, the death of Christ would only have made matters worse since he was murdered by human beings![4] This is rather more than the mere debating tactic it appears to be on the surface, since it reveals Abelard's interest in the actual human circumstances of the life and death of Christ

142

that can be lost in technical theory. There is only one possible motivation that Abelard can find for the Son of God to redeem us through the particular means of 'such numerous fastings, insults, scourgings and spittings, and finally that most bitter and disgraceful death';[5] that motive is the sheer love of God.

Though others had said this before, Abelard's originality is in the rigour and concentration with which he works it out. He affirms that when God revealed himself in the life of Jesus and reconciled us to himself by his death, he did not have to satisfy any prior conditions such as the demands of Satan or his own justice. He was simply satisfying his own nature of love. The very essence of God is love, and so the original act of creation and the new act of redemption were only 'necessary' in the sense that they fulfilled his own being. Since it is the essence of love to be 'ecstatic', moving beyond and diffusing itself, creation and redemption are fitting for God as a logical working out or 'intrinsic necessity' of his nature.[6] As God was moved to create human beings in the first place because he is love, planting within them his image which is chiefly character-ised by love,[7] so he was moved by love to restore them when they broke the bond of love that joined them to him. In the fine phrase of one interpreter of Abelard, Richard Weingart, this is 'the logic of divine love'.[8] Abelard seems here to celebrate the freedom of God without restraint, but, as we shall see, some of his difficulties might be resolved by being even more radical in affirming God to be 'the one who acts in freedom' (in Karl Barth's phrase).

Since, in Abelard's view, it is humankind that needs to be reconciled to God while God himself does not need to be reconciled to anyone, the love of God is the *means* as well as the motive of redemption. The need is for human beings to be changed, and Abelard believes that the love of God revealed and present in Christ will create that change. Indeed Abelard hints that the transforming effect of the love of God is so potent that the human state will not simply be restored to its pre-Fall glory, but taken to a new level altogether:

Everyone is made more righteous, that is more loving towards God, after the passion of Christ than he had been before, because a realized gift incites greater love than that which is only hoped for. Therefore, our redemption through Christ's suffering is that

143

supreme love in us which not only frees us from slavery to sin, but also acquires for us the true liberty of sons of God.[9]

It is clear from such expressions as 'made righteous', 'incites', 'frees us' and 'acquires for us' that Abelard believes the revelation of God's love to have a redemptive impact on its own account. To say that love 'kindles' love means that it generates it within; it is no mere matter of *our* imitating Christ. Abelard can certainly say rather subjectively that Christ shows us the love of God 'to *convince* us how much we *ought* to love him who spared not his own Son for us';[10] but elsewhere he speaks more objectively of God's action, in that 'Christ died for the wicked so that love might be *poured out* in our hearts',[11] and that 'Redemption *is* that supreme love within us, through Christ's suffering . . . so that we do all things out of love rather than fear.'[12] The severe criticism of Abelard in his own time by Bernard of Clairvaux therefore seems to lack perception; writing to Pope Innocent II Bernard is the first of a long line to accuse Abelard of holding a merely exemplary view of atonement:

> He holds and argues that it must be reduced just to this, that by his life and teaching [Jesus] handed down to men a pattern of life, that by his suffering and death he set up a standard of love. Did he then teach righteousness and now bestow it; reveal love and not infuse it?[13]

To these rhetorical questions Abelard was actually, like Bernard, offering a 'no'. Abelard's point is that Christ *did* 'infuse' love in us (though he prefers the phrase 'poured out' love), precisely *through* revealing it. Bernard is complaining that Jesus must have done something objectively and decisively for us in order to restore us to God; Abelard's point is that the demonstration of God's love is at the same time restorative, and so an objective act. Since, as we shall see, Abelard did not altogether succeed in making clear how this might be, Bernard is certainly exposing a weakness in his thought. But Bernard himself is deaf to any other objectivity than the kind he is familiar with.

Abelard's interest in the human life of Christ, and in the pattern which his teaching and works provide for us, is thoroughly characteristic of his time. Bernard and Anselm, among others, call upon the Christian disciple to imitate the example of Christ. Peter Damian exhorts the monk to follow 'Christ the poor man', and the discipline of imitation rises to a pitch in the slightly later work of Thomas à Kempis, who urges all to 'conform themselves to the crucified'. But alongside the setting forth of a pattern by Christ these theologians affirm more objective redemptive work – usually the satisfaction of God's honour or the meeting of the devil's rights. Bernard's mystical heart, however, is really in another kind of objective act of Christ; commenting on the text from the Song of Songs that 'thy name is as oil poured forth', Bernard explains that 'the plenitude of his divinity was poured forth when he dwelt in bodily form upon earth'.[14] He believes that God revealed his love by pouring divine life into human nature as a whole, changing it once and for all. This is why he accuses Abelard of forgetting that love was not only revealed but 'also' infused. However we are bound to ask how in practice human nature could have been universally transformed by a single act of transfusion.

By contrast Abelard's perception is that the showing forth of the love of God in the life of Christ is at the same time the pouring forth of love into the one who beholds it. Christ 'illuminates' us by his teaching, and by such aspects of his life as patience in suffering, discernment into evil, persistence in prayer, perfect obedience to God, humility in the face of malice and finally his selfless sacrifice for others in death: 'Dispelling our shadows with light, he *showed* us, both by his words and example, the fullness of all virtues, and *repaired* our nature.'[15] As Abelard moves from the word 'showed' to 'repaired' he is trying to express his insight that the love disclosed is at the same time the love which recreates. Similarly in the famous passage with which we began, often taken as summarising his thought, he moves from the phrase 'teaching us by word and example even unto death' to speaking of 'our hearts . . . enkindled by such a gift of divine grace'. Abelard is not simply saying that the *revelation* of love saves us; he is saying that *love as it is revealed* saves us.

If we ask how this happens, then the first clue Abelard offers is the power of the *story* of love. Writing to Héloïse, Abelard urges her to imagine herself to be one of the bystanders on the path of Christ's passion:

145

Are you not moved to tears of remorse by the only begotten Son of God, who for you and for all mankind, in his innocence was seized by the hands of impious men, dragged along and scourged, blindfolded, mocked at, buffeted, spat upon, crowned with thorns, finally hanged between thieves on the Cross. . . Keep him in mind. Look at him going to be crucified for your sake, carrying his own cross. Be one of the crowd, one of the women who wept and lamented over him. . . . In your mind be always present at his tomb, weep and wail with the faithful women . . . prepare with them the perfumes for his burial. . .[16]

The setting of this passage in the life of Abelard and Héloïse, one of the most famous love stories of the Middle Ages, is no mere incidental piece of biography. Following the catastrophic outcome of their secret marriage and the shameful revenge inflicted upon Abelard, the lovers had both retreated to the enclosed religious life. Thirteen years later Héloïse – now an esteemed abbess – was prompted to write to Abelard after reading his *History of My Misfortunes*. In the astonishing series of letters that followed, Héloïse passionately recalls their former love ('queens and great ladies envied me my joys and my bed'), reveals a heart still torn apart with longing for Abelard, and rebukes him for failing to write to her with comfort and spiritual counsel. Héloïse is imaginatively reliving the story of their love, and in telling it (in detail) to herself she feels both grief and grievance. Abelard thus takes up the human experience of telling a story and the human gift of memory, and applies it to the narrative of the cross; Héloïse is to enter into *that* story with the same imagination, for 'It was he who truly loved you, not I'. With psychological discernment, Abelard points out that their human love was actually marred by her fear of him;[17] elsewhere in his theological treatises he finds that the love shown in Christ is a new motivation for obedience to God, replacing the fear promoted by law.

Holding the picture of Christ, teacher and sufferer, in the imagination *can* have a merely emotional effect. Abelard trembles on the edge of this when he expects Héloïse to be moved to tears, and much medieval devotion is over-subjective, especially when it invites the onlooker to pity Christ. But Abelard clearly has an intuitive perception into a psychological mechanism at work which depends upon the impact of an objective event, and in which a deep change takes place in the mind. While all modern theories of atonement that find the cross to be an enabling event have a family-likeness to Abelard's thought (as we have seen), those that stand closest to it are those that use psychological insights to explore the profound change which the story of the cross can effect in the diseased ego.

Reinhold Niebuhr, for example, lays stress upon St Paul's coupling of the words 'wisdom' and 'power' when he describes the cross of Jesus.[18] There is wisdom in the cross, though the world counts it foolishness; that is, we *learn* from God's final revelation there of both his love and his justice. As we have already seen, without justice in the cross love becomes merely sentimental. But this disclosure of the meaning of God's love and justice, and the 'apprehension of truth' through faith, is at the same time a 'power'. For when 'we understand the possibilities and limits of our lives from beyond ourselves', this understanding has the power to shatter the self-centred self. 'The invasion of the self from beyond the self', comments Niebuhr, 'is therefore an invasion of both "wisdom" and "power", of both "truth" and "grace".'[19]

The Pauline statement that 'I am crucified with Christ' can thus be translated as 'My ego is shattered by the crucifixion of Christ'. In describing how this happens in the psyche, Niebuhr draws attention to the human faculty of self-reflection. We are able to rise above our present situation, telling ourselves the story of our past life; the gift of memory frees us from the prison of the present and together with hope it allows us to transcend time. Now, at the point when we transcend ourselves and survey the past, we become anxious, caught as we are between our freedom and our limitations. Instead of dealing with anxiety through trust in the One who transcends us, we adopt strategies to cope with it. We refuse to take responsibility for our past, making excuses for ourselves; the self, with its will to power and its pride, drawing everything in to its own centre, begins to change the story to justify itself. 'We deceive ourselves and the truth is not in us.'[20] In the moment of reflection then the self needs to be broken of its self-will and its evasions of the truth, and the hammer blow is delivered from outside itself by the revelation of the cross. As the self seeks inauthentic ways to deal with its anxiety, it needs to be turned towards the way of trust in God.

The cross achieves this by revealing the love of God and his verdict upon human life (his wrath):

> The self in this state of preoccupation with itself must be 'broken' and 'shattered' or, in the Pauline phrase, 'crucified'. It cannot be saved merely by being enlightened. . . The self is shattered whenever it is confronted by the power and holiness of God and becomes genuinely conscious of the real source and centre of all life.[21]

This account draws upon psychological insights into the tendency of the self to 'rationalisation', an adjustment of the truth to suit itself and to conform to social expectations. In its evasions and stratagems, the self cannot strengthen its own will to goodness. The only solution lies in a disclosure of truth breaking in from outside the self, and the cross has such power since it reveals a love which does not resort to any of the strategies for survival at which the self is so adept. The agape, the sacrificial love revealed on the cross, does not expect immediate reward within history. Though it has the power to draw out a response from other selves, it does not insist on getting a response as a condition of its self-offering.[22]

Niebuhr's linking of 'wisdom' and 'power' thus provides a psychological mechanism to support Abelard's perception that the revelation of love's truth is at the same time a generation of love. The self which is absorbed in itself needs to be shattered at its centre by an event from outside itself – which for us here and now means hearing the story or seeing the image of the cross. Talk of 'shattering' the self is of course a metaphor, and unless balanced by other metaphors may not be totally true to the life of the psyche. Niebuhr is really talking about the breaking of the *self-centredness* of the ego, not the ego itself. This, after all, needs to be healed and not destroyed. This is the centre of an account of atonement worked out by R. S. Lee,[23] in somewhat closer relation to Freud's theories of the ego and the super-ego. For Lee, identification with Christ (an *imitatio Christi*) promotes the growth of the ego in dealing with the real world. Once again he shows the link between perception of truth, or what is real, and the transforming of the self.

Lee follows the usual Freudian description of the growth of the super-ego, or the stern moralistic voice of conscience and guilt within the self, under the pressure of the Oedipus complex. The ego attempts to control the animal desires of the id (notably the desire to possess the mother, in the Freudian theory), by creating within itself a dominating image of the Father. The hapless ego then finds itself continually under criticism from this dictatorial super-ego. Whether or not we accept this particular account of the growth of conflict within the self, Lee is surely right to see the need to integrate the moral demands of the self (the super-ego) with the activity of the ego in gathering knowledge about the world and learning the skills of adapting itself to everyday life. He is also surely right in perceiving that trust must grow between the child and the father, and ultimately between the human child and the heavenly Father, if the self is to develop in a healthy way.

Lee pronounces that 'It is not the super-ego that leads us to the living God'; in the more familiar terms of Paul, the moral law cannot bring us peace with God. Rather, 'the ego must present [God] to the super-ego'.[24] The ego finds God and trusts him as the ultimate reality of the world, and from this perspective it can correct and shape the moral ideals of the self. Again in the terms of Paul, 'Christ is the end of the law' – the truth of God revealed in Christ is what the moral law is aiming at. Lee suggests that the ego always tries to correct the moral tyranny of the super-ego, to extend its view of what morality is, by finding models with which to identify itself. Not only admirable people in real life, but the heroes of literature and drama provide the ego with a range of characters 'in whom to live an imaginary life . . . Every such identification means that he takes a fresh character into himself and modifies his ego-ideal accordingly.'[25]

Now, Christ calls his disciples to identify with himself and his way of the cross, and the pattern of his life shows all the features that the ego needs for healthy development. Jesus is 'at one' with the Father; he is not in conflict with a dominating father-figure (the super-ego), but finds a true morality in obedience to the will of a Father in whom he trusts, even in the darkness of Gethsemane and Calvary. At the same time Jesus finds the reality of God in the whole area of the world which it is the function of the ego to explore; Jesus is interested in every aspect of life, discerning the kingdom of God through the growing of grass and corn, the building of a house, the jobs of shepherds, the hazards of travelling and the cares of housewives. When we take the character of Jesus into our imagination we are therefore absorbing a model which enables both ego and super-ego to find true fulfilment. Moreover the story of Jesus makes clear that when he calls people to identify with him, he also gives them the necessary freedom to be themselves. He gave his disciples no list of rules, but called them 'friends'. This is the love that does not attempt to appropriate, which does not leave the ego in childish dependence upon its role-model, but releases into the freedom of the sons of God.

These two modern interpretations of atonement supply insights into psychological processes through which the story and image of Christ – teacher and crucified one – can transform the mind. Whether 'shattering' the self-centredness of the ego or healing the conflict between conscious and unconscious levels of the mind, the theories show that the effect of revelation is much deeper than a mere moving of emotions. It is significant that in the fine hymn 'When I survey the wondrous cross', which sums up the whole tradition of contemplating the passion of Christ, Isaac Watts uses the device of *metonymy* in which the cause stands for the effect. In Christ's death, love is the cause, blood is the effect, and with a compression of meaning it is love which thus flows down (love and sorrow = blood and water). This pouring out of love is linked convincingly, though with no rational explanation, to an effect in us: 'and pour contempt on all my pride.'

> See, from his head, his hands, his feet,
>   Sorrow and love flow mingled down;
> Did e'er such love and sorrow meet,
>   Or thorns compose so rich a crown?
>
> (Isaac Watts)

First problem: the limits of individualism

Yet as they stand, the accounts of Niebuhr and Lee raise a number of questions that are already prompted by Abelard's own presentation of the power of divine love to kindle the heart. In the first place this approach seems highly individualistic, and does not immediately translate into the atonement of the individual within the setting of a social group, and even less into the reconciling of whole social groups themselves. In contrast, Bernard's vision of atonement centres upon an infusion of divine love into human nature *as a whole* through the advent and death of Christ. Bernard in the western church is here echoing the eastern tradition of *theosis*, that is, 'divinisation' in the sense of incorporating human nature into the fellowship of the divine life.

The eastern thinking on this matter goes back at least as far as Athanasius, who found the heart of atonement to lie in the restoring of the divine image in us through the becoming man of the divine Son. 'No other could raise up a mortal being as immortal, except our Lord Jesus Christ, who is life itself,' writes Athanasius.[26] Later Greek thought defined this more closely as the 'hypostasising' of human nature by the Logos, or our achieving of true 'personhood' through union with the person (*hypostasis*) of the Logos. In the thought of St Maximus, for example, the uncreated divine person of Christ absorbed into himself all created but sin-scarred human nature so that we might in ourselves 'unite, by love, created with uncreated nature' and become 'divine by grace'.[27] This is the fulfilling of God's purpose in bringing the world from nothing and endowing human beings with his image of eternal life.

But how does the 'divinising' of one particular human nature in Christ *extend* to the transforming of our natures? At times Athanasius and those who followed him seem to conceive of human nature as a kind of universal reality in which all individual human beings participate, so that the divinising effect of the Logos in Christ would be naturally communicated to all humankind who are his kin and flesh of his flesh. Thus Athanasius can write of the incarnation as actually changing the direction of our wills: 'Since the Word became man and appropriated what belongs to the flesh, these affections no longer touch the body because of the Word who assumed it, but have been destroyed by him.'[28] In our world it is no longer possible, however, to think in terms of individuals participating in universals as Platonist philosophers did. The link between the particular human nature of Jesus and ours must be understood in some other way.

Thus when we contrast Abelard with his contemporary in the West, Bernard, and even more with the eastern strain of *theosis*, we find a clarity in Abelard's account of the transforming power of

God's love; it happens as the self comes into confrontation with a story of unique revelatory force. But we also find a weakness. The other traditions are attempting to express the conviction that something has happened, objectively, to change the state of human life as a whole; something has happened in the corporate human existence which is there before us and in which we are all bound up. Abelard's attention is focused upon the individual person, and the intentions of the individual mind. This view of the atoning act of Christ fits in with his understanding of the problem with which atonement deals; sin, as he explains in his *Ethics*, is an interior quality of the soul, and in particular an attitude towards God. Neither natural vices nor evil desires, nor even evil actions are sinful in themselves; what makes something a sin is the intention behind it, the spirit in which it is willed or done. Sin is to be defined as 'actual contempt towards God or consent to evil'.[29] This is well illustrated, according to Abelard, by the different roles played by God and Judas in the crucifixion. Both handed over Christ to his enemies, and brought about the act of salvation; but Judas' deed could not be called good because of his malicious intention. 'Thus the betrayer did what God also did, but surely he did not do it well? . . . Although what was done was good, it was certainly not well done.'[30]

Abelard is surely right that sin is a matter of the rebellion of our hearts against God, not some impersonal debt to be paid off outside us, but rather a broken relationship to be healed within us. Salvation must be a healing of our wills which are resisting God here and now in the present. In this sense atonement must deal with the individual mind and its attitude towards God. But, as became clear in our discussion of the 'principalities and powers', there is also something more corporate about sin. It has results in damaging the lives of others, and works its way into the network of relationships with which we are (in a striking Old Testament phrase) 'bound up in the bundle of life'.[31] We must then try to understand the cross as having some effect upon the whole structure of human life and society. The eastern tradition attempts this with its stress upon divinisation and the gift of incorruption to corrupted human nature, even though it leaves us with the problem of connecting the particular (the nature of Jesus of Nazareth) to the universal (us).

Second problem: the event and the spirit

Actually Athanasius and his successors do offer another explanation for the link between the new creation in Christ and us:

> By grace [God] becomes the Father of those whose Maker he already is; he becomes this when created men receive, as the Apostle says, the Spirit of His Son crying, 'Abba Father' in their hearts. It is these who, having received the Word, have gained power from him to become God's children. Being creatures by nature, they would never have become sons if they had not received the Spirit from Him who is true son by nature.[32]

The Holy Spirit of God, on this view, applies to us the renewal of the divine image in Christ's nature. In the concept of developed eastern thought, the Spirit communicates the divine personhood (*hypostasis*) of the Logos to our natures.[33] The Spirit bridges the gap. But there is a danger of a merely superficial appeal to the idea of Spirit here, like summoning a *deus ex machina*, a deity rising from the machinery of the stage to confound the actors and to put the plot to rights. All can too easily be explained by invoking the mysterious activity of the Holy Spirit, God's active and gracious presence in the world. It is another step to make clear that the Spirit is indeed, as Athanasius asserts, 'from Him [Christ]'; in other words we have to clarify the causative link between the present acts of God to restore and adopt human beings into his family, and what is claimed to be the special activity of God in one human person in the past. This is a point to which we shall return, but for the moment we must notice that Abelard too appeals to the inner working of the Holy Spirit, and that much of his language of the infusing of love into the human heart is in fact related to the Spirit: 'Christ . . . sent the Holy Spirit; that is, he poured out his pure love into us by which we love him sincerely for his own sake.'[34]

Abelard's identifying of the Holy Spirit as love underlines that he is not simply urging us to copy the love of Christ by our own efforts; it emphasises Abelard's attempt to talk about the creative power of God's love to generate love within us. Love he understands to be the special characteristic of the Holy Spirit within the Trinity, and it is the Spirit who reactivates the love of human beings for their Creator. There is no question of our love for God being a product of our own good works; it is 'the love of God, which we call the Holy Spirit, infused into the heart of man', which 'vivifies the heart by moving us to do work productive of good.'[35] The statement of Paul that 'the love of God is poured forth in our hearts by the Holy Spirit' (Rom. 5:5) is a key one for Abelard, and he quotes it to explain the statement that redemption consists in the inciting of love within us.[36] But the way that Abelard understands the relation between the Holy Spirit and this kindling of love in the human heart must, for all this, be accounted a second major weakness in his thought.

We have seen Abelard's great insight to be that the revelation in Christ, when received by the human mind, is at the same time an actual infusion of love. The exhibition *is* a restoration. The manifestation *is* a transformation. This is what Abelard is struggling to understand for himself and to express. But when he analyses the operation of the Spirit in this, he finds a *sequence* in which the Spirit prepares the human mind to perceive the revelation of love for what it is, or grants the saving faith which results in works of love:

> The Spirit creates light first through his inspiration of faith, then hope, and finally love, by so perfecting man in works of love that he lives not only for himself but also for others ... The Holy Spirit, inspiring those whom he pleases, begins the spiritual building of the soul from this foundation.[37]

The last sentence indicates the end-point of this line of thought; the freedom of God to love as he desires is shown in his predestination of only some to salvation ('those whom he pleases'). In a double divine decree, while some are elected to redemption, the rest of mankind are elected to reprobation. It may seem very odd that a theologian who exults in the unbounded generosity of the love of God should be willing to consign little children to damnation, though it be of the mildest kind; but it is a logical consequence of equating the preparatory movement of the Spirit in the human heart with the complete work of love, recreating and turning the will to love of God. If the prevenient work of the Spirit is the kind of infusion of love which actually *justifies* the sinner, then since it is

154

an empirical fact that all men do not show love for God, the conclusion follows that only some have been elected.

Rather we ought to think of the mysterious work of the Spirit, deep beneath the surface of human life, in a more complex way; we need, for example, to enlarge our minds to think of God as being humble enough to tolerate resistance to his love which is shed abroad in our hearts. On the other hand we must try to follow, more closely than Abelard does, his own deepest insight that the love of God is somehow poured out *from the event* of Christ. The work of the Spirit who is love is actually bound up with the act of revelation, not simply laying the ground for it. As Abelard himself sees, it is the manifestation of love in Christ by which 'everyone is made more righteous': 'the showing of his justice, that is his love, justifies us in his sight'.[38] Yet when he comes to consider how love *can* be poured out from the cross, justifying love simply becomes the prior condition for noticing the revelation.

Thus the pouring out of the Spirit of love becomes separated from the actual act of love in Christ. It is a detached event, and does not seem to need the life or death of Christ at all. But how can love be 'poured out' from an event in the past? Abelard tells us this is so, but is not really able to tell us how. I intend to offer an answer by the end of this chapter, but we can only approach it by observing a third weakness in Abelard's own thought about redeeming love.

Third problem: why was love shown in a death?

If the 'showing of love' in Christ has power to reconcile, we must still ask why love should be revealed in a *death*. It is easy to see the love of God unveiled in the compassionate deeds of Jesus, and his teaching about the caring heavenly Father, but the sight of a man dying by means of a prolonged and agonising torture does not immediately arouse a sense of the love of God. Abelard quotes the text of John 15:13, that 'Greater love has no man but this, that a man lay down his life for his friends', but for such an act to demonstrate how much one loves there must be a reason why it is needed. Abelard affirms that God has freely chosen to display his love in this way – but why in a death?

155

I believe that it is to find an answer to this pressing question that Abelard returns to the range of traditional images and theories of atonement which he has previously found to be unsatisfactory. Expositors of Abelard often express surprise that, having propounded his own theory of redeeming love, Abelard still resorts to images of sacrifice, merit, expiation, purchase, and the defeat of Satan that he had previously weighed and found wanting. It is even suggested that, where these appear in his commentary on the Epistle to the Romans, he is merely recording the views of past theologians as a good commentator would, without necessarily adopting them. However we notice that, both here and in other places, he uses them in a way that does not conflict with his own fundamental view of atonement. He is not inconsistent, but there is a curious untidiness about his thought; he is unable to integrate these other metaphors of atonement into his main idea.

In portraying the crucified Christ as a sacrifice, for instance, he shows consistency by refraining from mentioning any notion of appeasing God. Christ sacrifices himself, as both priest and victim to the altar, in an act of love 'for us'; but Abelard offers no explanation as to how the death might *be* 'for us'. Similarly, using the language of expiation he affirms that Christ bears our sins in his body, dies under the curse of the law and submits to the wrath of God against sin. Through this he lifts the punishment for sin with which we are threatened, but Abelard does not attempt to explain *how* this happens, except to attribute it to Christ's sinlessness and to the power of love to cancel the command of the law. He says nothing of any satisfaction offered to God, and though he quotes the word *propriator* from the Vulgate (Latin) translation of the New Testament,[39] he does not define or expound it. Asserting that Christ has indeed achieved a conquest over Satan, he refuses to accept that the devil has any rights, either in law or fact, and denies that a ransom has been paid to him. How the death of Christ constitutes a victory is not explained, but conquest is interpreted as the winning of freedom from sin and release from fear in death. Nor has any ransom been paid to God; where Abelard uses the language of 'purchase' and 'price' it is simply to underline the cost of redemption to God.[40]

Thus Abelard heaps together a glittering pile of traditional images – sacrifice, purchase, penalty, curse, victory – and in line with his view of atoning love he removes any elements of satisfaction or appeasement from them. They are all about *death*, and in this way Abelard seems to be explaining why the death of Christ was a central part of the revelation of divine love. But, on closer examination, Abelard has still not made clear why a death should be such a demonstration of love; he simply uses the images in an impressionistic way, drawing on the emotive power of their link with death. With these traditional images of death, Abelard can certainly express the initiative which God takes in his love, and the cost of forgiveness to God. But his references remain untidy, not properly integrated into the mainstream of his thought.

There is, of course, a straightforward answer to the question as to why the love of God is demonstrated finally in the death of Christ: it is because God himself undergoes the bitter depths of human experience in the cross. God, we may say, shows his love by enduring to the uttermost the estrangement of his own creation. This is the depth of God's identification with us. But Abelard, like others of his time, is not able to give this answer. He is working with the presupposition that the divine nature cannot suffer or change in any way, so that it is only the *human nature* of Jesus which literally suffers in the cross. Following the tradition of a 'two nature Christology', Abelard explains that when God assumed humanity the divine and human natures were united in one Person, so it is permissible to interchange the titles given to God and man in Christ. Thus we can certainly say that the Son of God was born of Mary, and even that 'the Lord of glory was crucified'; but we must interpret this as 'the man or body assumed by him was fastened to the stake'.[41]

Since, according to Abelard, the eternal Word or Son of God shares the impassibility of God within the Trinity, then strictly it is only in his humanity that Christ fears, prays, suffers the agonies of crucifixion and endures mortality. In his humanity Christ suffers a more terrible death than any other man, since through union with the Logos he knows more than any other man about the depth of the horror of death; but still suffering and death does not actually touch the divine nature. Abelard, for all his celebration of the freedom of God to love, restricts his freedom at this point. God is not free to endure suffering and death, because the divine essence must be always impassible and immutable. We recall that Abelard grounds the redemptive acts of God in the 'inner necessity' of his nature; that is, the essence of God as love dictates his actions. Likewise the same nature lays down the limits for acts of love; for God, love cannot be unto death.

The One who loves in freedom

With this view we may compare the insight of a modern theologian, Karl Barth, who finds the ultimate lordship of God to lie precisely in his freedom to be and to do what he chooses. God is 'the one who loves in freedom', and he is not constrained by any nature apart from the one he determines for himself.[42] He is free to be conditioned by his own creation as much as to remain unconditioned by it; in short, 'God is his own decision'.[43]

What he has decided, Barth declares, is known to us in God's revelation of himself. His being corresponds to his acts, and in unveiling himself in the world he tells the truth about himself. Since we find God in Christ, and Christ is on the cross, we know that God has freely chosen to humble himself, to endure suffering and to face death (though not to be defeated by it). If our philosophical ideas tell us that all this is not worthy of God, and that he must be 'wholly other' than us, then 'such beliefs are shown to be untenable, and corrupt and pagan, by the fact that God does in fact be and do this in Jesus Christ'.[44] It is a majestic theme of Barth's theology that the true nature of divinity is seen in abasement and service; God is never more the sovereign Lord than in the cross. Our thoughts about what is proper for God must be guided only by what he has shown us of himself in Christ.

This in turn leads us to see love itself in a slightly different light from the one Abelard places it in. For Abelard the love which the life and death of Christ creates in us is completely disinterested, expecting no reward. God is to be loved purely for his own sake, and not because of the blessedness that comes from him, or even because of his own love for us. It is, Abelard judges, a matter of self-interest 'if I love God because he loved me and not because he is such as is to be loved above all else regardless of what he does to me'.[45] As I have already commented, love does indeed take the risk of getting no return for its expense; the self-giving love hymned by Paul in the New Testament (agape) does not calculate any gains but spends itself extravagantly. However, unless we allow the other person within a relationship to give to us as well as to receive from us, even this love can become a form of domination. The attitude that says 'You can do nothing for me' can destroy relationship and diminish the other. If love is a mutual giving and receiving, then there is bound to be an element of desire and self-fulfilment (*eros*) in love, as we allow a friend or lover to make their own contribution to the relationship. We are the richer through their qualities and their self-giving. In giving ourselves away we thus receive ourselves back, or in the gospel text, 'He who loses his life . . . will gain it.' Abelard is surely right in his emphasis, but he does not sufficiently allow for the dimension of *eros* in our love for God and our neighbour. A total stress upon self-giving love reflects a view of divine love which belongs with impassibility and immutability. If God cannot be affected in any way by his creation, then he cannot gain anything from it; strictly his bliss cannot be increased by fellowship with his creatures. They can do nothing for him; it is only their joy which is fulfilled, and not his.

But if we take seriously the freedom of God to love, then we can say that he desires fellowship with us, and that by his own eternal choice his being is enhanced by relationship with us. It is not that there is a need for fellowship with others thrust upon him which he has to satisfy, but that out of his freedom he determines to be in need. The One who owes nothing to anyone else for his existence, nevertheless humbly chooses not to be totally self-sufficient in the life he enjoys. The seventeenth-century poet Thomas Traherne saw the logic of saying that God finds joy in his creation: incredible though it is to us, 'Want is the fountain of all His fullness . . . Infinite wants satisfied produce infinite joys.'[46] The 'want' of God is eternal because God's choice cannot be sundered from his very being. We may say, again with Karl Barth, that God has an 'eternal covenant' with man, that God opens the fellowship of his triune life to his creatures in a primal decision upon which he will never go back and behind which we can never penetrate.[47]

We may then follow through the main thrust of Abelard's view of atonement, further than he could. The death of Christ 'exhibited that love than which there could be nothing greater' because God suffered there to bring many sons to glory and thus to complete his joy; both the pain and the fulfilment of bliss show the humility and the weakness of God, freely assumed in love. As we have seen, the element of judgement in the cross is not altogether absent from Abelard's thought, but it must have a more central place if love leads God to endure the desolation which is his own verdict upon humankind. The revelation of such a deep identification with the predicament of humankind has, at the least, a psychological effect upon us. As Paul Tillich suggests, we would not have the courage 'to accept that we are accepted' in spite of our awareness that we are unacceptable, unless we knew that God had participated in our estrangement and loss. It is this participation that quietens our anxiety and gives us assurance.[48] But we must surely say more than this about the revelation of love if it is at the same time an imparting of love.

The transforming presence

The humble love of God, in which he opens himself to pain and joy in the world, is not just revealed like a fact in a scientific textbook. The revealing of his love *is* at the same time God's opening of himself, for revelation can be nothing less than the self-unveiling of the being of God. Revelation, as Karl Barth puts it, is 'the Person of God speaking', not a message about him.[49] If revelation were the communication of certain statements from God to us, then we would have God under our control; we could analyse and master such a word of God, and God would no longer be free. As Moses wanted to gain power over God by possessing his name in the ancient story (Exod. 3:13), so we would possess the divine word. But God remains the sovereign Lord if the 'Word' of God is nothing less than God's expressing himself, an act in which we encounter him and in which he remains free always to surprise us with new things. Human words are then called to witness and respond to this Word, and part of the witness is the gospel story itself. Thus God is 'revealed' in the life and death of Jesus in the sense that human beings meet him there, either in the historic event or through the story as it is told now.

Only God can link the revelation of love and the outpouring of love, because revelation is always an encounter with the 'person of

God speaking'. To encounter a God in whose heart is a cross is bound to affect the human personality. But in what sense can the crucified Son, through whom the Father is known, be present with us today to mould us to the pattern of his death and life? Abelard speaks not only of Christ's teaching us by word and example; commenting on Paul's saying that the love of God is poured into our hearts, Abelard explains this as the dwelling of Christ in the soul.[50] Naturally Abelard associates this presence of Christ with the sacraments of baptism and Eucharist. In baptism the soul is united with Christ, and rises from the baptismal waters like a bride going to the embrace of the bridegroom.[51] In his understanding of the Eucharist Abelard lays particular stress upon the communion of the receiver with Christ, and especially upon a sharing of the pattern of Christ's sufferings: Christ, he comments, bids us to his table as if inviting us 'to suffer together with me'.[52] Here it might seem we have reached the end of our quest for the link between past event and present salvation, but an appeal to the sacraments does not simply resolve everything. The bread, wine and water of Eucharist and baptism focus the presence of God in the whole of creation; though God gives himself to us in an intensified way in the sacraments, and though they provide a place of encounter with the person of Christ crucified and risen, this gift and meeting belongs in some way to the whole of life in the world. This means that we must be able to speak about the presence of Christ in a way that is not *exclusive* to the sacraments, although they focus it.

It was Friedrich Schleiermacher in the nineteenth century who firmly located the influence of Christ's personality in the context of a community. He is the heir of Abelard in so far as he found the atoning power of Christ's life and death to lie in the transforming of human attitudes to God, but more clearly than Abelard he stresses that the presence of the Redeemer cannot be separated from the community of his followers. Schleiermacher believed that a sense of 'absolute dependence' was a universal characteristic of all human experience, and that this was in fact a consciousness of God who is the 'whence' towards which this dependence leans. While human God-consciousness has become confused and broken, Jesus Christ had perfect God-consciousness, and it is this which he communicates to his disciples. His reconciling activity is the assuming of sinners into vital fellowship with himself and so into the blessedness of his own consciousness of God. Schleiermacher's great insight was to realise that if God was present in Christ, and if this presence actually had the power to *form* other human personalities, then Christ must bring about a new kind of 'corporate life' between himself and those whom he transforms, and also between those who are seized by his influence:

> Hence, just as the redemptive activity of Christ brings about for all believers a corporate activity corresponding to the being of God in Christ, so the reconciling element, that is, the blessedness of the being of God in him, brings about for all believers, as for each separately, a corporate feeling of blessedness.[53]

However, in considering the power of Christ to shape our personalities, Schleiermacher believed that the decisive moment of atonement lay in the fact that Christ's communion with God remained undisturbed and unbroken by his suffering and death. On this view the cross tests and authenticates the strength of the blessedness which Christ imparts to us. Schleiermacher therefore is also the heir of Abelard in failing to take the God-forsakenness of the event seriously. Further (and not unconnected with the previous point) it seems clear to us in our modern age that Schleiermacher was altogether too confident about a universal religious experience, and has little to say to the sense of loss of God-consciousness among people today that has been called 'the death of God'. In this century Dietrich Bonhoeffer – theologian and martyr, who was hanged in a Nazi prison – has dared to face the implications of a secular world in which God no longer seems necessary to explain anything. Like Schleiermacher he finds the atoning power of Christ to lie in his 'taking form' in the world today, and in his 'conforming' of others to himself. The cross, however, has a much more central part in all this, as an event in which Christ knew real loss and alienation.

Bonhoeffer directs us to ask, '*Who* is Christ today?' and '*where* is he present?' These are the important questions regarding Christ and redemption, since 'It is an impossible question to ask how the man Jesus, limited by space and time, can be contemporary with us. There exists no such isolated Jesus.'[54] Bonhoeffer's point is that the presence of Christ in every age is simply a given reality, because he exists for the sake of others. Christ is *pro me* ('for me') as Luther con-

162

stantly affirmed, and this is not a quality added to his person but the very definition of his being. As 'the man for others' Christ must be a 'corporate person', present in the human community. When we find the form and the place in which Christ is present, then we discover the power of Christ to shape our lives to his pattern, into that costly discipleship which is the true imitation of his love.

Christ is 'for us', and so lives a life that includes us, because the God who is always 'for us' is uniquely present in him: 'This isolated God does not exist. . . Who is there, present in time and place? The answer is, "the one person of the God–Man Jesus Christ" . . . in the man Jesus is God *God.*'[55] God's nature is fully relational; he is ecstatic love, love that goes out beyond the self to another. The deepest reality is personal, and to be a person is not to be a self-contained individual but to live in relationships. 'Being is communion', states a modern Orthodox scholar, John Zizioulas, recalling that the early Greek Fathers caused a revolution in philosophical thinking when they created the Trinitarian confession of 'One God in three Persons (*hypostases*)'.[56] By equating the term *hypostasis* (meaning 'being' or 'reality') with 'person' (*prosopon*) they made clear that to be personal is not merely a quality added on to the nature of someone, but that to live in relationships is the very centre of his essence. In our distorted, fallen existence *we* may begin by thinking first of someone's being, and then of the relationships in which he loves, works and plays; but for God, to be and to relate is the same. Thus if this God is fully present in Christ, regardless of the exact way we define the incarnation, Christ must be a fully relational reality. In Jesus Christ there is a new kind of human being, who could not and cannot exist except in relation to us. 'The only way for a true being to exist is for being and communion to coincide.'[57]

Though a man who is totally personal in this way challenges our notions of how things are, yet to some degree we experience the personal world of communion and relationship all the time, and poets and novelists have given us visions of what it might be like to be fully interpersonal. The contemporary novelist Doris Lessing, for example, writing in the genre of science fiction portrays a superior civilisation in which the one can represent the many in a new commonwealth of love: 'The Representative swept on and up, like a shoal of fishes or flock of birds; one, but a conglomerate of individuals – each with its little thoughts and feelings, but these shared with the others, tides of thought, of feeling, moving in and out and around, making the several one.'[58]

Where and *who*, then, is Christ the representative for us today? In his earlier work Bonhoeffer gave a similar answer to Schleiermacher: 'Christ exists as the church.' By this he meant not that the being of Christ is exhaustively emptied into it but that the church is now the form he takes in space and time. Indeed with his startling image of the church as 'the *body* of Christ', the apostle Paul had already portrayed the risen Christ as leading a life which overlaps with and includes the community of his followers. Bonhoeffer's deep insight, which takes him much further than Schleiermacher, is to draw this firmly into the orbit of the cross. The Christ who takes form as the church is 'the whole Person, the one who is exalted and *the one who is humiliated*'.[59] He is present not only as the exalted Lord, but as the one who went about incognito in Palestine, 'as a beggar among beggars, as an outcast among outcasts, as despairing among the despairing, as dying among the dying'.[60]

Bonhoeffer perceives that for Christ to take form as the church must mean the scandalous form of a crucified and humiliated one, because Christ must be hidden in his members who, while not any longer under the power of sin, yet remain sinners. One only has to think of the shameful record of the church of Christ – such as the medieval Inquisition and the modern silence when the Holocaust was taking place – to realise exactly how humiliated Christ must be. Christ is hidden also, his glory veiled, in the human word of preaching and the material bread and wine of the Eucharist. 'He is present as our creator, who makes us into new creatures. But he is present also as the humiliated creature in the sacrament, and in no other way.'[61]

In his final writings from his prison cell, however, Bonhoeffer widens his vision of the Christ who is present as the humiliated one, and so widens the scope of the imitation of Christ. We are to look in all the life of the world, in the secular world that lives 'as if there were no God', to discover *where* Christ is. For Christ must not be limited to being the answer to human problems and unful-filled desires; 'God is the beyond in the midst of life, in the centre', not on the boundaries. Christ is present in the midst of what people *can* do, not simply the one who steps in to what they cannot do.

Here Bonhoeffer makes a profound connection between the cross and the lack of a sense of God in the world today. On the cross God reveals himself as the one who has left aside his power and glory, since he reveals himself in a forsaken man who longs for God and yet is given no divine escape route. 'If we are speaking about the divinity of Jesus we must speak especially of his weakness.' So, Bonhoeffer concludes, Christ is now hidden and waiting to be found in places where God seems weak and powerless. This certainly means that God suffers with the forsaken and oppressed in our world, but it also means that God is 'there for us' in places where he appears to be redundant, where no one calls for a God to intervene, where human beings are exercising their freedom to be adult. There God suffers his humiliation, crucified 'at the hands of a godless world':

> God would have us know that we must live as men who manage our lives without him. The God who is with us is the God who forsakes us (Mark 15.34). The God who lets us live in the world without the working hypothesis of God is the God before whom we stand continually. Before God and with God we live without God. God lets himself be pushed out of the world on to the cross. He is weak and powerless in the world and that is the way, the only way, in which he is with us and helps us.[62]

Now if the believer is to imitate the pattern of Christ, he must participate in these sufferings of God. This means engaging wholeheartedly in the projects and concerns of the secular world, wherever these foster the life and love which Christ came to bring, whether or not religious talk is applied to them. It means being interested in those things which religious people often call 'secondary'. Bonhoeffer never rejected his earlier concerns for the life of prayer, exegesis of scripture and 'quiet meditation upon the life, sayings, deeds, suffering and death of Jesus in order to learn what God promises and what he fulfils'.[63] But this 'secret discipline' runs alongside the discipleship of action in the secular world, where Christ is also to be found. In a later chapter we shall be exploring the relevance of this for political engagement in particular.

So the presence of Christ, conforming us to himself, is intimately bound up with the cross whether he is met in the community of the church or the community of the wider world. The transforming presence of Christ is not simply illustrated by the cross; it can be said to come *from* the cross in that it is the God who experienced the cross who is present to us. To meet this God is to be summoned to enter the interweaving of relationships which is God's own life. Talk of God as Trinity is not really to make a picture of God that can be painted either in the mind or on canvas or in glass. It is not a way of making God an object of our analysis, but rather a language about *sharing* in God. In praying to the Father we find that our words are fitting into a movement of relationship that is already there before us, like that of a conversation between a Son and a Father; so, as St Paul says, we offer our 'yes' to God through the Amen which Christ speaks as the faithful son to the Father.[64] In giving ourselves away to others, we find ourselves leaning upon a movement of self-giving and mission that is far deeper than our own, as we share in the 'sending' of the Son *by* the Father. In our suffering we find ourselves supported by a movement of suffering love which is more terrible than our own.

The dimension of the Spirit

But we must also speak of relationship in the Holy Spirit. Abelard, as we saw, was not really able to associate the love of the Spirit with the cross of Christ, and so the pouring out of the Spirit became dissociated from atonement. Nor is it enough with Augustine and many successors simply to speak of the Spirit as the 'bond of love' between the Father and the Son. This empties the Spirit of his own personal identity which the worshipping church has wanted to recognise through the ages. Moreover if we think of encounter with God as 'participating' in the relationship within God, then ideas of 'bond' or 'communion' cannot be limited to the Spirit alone. Yet experience of God does lead believers to associate 'fellowship' in a particular way with the person of the Spirit; he is the 'spirit of unifying', the 'go-between God', the one who prays within us 'with groans that cannot be articulated' (Rom. 8:15,26).

This last phrase of the apostle Paul perhaps supplies us with the clue to the particular work of the Spirit in atonement. It cannot simply be a matter of 'applying' the past atoning work of Christ to us, since God as Father and Son as well as Spirit is present to transform our personalities here and now. But Paul reminds us that there is a dimension in our participation in God that is not satisfied by talk of a Father–Son relationship. Another metaphor – a 'breathing' (spirit) like the gentle movement of air in our bodies or the strong wind blowing outside us – is needed to evoke those depths of personal experience which are more to do with moods, intuitions, non-verbal communication and empathy. There is a dimension of sympathy which 'cannot be expressed'.

Of course all human language about God is analogy, corresponding to the truth and yet falling short of it. But we do find that the image of Father and Son drawn from everyday life can conceptualise our experience of God's activity, and we have seen how theories of atonement can appeal to different aspects of the relationship between Father and Son to 'explain' our experience of being reconciled. Yet in all these processes of victory, obedience, penalty and sacrifice there remains something mysterious, something to do with the depth of personality for which we can only use the range of impressionistic images which the scriptural writers supply for the Spirit – a breeze blowing gently, a gale uprooting everything in its path, a breath stirring, oil trickling, fire warming and fire burning, water refreshing and water in which we are totally immersed, wings beating and wings brooding.[65]

These images appear to be impersonal because they do not use the terms of human family and society. But they surely evoke another *level* of personality, reminding us that the personal relationships within God cannot be exhausted by filial and paternal characteristics. I agree with those feminist theologians who refuse to view the Holy Spirit as the token female within the Godhead, though language about the Spirit has often been marked by female qualities; but the point is that to speak of the outpouring of the Spirit or baptism in the Spirit is to make clear that we cannot reduce the terms 'Father' and 'Son' to the male characteristics that belong to fathers and sons in human life. Indeed as soon as we speak of a 'corporate personality' of Christ as we have been doing, we have lost the concept of an exclusively male individual. Paul, we notice, needs to use 'Spirit' language when he speaks of our being included 'in the body of Christ' (1 Cor. 12:13). It is also the images of Spirit, briefly mentioned above, that enable us to think of the reconciling work of God as reaching into the whole of creation. Again Paul describes not only human beings but all creation as 'groaning' in the 'travail' of hope for final redemption, and immediately speaks of the Spirit as uttering 'sighs too deep for words'.[66] The implication is surely that the sighs of all creation are taken up into, and transformed by, the being of God.

To speak of the creative influence of the divine personality upon our personalities, we need to speak of the fellowship of the Holy Spirit as well as the love of the Father and the grace of Christ. The Holy Spirit is not alone fellowship, any more than the Father is alone love, but we may say that there is a movement within the being of God that is always opening up the hidden depths of fellowship. In the same way, the Spirit in scripture is associated with the future, breaking open history with the challenge of something new. God is Holy Spirit, a breath whose origins cannot be traced, a wind that blows where it wills.[67] This is the one who loves in freedom.

Part III

Experiences

8

The cost of forgiveness

In his play *The Tempest* Shakespeare invites us to imagine an island where one man, by his magic arts, has gained complete control over his natural surroundings. Prospero, the rightful Duke of Milan, had been supplanted from his dukedom twelve years before, and after being abandoned to the sea with his young daughter Miranda, had been cast ashore on this island. Now the sea has brought his enemies who conspired against him within the orbit of his power, and by his magic he pitches them into a storm which apparently wrecks them on his shore. Through exposure to the elements, their wandering exhausted through the island, and the tragic loss (as they believe) of Ferdinand, the son of the King of Naples, Prospero is giving his enemies space to learn repentance. The wise Prospero has mastered not only the natural elements but his own heart, and when those who wronged him are powerless before him he offers forgiveness rather than revenge. Ferdinand, who has been kept safe, meets and loves Miranda and Prospero has his dukedom restored to him. Passing through a water of cleansing all can die to their old lives and can experience a new world. Yet one character at least refuses to be reconciled.[1] Antonio, the wicked brother of Prospero, remains silent in the face of forgiveness, declining to choose the good. With great perception, the modern poet W. H. Auden makes him speak thus:[2]

> Your all is partial, Prospero,
>   My will is all my own:
> Your need to love shall never know
> Me: I am I, Antonio,
>   By choice myself alone.

Blockages to forgiveness

Through the experience of this play we come to see that even if a man might control nature and his own passions, he could not force love and forgiveness upon other persons. They have to repent and receive, and the one who wants to forgive must enable the other to accept his offer and win him back into fellowship freely. The blockage to relationship lies in the attitude of the offender, and faced with this all the magic books and wands in the world can do nothing. Setting sail for Milan, Prospero breaks his magic staff and buries his book of spells fathoms deep, knowing he must face the unknown hazards of human personalities once more. The king of the island is vulnerable in real life to forces that he can never control.

> ... like the baseless fabric of this vision,
> The cloud-capp'd towers, the gorgeous palaces,
> The solemn temples, the great globe itself,
> Yea, all which it inherit, shall dissolve,
> And, like this insubstantial pageant faded,
> Leave not a wrack behind. We are such stuff
> As dreams are made on; and our little life
> Is rounded with a sleep.[3]

Prospero knows that the island is an interlude, a play or dream which must end. Life itself is surrounded by death, like an island set in hostile seas, and throughout life there are other elements of chaos that love and wisdom must face, the darkest of these lying in the personalities of human beings.

Forgiveness is a costly and difficult matter both for the one who offers it and the one who receives it, because true forgiveness aims for reconciliation, and this means the removal of barriers to relationship. Early on I referred to forgiveness as a 'shattering' experience, and stressed that when atonement is understood as an act of divine forgiveness it must be an event that happens here and now.[4] Forgiveness is no mere legal pardon, as became clear in our analysis of the New Testament concept of 'justification'; it is not an impersonal notice of acquittal which could be issued long ago and left lying around for us to pick up in due time, but a healing of relationship that must involve us *now* as the ones who are estranged. The theme which has continually emerged from our exploration of the images of atonement is that the cross is a creative act, a past event with power to change human attitudes to God and to each other in the present; this creativity is at the very heart of forgiveness, as can be seen if we reflect upon what it involves in human relationships.

The journey of forgiveness

We notice that in any act of forgiveness there is a change that takes place in both the participants, in the forgiver as much as in the one who is forgiven. For true reconciliation there must be a movement from both sides. Naturally the offender has to move in sorrow and repentance towards the person he has hurt, but the forgiver also needs to move and experience change within himself, even when he is totally willing to forgive. In human acts of forgiveness this movement is often partly a matter of recognising that he himself has contributed something to the breach. In situations where an established relationship has been broken – in the family, between friends or colleagues – the forgiver may have been the one mainly injured, but in human relationships no one is an entirely 'innocent party'. So the forgiver also needs to be forgiven, and must move in his attitude to accept this. However there is another kind of 'change' in approach to the other, which is also appropriate for God who is perfect in his relationships, as we are not. Borrowing a phrase from H. R. Mackintosh, we can say that the forgiver must 'set out on voyages of anguish';[5] he must make an agonising and costly journey in experience.

The first part of the journey of forgiveness is a voyage of discovery, an active movement in which awareness is awakened. If the forgiver is aiming to heal a broken relationship, he cannot just forget about the offence done to him. In fact it would be far more comfortable to put the hurtful affair out of mind and to resolve never to meet the offender again. But there is a brokenness in relationship that has to be faced up to if it is going to be healed, and so the forgiver needs to bring the injury done to him back to mind, and has to live again through the pain of it. This voyage must go far, to the very

173

point of thinking himself into the mind of the offender, feeling with the guilty person, standing in his shoes and making a deep effort to understand why he said or did what he did. Only when the forgiver has made this costly journey of sympathy into the experience of the other can he go to him and say 'I forgive you'. As soon as he says this, he has brought the offence out into the open, pulling it from the darkness in which it has been festering into clear daylight. Now the offender must embark upon his own voyage of discovery; he has been shaken into awareness of what he has done, and there can be no healing unless it is faced up to and sorrowed over. There is no need for the forgiver to utter words of recrimination; the word of forgiveness itself is a word of searching judgement, reminding them both of the hurt and wrong that lies between them.

After the stage of discovery in the voyage of forgiveness comes the journey of endurance. This is a passive mood, submitting to the consequences of acting to awaken the sleeping wrong. The forgiver must absorb the hostility of the other, to bear it and receive it into himself. By offering the word of forgiveness he has taken the first step across the gulf which separates the two who are apart, and so he has exposed himself to attack. He has made himself vulnerable, laying himself open to aggressive reactions. The offender is resentful at having the offence recalled; he fears blame and so wants to justify himself by blaming the other. He is angry with the one who offers forgiveness, saying (or at least feeling), 'How dare you say that you forgive me! What presumption! It's as much your fault as mine.' If there is to be reconciliation the forgiver must not react to justify himself or to accuse the other; he must not argue the case, but rather bear patiently the hostility of the other, drawing out the venom of his anger. He has acted to bring the matter out into the open in the first place; now he must neutralise the hostility by submissively bearing with the other in love.

Through the twofold journey of action and submission, provoking and absorbing, the forgiver is actually discovering how to win the offender back into relationship. Through identification with the feelings of the other, he is learning how to enable the other to accept his forgiveness. The inner change the forgiver undergoes is a sympathetic entering into the other's life, and his approach to him is shaped by this experience. Forgiveness takes the form of a painful voyage like this because of the nature of the problem to be overcome; there is a blockage in the offender's attitude to the relationship which makes it hard for him to accept forgiveness. As Mackintosh puts it, forgiveness is a 'shattering experience' for the one who is forgiven as much as for the one who offers it. It is a humbling and disturbing gift, and it is not at all surprising if (like Shakespeare's Antonio with whom we began) it is declined. The offender will only be enticed to accept it if he experiences the forgiver as a certain kind of person, not as a harsh critic or judge of his actions, but someone who has truly drawn alongside him and feels with him. Forgiveness is thus a creative act, 'calling a fresh situation into being' (Mackintosh).[6]

Forgiveness through the life and death of Jesus

The experience of forgiveness in human relationships helps us to interpret the cross of Jesus as God's great offer of forgiveness to human beings, creating a new situation universally. In it we can trace the same twofold journey of discovery and endurance, or moments of action and submission. In the first place there is the voyage of discovery, as Christ enters into the experience of those who have offended against God and life itself, and have propelled themselves into a situation of estrangement. In death Christ identifies himself with human beings at the lowest point of their existence, immersed into utter forsakenness. Though himself living in tune with the Father's mind, he consents to participate in the alienation which is the lot of a humanity which has lost communion with God. He stands with the guilty under the weight of the verdict which God passes upon rebellious human life. God's judgement, as I have argued, is his underlining of the momentum and consequences of human sin, so that Christ enters the realm of death in its most bitter form, as the place where all relationships are broken. The various words of Christ from the cross which the evangelists place in their narratives interpret the event: the plea 'Father forgive them' does not conflict with the awful cry 'My God why have you forsaken me?' but brings out its meaning, since forgiveness is nothing less than a voyage into the dark void of the guilty life.

At the same time the cross brings all humankind to discovery of its condition, bringing clearly out into the open the vicious nature of human sin, and the end to which it leads. This is what it looks like for man to sin against his neighbour, to crucify love. Further, this is what death looks like when humankind is estranged from the source of its life in God. As the forgiver plumbs the depths of the offenders' lives, he provokes the guilty into awareness of the wrongs they would prefer to hide. The initiative he takes in identifying with them calls for a response; empathy becomes judgement.

This pattern seems to have been characteristic of the way that Jesus, in his whole ministry, offered God's forgiveness of sins and acceptance into the coming kingdom of God. Even if we had no examples of Jesus actually speaking about forgiveness,[7] the offer would be unmistakable in the way he acted. Without waiting for them to repent first, he welcomes into his company those whom the respectable religious establishment reckoned as grievous sinners or definite outcasts from God's kingdom. He takes the initiative, entering sympathetically into the lives of tax collectors (extortioners and quislings as they were), prostitutes, beggars and those who were too ignorant to keep the religious laws properly, in order to entice them to an obedient response to God's purpose.[8] By sharing table fellowship with them he is sharing their life, and offering them a place at the Messianic feast, the festival of joy that would be ushered in by God's new creation of all things at the end of the age. Though Jesus hopes the sinners will repent, he offers forgiveness on God's behalf without prior conditions. Moreover, as I have already suggested, the repentance that he expects to follow forgiveness is of a kind that traditional religion would not regard as repentance at all, being essentially trust in himself as the agent of his heavenly Father.[9]

Justifying his scandalous behaviour, Jesus tells the parable of the lost sheep, in which the shepherd takes the first steps in finding those who are straying.[10] Such unconditional forgiveness may seem to be immoral because it takes no account of transgressions. In modern times Bernard Shaw put this instinctive feeling into words: 'forgiveness is a beggar's refuge; we must pay our debts'. H. R. Mackintosh admits that 'there is something in forgiveness that baffles common thought', but adds perceptively that 'the difficulty of understanding lies in the fact that it is creative'.[11] Forgiveness takes a risk; it calls out and enables the response of goodness but cannot guarantee results. When Jesus asks for hospitality from Zacchaeus, the notorious tax collector of the Jericho area, he does not first require him to return what he has gained through fraud and extortion, though this is the happy outcome.[12] He accepts from a prostitute the intimate act of her anointing his feet and wiping them with her hair, without first establishing whether she has given up her trade, and pronounces the forgiveness of God without further enquiry.[13]

Forgiveness also takes the risk of provoking antagonism and hostility. Thus the second stage of the journey of forgiveness, the voyage of endurance, is no less characteristic of the ministry and the death of Jesus. Through participating in the lives of sinners, Jesus evokes resentment from the religious authorities. It seems that Jesus also shared table fellowship with scribes and Pharisees, but on the whole it appears that they refused to accept a forgiveness pronounced by one who believed in sharing the banquet table of the kingdom with those who were still outcasts and ritually unclean. A simmering hostility comes to a head with the trial and crucifixion, where we see Jesus drawing out the venom of hatred from priests, soldiers and the crowd. Having provoked antagonism, he absorbs it – for the most part in patient silence: 'consider him who endured from sinners such hostility against himself'.[14] The fact that the common people consented to the death, despite the frequent popularity of Jesus with the crowds, shows how vulnerable someone becomes when he identifies with others. Jesus developed no demagogic mystique to protect himself;[15] by his openness he was the more in danger of rejection – either because he disappointed expectations or because his warning that the Temple would be destroyed was more than even the non-pious could take.[16]

Our tracing of the twofold journey of forgiveness, as experienced in our own relationships and as displayed in the ministry of Jesus, illuminates the main themes of atonement that have emerged throughout this study. In speaking of Jesus as the Son of God Christian faith affirms that God the Father of all has committed himself to Christ as the unique representative of his forgiving love. Since he has identified himself with Jesus in both act and being, we may say that the Father himself embarks upon the agonising journey of discovery that forgiveness entails. Far from simply forgetting about the sins of the world he journeys deeply into the heart of the human tragedy. It is as if the Father is not content to go out on to the road to await the return of the prodigal son, but actually takes the path into the far country to fetch the wayward son from the pigsty. In exploring the great images of atonement – victory, sacrifice, justice – we have already seen that the participation of God in human life is a creative act, enabling us to respond in repentance and in cooperation with God's liberating Spirit. In thinking of the nature of love we have already seen that God can open himself to experience something 'new' at the cross.

Now, these insights are illuminated profoundly by the experience of forgiveness. Through the twofold journey of forgiveness, through the stages of awakening awareness and absorbing hostility, the forgiver is learning how best to win the offender to himself. The fruit of this agonising journey is the ability to draw a hostile and stubborn heart into forgiving love. Though talk of God's 'learning' can only be a metaphorical way of speaking of his taking new human experience into himself, yet there is surely a hint that God's Spirit is able to wrestle with human spirits today and draw them into reconciliation because he has made the journey of discovery in the cross. God's approach to us is shaped to our needs because it is marked by the experience of Calvary; the God who comes to us here and now is the one who was *then* in the cross and who has been marked eternally by it. God is indeed always offering forgiveness, but the cross was a unique situation for him. Nowhere else has there been a man so awake to the state of human sin and so consenting to God's verdict upon it. Such a oneness of mind and feeling between Jesus and the Father must in turn have meant that God was, in this victim, more immersed into human antagonism towards goodness than anywhere else. At the cross was a new situation for the forgiving God – a unique experience of human hostility and a unique human response. Thus here as nowhere else God is drawn into human flesh and stands where humankind stands.

In this one past event the God who was and is always willing to forgive gains through the cross that experience of the human heart that gives him a way into our hearts. There is an objective 'change' in God, not with the effect of moving him from wrath to love, but rather with the subjective effect of moving us from rebellion to fellowship. Change in God (in the sense of new experience) thus makes change in us. Looked at from the human perspective, we

178

experience God as the one who sympathises with us, and so we are enabled to face up both to judgement and to acceptance.

If the experience of forgiveness illuminates the meaning of atonement, belief in an act of divine atonement in turn illuminates the experience of forgiveness. In particular the conviction that God himself participates in the consequences of human sin helps to resolve certain problems that arise in our quest for forgiveness in life, whether we are concerned with acceptance of ourselves or others.

The problems of guilt

Forgiveness only makes sense against the background of a sense of guilt, yet guilt feelings can themselves prove a barrier to the healing of personalities. So far we have traced our resistance to forgiveness to an attitude of hostility, but Paul Tillich rightly points out that the mood of anxiety is also a crippling and paralysing one, making it difficult to 'accept that we are accepted'.[17] Refusal to accept forgiveness is in fact compounded of both hostility *and* anxiety, in various mixes. A hostile reaction can be a way of covering up an underlying anxiety. Though this may take the stark form, particularly in neurosis, of the lament that 'I am too wicked to be forgiven', anxieties about guilt are usually more complex than this.

In the first place there is the difficulty of establishing our *responsibility* for acts we have committed and that we know are wrong in themselves. In our age psychology and sociology have made us well aware of all the factors that condition and shape us in our being and actions. As soon as we begin to trace the reasons for an act which is harmful to others and destructive of human fellowship, we find ourselves caught in a maze which stretches back and around in all directions. The hidden persuaders are endless in number – bad housing, unemployment, the class struggle, pressures to which we were subjected by parents and teachers in growing up, aggressive instincts inherited through our genes, and the influences at work upon us while we were still in the womb (whether the mother took drugs, smoked or played soothing music to the foetus are all claimed to have an effect on the personality). At the beginning I suggested that the tension between these limits and our freedom produces anxiety, and that sin is a false attempt to cope with anxiety. Here we should notice that the very fact that we are wrapped around by such constraints makes it difficult to see in what way we are agents of our own downfall.

There is of course no problem for those who adopt a totally behaviourist view, and are simply content to record varieties of human behaviour without making any moral judgements. This reduces the torturer, the sadist and the rapist to the level of rats in a laboratory maze, and takes a merely scientific interest in comparing their aggressive reactions. I am not concerned here with those who deny human guilt, but with those who *do* feel guilty and ill at ease with themselves, but cannot honestly sort out where their own responsibility lies. They feel trapped in a determined universe, the victim of pressures and circumstances beyond their control; yet they will not be content with being told that their sense of guilt is an illusion. They *know* they have played their part in the human tragedy but cannot explain exactly how. They need forgiveness, but they are not sure what they need it for. Because they cannot explain how things have come to happen they find it hard to open themselves to the good news that they have been forgiven. Invited to participate in corporate prayers of confession in church services, they cannot fit themselves into the general picture of having 'erred and strayed like lost sheep'. The words remain detached from them.

Sammy Mountjoy in Golding's novel *Free Fall* is typical of the person with this problem, asking 'What am I looking for? I am looking for the beginning of responsibility'.[18] Sammy, although a successful artist, is disgusted with himself and what he has become as a human being; in particular he is laden with guilt for his treatment of Beatrice Ifor whom he exploited and degraded sexually, and then deserted despite all his promises to her. Tipped into mental illness, she has become what he wanted her to be – simply a body to be used, not Beatrice but only 'I-for' (existing for-me). He finds his own nature to be unendurable, but he cannot find the *cause* for his behaviour. Recalling, like a series of pictures, his growth from the innocence of childhood into young manhood, he is asking 'where did I lose my freedom?' He cannot see how he could have avoided deserting Beatrice, given the kind of person he had become: 'I had given away my freedom. I cannot be blamed for the mechanical and helpless reaction of my nature.'[19] When, then, did he freely fall and cease to be free? He finally believes he has found the critical moment in a decision he made as he left school. The answer to his headmaster's question 'What is important to you?' is spoken within himself; it is 'the white, unseen body of Beatrice Ifor, her obedience and for all time my protection of her; and for the pain she has caused me, her utter abjection this side of death'. A voice within him asks 'What will you sacrifice?', and he replies 'everything'.[20]

Sammy believes he has found the point of self-damnation in which he fell freely, never to act freely again. Yet the novel tells us that Sammy still cannot find forgiveness, searching through the portrait gallery of his life. It leaves us with the impression that the answer is unsatisfactory; reducing everything to this one moment does not do justice to the complexity of his being and to the influences that brought him to that decision.

Associated with this perplexity are others. How can we reckon not only the cause of our actions but their effects? Like a stone thrown into a pond, the ripples spread out far beyond the centre. How can we count the ripples? Are we responsible for all the consequences of our actions? When our anger with another person upsets him and contributes to his loss of concentration when driving, are we responsible for the accident? When we fail to spend five minutes with a lonely person, are we responsible for her suicide attempt? When we buy a packet of coffee which someone has harvested on a wage scarcely above starvation level, in order to give the middle-men a fat profit, are we responsible for keeping the unjust system going? As human beings we are enmeshed in a web of broken lives, and there is a fall-out from our sin in which others are caught. There is a moment of scientific carelessness at Chernobyl, and thousands of miles away someone will die of cancer. There is a moment of sexual infidelity in a secret room, and far away a haemophiliac child eventually dies from AIDS. There is a maze not only of causes but of effects in which we can wander in bewildered guilt.

Compounded with these uncertainties is the difference between true and false guilt. Some actions for which we feel guilty may in fact not be wrong at all, but simply infringements of a social code or taboo which has been foisted upon us. We feel guilty at not conforming to expectations of parents or others in authority, and we fear that we shall lose their love by displeasing them. This is what psychiatrists call 'functional' guilt, and it should be distinguished from 'value guilt', or the sense of betraying a real moral standard. Yet the boundary between these two sorts of guilt is not at all clear-cut. The psychiatrist Paul Tournier points out that there are many instances in the lives of the saints of merely 'functional' guilt becoming the occasion for an experience of divine grace; 'Medical practice', he concludes, 'makes us very reserved before this great mystery of the sense of guilt.'[21]

Faced with these perplexities the Christian doctrine of atonement offers the glimpse of a way through, affirming as it does that God enters the depths of our experience in accepting love. Here and now God addresses us, and offers us the possibility of a way forward into a life of freedom from our past history and our present character. 'I am responsible in that I have the possibility of rejecting or accepting this freedom,' declares David Jenkins.[22] That is, responsibility lies first of all in *responding* to what is offered in the present, rather than in an exact calculation of what can be laid to my account in the past. I am guilty in that I discover through this offer that 'I am in a situation where I ought not to be'. Guilt is the awareness that 'I am not what I can be', that I am falling short of my human potential. So forgiveness enables us to face the reality that we are in a wrong situation, which is a wrong relationship with God. Responsibility lies, not in a catalogue of debts, but in how we respond to this awareness.

This cannot, however, be all that there is to be said about responsibility. It is certainly the right point from which to start, releasing us from the winding labyrinth of tracing the causes and effects of our actions. It also reminds us that atonement happens here and now. But as persons we do not just exist in the passing fragment of the present moment; we have a past which makes us what we are. True guilt is not only the sense that 'I am less than I can be', but also 'I need not have done what I did'. From the perspective of responding to the present challenge of God's love and freedom, we can begin to repent for the past. Yet we do not need to establish exact accountability for forgiveness to make sense. We do not have to explain everything to repent with integrity, in a way that truly belongs to us. We do not have to search into every dark corner of our sin. For the doctrine of atonement tells us that in Christ God has trodden every step of the maze which baffles us; he

182

has counted all the ripples on the dark surface of the waters. Since God participates in human life at its depths he knows all the factors that perplex us, not as some abstract truth but as hurt which he absorbs into himself. From that first-hand knowledge of our lives, aware even of the depths that remain hidden to us, he offers acceptance.

As guilty people we can have the courage to accept that we are accepted, because God has taken all the consequences of our actions upon himself. The point is not that justice has been appeased, but that the one who offers acceptance does so from the situation of knowing the whole truth about us, and being most wounded by it. God knows how much we are implicated in the wrongs under which humanity groans, and accepts us as we are. There is no question then of repentance being a kind of payment for wrongs done, so that it has to match evil exactly. We can be generous in our penitence as God is generous in his forgiveness. It was right, for example, for the Protestant churches in Germany to pass a resolution in 1945 confessing their guilt, even though they had sinned more by omission than commission during the Hitler era. It is right in Christian worship to confess guilt for poverty and hunger in the world; even if we are not directly responsible, we are part of the human family and linked together in ways that pure logic can never unravel.

Difficulties in forgiving others

As acute as the problem of accepting forgiveness for oneself are problems involved in forgiving others, which trouble us even when we *intend* to be charitable. Even when we seriously want to follow the command to forgive one another as Christ has forgiven us, we find real blockages in our way. The first kind of difficulty is memorably expressed in a story by Dostoevsky, writing out of his experience of the terrible suffering of the peasants in nineteenth-century Russia. In *The Brothers Karamazov* he relates how a peasant boy threw a stone in play and by mistake hurt the leg of a hunting dog belonging to the lord of the manor; the next day the landowner had the boy hunted and torn to pieces by the pack of hounds in full sight of his mother. Ivan protests:

I don't want a mother to embrace the torturer who had her child torn to pieces by his dogs! She has no right to forgive him! If she likes, she can forgive him for herself, she can forgive the torturer for the immeasurable suffering he has inflicted upon her as a mother; but she has no right to forgive him for the sufferings of her tortured child. She has no right to forgive the torturer for that, even if the child were to forgive him! . . . Is there in the whole world a being who could or would have the right to forgive?[23]

The problem is how one can forgive on behalf of others, to forgive injury done not alone to oneself, but to someone else. Surely only the person who has actually been injured has the right to forgive. It is understandable how, in response to the unspeakable horror of the Holocaust in our times, Jewish opinion has stressed the need for justice and has found talk of forgiveness strictly meaningless. Echoing the protest of Ivan, one Jewish rabbi recently spoke thus in a BBC television programme, urging the rightness of prosecuting Nazi war criminals even forty years afterwards:

The question is, *who* is to forgive them? They must go to those they have hurt – but they are dead. What am I to say? I do not hate you? I forgive you? I can say the first but not the second. I do not deal in handing out pardons.[24]

A woman survivor from Auschwitz spoke for many in the same programme when she said, 'I cannot forgive them. That would be no longer to remember those who died.' A poet and playwright who perished in the death camps describes the butchery of children in Warsaw and pleads in a lyric to his wife: 'Don't let oblivion heal our eternal wound . . . I charge you with my wrath,/Bear it, as you bore my sons.'[25]

Justice seems to cry for us to bear wrath against the torturer. Even in less apocalyptic scenes of the sexual abuse of children or cruelty inflicted upon elderly people in institutions that are supposed to be caring for them, forgiveness by relatives and friends of the victims seems somehow presumptuous. Ivan's question remains, yet his brother's answer must also be heeded:

You said just now, 'Is there a being in the whole world who could or would have the right to forgive?' But there is such a being, and he can forgive everything, everyone and everything and for everything, because he gave his innocent blood for all and for everything. You've forgotten him, but it is on him that the edifice is founded . . .[26]

In the light of our study, we may interpret the phrase 'he gave his innocent blood for all' in this way: in Christ God is exposed most deeply to the suffering of the victims of our world. He has the right to forgive because he is the sympathetic Creator who shares the lives of his creatures, experiencing the agony of all those who suffer and receiving their hurt as his own. This did not happen only at the cross, but happens continually as God identifies himself with the weak and oppressed. However, at the cross his being was drawn most closely into the pain and desolation of the victim because of the closest union between himself and this human Son, so that his universal sympathy is always grounded in this particular experience. Thus we may say again that God is 'enabled' to forgive through the cross; he gains the right to forgive.

The follower of Christ also gains the right to pronounce his forgiveness. This is what it means to 'forgive' the one who injures someone other than oneself. We may forgive directly for the hurt caused to ourselves, and for the rest we may say, 'God offers him forgiveness through Christ, and I consent willingly to that offer.' Justice is then not neglected, for we have seen that forgiveness must be completed in the repentance of the offender; the offer is unconditional, but the offer is itself a form of judgement, awakening the wrongdoer to his offence. Forgiveness aims at reconciliation, and that requires the offender to come back into the relationship in sorrow and penitence. Atonement is not simply the issue of a pardon; it is a process of healing in a person's life; forgiveness is offered without conditions, but it must be accepted for *atonement* to take place. Ulrich Simon has a stern but important warning to make when he considers the 'never-ending machinery which finds its sole *raison d'être* in the administration of death':

Christians can become involved in deadly sin when they wish to extend the atonement of Christ to the perpetrators of unrepented

185

evil ... the book of judgement cannot be so lightly closed, and all our moral instincts are outraged if the pardon of devils and devilry is envisaged as a Christian virtue ... the deaths of the tormentors do at last vindicate the truth.[27]

We must add however that the forgiveness of God is boundless, and we cannot know through what processes of judgement the human devils may come to face the truth about themselves in agonising sorrow, and be won back to the Father's house. Nor can we limit the scope of the searching love of God to the boundary of death; we cannot know over what precipices of the mind the Shepherd will travel in eternity to reach the lost.

A second problem involved in forgiving others seems less serious, but blights many relationships. It is well expressed in a scene from T. S. Eliot's play *The Cocktail Party*, when Edward has just told the strange guest that his wife has apparently left him:

UNIDENTIFIED GUEST   Do you know who the man is?

EDWARD   There was no other man –
None that I know of.

UNIDENTIFIED GUEST   Or another woman
Of whom she thought she had cause to be jealous?

EDWARD   She had nothing to complain of in my behaviour.

UNIDENTIFIED GUEST   Then no doubt it's all for the best.
With another man, she might have made a mistake
And want to come back to you. If another woman,
She might decide to be forgiving
And gain an advantage ... .[28]

There is the constant temptation to use our forgiveness as a means of gaining an advantage, using our apparent generosity for our own ends. It may be in order to gain an advantage over someone else, as the Unidentified Guest ironically suggests; we can adopt an insidious kind of moral blackmail, reminding someone by hint or look that we have forgiven them, and so they had better be grateful by doing what we want. Or we may simply want to gain an advantage for ourselves, to make ourselves more secure. We may forgive with the expectation that a beautiful relationship is bound to flower from our action, forgiving in order to gain a friend as a reward. Or it may be that we want to be looked up to as a magnanimous person and be generally liked, to build an image of ourselves as 'a person who never bears grudges'.

In all these ways we attempt to avoid the pain in the journey of forgiveness. Seeing that forgiveness makes us weak and vulnerable to the attacks of others, we fear that we are giving ourselves away and losing ourselves. We ask, in trepidation, what will happen to us as persons if we go on forgiving, whether people will see us as an easy target and trample over us. To these fears Jesus speaks the word of the gospel of forgiveness: 'He who seeks to keep his life will lose it; he who loses his life for my sake will find it.' As a matter of fact it is those who have given themselves away in the most spend-thrift manner who stand out in history as the most vital personalities – from Francis of Assisi to Simone Weil and Mother Teresa of Calcutta. Above all this is the pattern of the cross and resurrection, which gives us the courage to believe that to give oneself away in forgiveness is to become more truly oneself.

Forgiving love does not calculate. It is full of hope that it will win response, but this is not an exact calculation; what forgiveness may achieve is unknown. This element of risk is always at the heart of relationships, for they begin with a journey into the unknown. As Daniel Day Williams perceives, speaking of a 'pilgrimage of love', 'What love may do and will do . . . lies ahead, can only be known partially in the history of love until the end.'[29] Even within the family the mystery of another's personality means that there is always a journey of discovery into strange territory. A still more daring voyage is the experience where people meet from different cultures and societies; friendship with a stranger has rich possi-bilities, promising wider horizons of understanding and more complex patterns of relationship. But in meeting with a stranger there is also the sense of having one's own identity and one's belief about what is 'normal' challenged, and so an urge for self-preservation develops which can lead to a breach in relationship. In the remaking of the bond through forgiveness, even more than in its first creation, there will be a strong element of uncertainty about how things will turn out.

But to take steps into the unknown, with forgiving love, is to grow as a person. The cross of Jesus assures us of this, revealing the story of God himself as one who goes on pilgrimage and thereby becomes even more truly himself. In creating humankind God freely chooses to come out of self-sufficient isolation to make covenant with one who is a stranger to his being. F. W. Dillistone contrasts such a picture of God with one who is merely a god of the natural world or of humankind in general:

> In a very real sense Yahweh, the God who reveals himself to the chosen men of the Old Testament, is a *stranger* God . . . Yahweh went forth from the familiar circle of divine existence seeking the man, the succession of men, to whom He could relate Himself as friend to friend.[30]

When humankind has broken this relationship God takes an even greater step into the unknown in the cross, experiencing a disturbance of relationships within his very being as the Father suffers for a moment the loss of the Son and the Son endures forsakenness. Here God becomes strange to himself, taking estrangement and desolation into his very being, in order to offer forgiveness to humankind. Through this journey of forgiveness God does not lose himself, but fulfils his desire for fellowship, humbly allowing his being to be enriched through relationship with others. Yet he does not calculate what he can achieve. In the resurrection of Jesus he assures us that he has overcome the threat of death which he confronted in the cross, but even in resurrection there is an element of the unknown. The resurrection of Jesus points forward to the new creation at the end of history, and promises that all created personalities will be transformed with a new quality of life and finally glorify the Father; yet on the way to that future God wants and waits for our response.

Thus the meaning of 'resurrection' itself, the final destiny of human beings, depends in some way upon the unknown factor of our response to God. The *fact* of the end is certain, and yet the *content* of that final triumph is left open, making space for our cooperation with God. A personality is not a standard product, made on a cosmic assembly line; personalities become what they are through their choices and acts. What it will mean for personalities to come to the fullness of their human potential cannot be something that is fixed in advance. So in creation and in forgiveness God embarks, through his own desire, upon a voyage of discovery. He invites us to join him in forgiving others, promising that we will not lose ourselves in the process. But he does not promise that we shall remain the same.

9

Political engagement

'The philosophers have only interpreted the world; the point is to change it.'[1] This thesis of Karl Marx has seemed remarkably apt to 'theologians of liberation' in the Third World, in their thinking about the question of salvation. It summarises their protest against analysing the nature of sin without changing the sinful structures of society, against spinning theories of atonement without acting to free the oppressed. The saving work of Christ is, they believe, all too often consigned to a safe area of doctrine and not allowed to become a powerful motive in transforming the actual situation of people today. The first conference of Latin American bishops at Medellin in 1968 set the tone when it declared that:

> The centre of God's salvific design is Jesus Christ, who by his death and resurrection transforms the universe and makes it possible for man to reach fulfillment as à human being. This fulfillment embraces every aspect of humanity: body and spirit, individual and society, person and cosmos, time and eternity.[2]

My concern in this chapter is not to explore in detail the social and the individual fulfilment of which the statement speaks; that would be to present a whole theology of liberation. My aim is the more limited one of asking how the past event of the cross of Christ, as the atoning act of God, is related to the experience of engaging in politics today. When we set the death of Jesus in the context of his life, recognising it to be the result of his conflict with the structures of power around him, we cannot but conclude that atonement must have *something* to do with reconciliation and freedom in society. Otherwise God's presence and activity in a death like this would have been quite arbitrary.

Theologians in Latin America like Leonardo Boff have in fact been impressed to find that 'the social-political situation of Jesus' time contains surprising parallels'[3] with their own situation. They have in mind the situation óf being dependent upon 'a centre situated abroad', together with associated political and economic oppression. For the Roman Empire of the first century, we can in our century substitute foreign corporate investment, a new empire of world banks and multi-national corporations.[4] The lament of Latin American theologians has been that development, western style, has led to a situation in which an élite class in their countries has become dependent upon the demands of the international money market, and has met these demands by exploiting the labour of the poor.[5] No less oppressive, either in the time of Jesus or today, is the domination of people by religious structures of power. Though a faithful son of the Roman Catholic Church, Boff has to note with sorrow that authority in the church has been indebted to age-old patterns of 'Roman power and the feudal structure'. As a consequence, even when taking up the cause of the poor, 'the church seems to be conformable with authoritarian regimes; it never questions their legitimacy, only their abuses'.[6] Nor is Protestantism, which is a fast-growing movement in Latin America, exempt from repressive behaviour. As Rubem Alves notes, the affirming of an inner freedom of the individual can result in a failure to challenge social structures: 'on the social level, individualism functions to mask and justify a situation of oppression'.[7]

Any attempt to speak of engagement in politics must connect with one's own context. We need to learn from the insights of 'liberation theologians' of the Third World, since their countries have become hapless social laboratories in which various types of oppression are being tested in the starkest form today. But those of us who are citizens of western democracies must attend to the patterns of domination within our own societies, and be ready to be surprised by the ways that the practice of Jesus relates to our own political commitments. If political action can be understood as a vehicle (to say the least) through which the liberating and reconciling work of God can be made manifest in our world, we must ask how well the various theories of the atonement alert us to God's work and enable us to participate in it.

The forsakenness of Christ

When the death of Christ is understood to be the outcome of his conflict with the religious and political powers of his time, his offending of both Jewish and Roman authorities, then the cross must be seen in the first instance as the reaction of human sin against divine love. Christ is forsaken as a consequence of his 'option for justice' and his 'preference for the poor'. He is crucified by the powers that are in rebellion against God's intention for human life. Though God can transform even the brutal cross into an instrument of his love, the cross is there in the first place as a negation of his rule, a final fling of the created against the Creator. As I have already observed,[8] this historical perspective hardly fits in with theories of atonement that present God as planning the cross as a mechanism for satisfying his anger against human sin. Here we must add a point of more political relevance: if the Father is envisaged as requiring the death of Christ as a reparation for his offended justice, the cross will only legitimise other patterns of oppression in our world. If the Father is an oppressor, for whatever apparently good reasons, this sets up a pattern in which oppression can always be justified as being for the ultimate benefit of society. If God is not only the supreme victim but also the supreme executioner, he will become the patron of human executioners and torturers.

For this reason Leonardo Boff is highly critical of those who interpret the forsakenness of Christ as an event in which 'God abandoned God and contradicted himself'[9] or in which 'the first person of the Trinity casts out and annihilates the second', following Luther's statement that 'No one is against God except God himself'. This, says Boff, amounts to the proposition that the Father is Jesus' murderer, and forgets that God takes up the cross in order to put an end to all the crosses of history.[10] Boff levels his criticism particularly at the theologian Jürgen Moltmann, who presents the Father as abandoning the Son for the very best of reasons; according to Moltmann, God causes a disruption in his own Trinitarian life in order to be the Father of those who are abandoned in the world. He does not forsake the Son to satisfy any retributive justice, but in order to be the Father of all the forsaken; those who are oppressed, rejected and dying can identify with God because there is death in the fellowship of God's own life. If people are to respond to the call of God to enter his divine life, they 'must be able to recognise rejection, the curse, and final nothingness in it'.[11] So they are taken into the grief of God and are liberated as they also find there the hope for resurrection that flows from the Spirit who unites the Father and the Son in love.

Boff, however, has a valid point in criticising Moltmann's language of 'God contradicting God'. Despite his best intentions, this places God on the side of those who inflict suffering as well as those who endure it. Moltmann does certainly involve the Father in suffering as well as the Son; he suggests that while the Son suffers the actual experience of dying, the Father experiences death in the sense of being bereaved of the Son. There is not only the forsaken-ness of the Son but the grief of the Father.[12] However, the Father is still depicted as directly *causing* the son to suffer and die, and so producing his own bereavement. It almost looks as if God the Father rejects the Son in order to provide us with someone with whom we can sympathise. We ought surely to think more consistently in terms of *participation* rather than causation. As we have already seen in thinking about 'the demands of justice', the Father in his love sends forth the Son to identify with human beings in all their estrangement from himself. As a result of that total immersion into the situation of human sin, the Son is brought to the cross by human hands, and thereby suffers the forsakenness that is the natural consequence of broken human lives. Since God confirms and supports these consequences in his justice, we *can* say that Jesus suffers abandon-ment by his Father. We *can* speak of an awful crevasse which is opened up within the relationships in which God lives. But we do not – and ought not to – draw the conclusion that the Father is directly *inflicting* rejection upon the Son. God does indeed take the 'disruption' and 'sinking into nothingness' of human life into his life, but he does not disrupt himself or 'contradict' himself.

Boff, in his concern to correct Moltmann, fails to consider *this* kind of disruption in the fellowship of the Trinity, and for his part he therefore underplays the desolation of the cross. He speaks of the mystery of the divine silence at the cross to which Jesus is exposed, and before which he hangs empty and helpless: 'The text speaks to us of a rending, wrenching cry from out of the hell of the experience of the divine absence.'[13] As does Moltmann, Boff finds the awfulness of the forsakenness by contrast with Jesus' previous experience of the nearness of the Father, and the nearness of the Father's kingship he had proclaimed and demonstrated in his ministry of liberation to the poor. Yet Boff cannot speak of the deepest scandal, the infinite shock of a gulf opening up within God's own life. The cross cannot therefore be found in the inner life of the Trinity as a shattering of relationships. The 'real reason' why God is silent in the face of suffering at the cross must simply be that God is suffering too, freely accepting weakness in solidarity with the world.[14]

True though this be, if it is all there is to say I cannot but feel the scandal to have been weakened, the silence to have been broken. If we understand the 'wrath' of God to be his confirming of the natural consequences of human estrangement, as I have argued above, and if we see Christ as participating in the deepest human predicament, then we can speak (with Karl Barth)[15] of God's suffering his own contradiction of sinful humanity; we need not speak of God's contradicting *himself*. To speak of the cross as entering the very life of the Trinity, and so of the cross as being 'intrinsic to divine identity' does not mean, as Boff fears, that we will lose all motivation for overcoming the crosses which human oppressors inflict. The shock of silence at the cross is God's exposure of his very being to non-being, as the Son is identified with those for whom the Father must, with infinite grief, confirm death as the goal of their own direction of life. This breach in God cannot be diminished, even by saying with Boff that Jesus turns his deepest despair into 'trust in the Mystery'. The cry of forsakenness cannot be abridged like this; it is not resolved, at the cross, into a word of trust, but rings out in all its starkness. But it is not the last word; the resurrection tells us that as God takes death into himself, he is not overcome by it. All hangs in balance as the being of God and death strike against each other; yet God sustains his being in the face of the threat of death, and makes it serve him.

Now when we take the silence of forsakenness at the cross as seriously as this, it has implications for political engagement. Another liberation theologian, Jon Sobrino, perhaps takes over the language of Moltmann a shade too uncritically, but he is powerfully impressed by Moltmann's perception that this event spells the end to all merely natural theology. The silence of God in the cross produces a crisis in our knowledge of God; in the face of this scandal we can no longer project God from human ideas of power and glory, envisaging him as the supreme case of a human ruler, the ultimate and immutable cause of our mutable world.[16] God has taken the identity of a slave. Sobrino, however, adds something characteristic of Latin American theology: we shall only find the *meaning* of the cross by entering into its experience, which means engaging ourselves with the cause of those who are poor and who suffer injustice: 'The cross ... does not offer us any explanatory model that would make us understand what salvation is and how it might itself be salvation. Instead it invites us to participate in a process within which we can actually experience history as salvation.'[17]

The cross itself is silent. The ministry of Jesus which brought him there has left open questions: who is right – Jesus or the authorities? Jesus himself finds no answer in the cross, and can only utter a great cry of forsakenness. In the resurrection God vindicates him, and in its light we can see that the unconditional love of God is in fact displayed in the cross; but we can only reach resurrection through dwelling in the silence of the cross with Jesus. As the apostle Paul puts it, 'If we are united with Christ in a death like his, we shall certainly be united with him in a resurrection like his' (Rom. 6:5). The point is that we do not simply follow through this sequence in our minds. God himself made the journey in real history, venturing on to a path in space and time. If he opens himself to us at the cross so that his Spirit takes us into the fellowship of the divine life, then we become 'co-actors' with God in history. We go on a journey with God. It is as we take on the cause of those who are crucified today – those who are victims of injustice, oppression and the economic system – that we can pierce through the darkness of the cross and discover both the love of God and a hope for the future. 'In Latin America', says Sobrino, 'the concrete mediation of the "death of God" has been the "death of the other human being" – that is, the death of the peasant, the native Indian, and so on.'[18]

Finding the meaning of atonement

In face of the deepest silence of God at the cross, confronted by the scandal of a brokenness in God's own life, we cannot penetrate the

195

mystery through mental processes alone. We need another kind of knowing, a mode of awareness which aligns us with the experience of God himself. This is what Sobrino calls 'an analogy of sympathy'. Through feeling sorrow for the oppressed, a grieving that takes the positive form of seeking to overcome the conditions that cause suffering, we find the revelation of God in the midst of his hidden-ness. Our knowledge of God and his Son is ultimately 'a knowledge based on sympathy within the very process of God himself rather than outside it. The Son reveals himself to us as the Son in so far as we follow his path.'[19] To engage in the historical adventure of liberating humanity is to enter into the mystery of atonement.

The claim that we can only *find* the meaning of atonement as we engage with the needs of those who are weak and oppressed today is grounded in the whole way that liberation theologians develop Christian doctrine. Their method is to begin from the actual situation (social, economic and political) in which they find themselves, and then to reflect upon it with the help of scripture and church tradition. A basic principle is that 'theology is critical reflection upon the praxis of liberation', or that theological concepts and theories are 'the second step'. Commitment to activity in the world (praxis) in the light of faith is 'the first act of theology'.[20] To take the side of those who are hungry and unjustly treated and to join their struggle for basic human rights is a matter of sheer obedience to the living God, requiring no further theological justification. Indeed (as Calvin argued) obedience is actually a form of *knowing* God, and conceptual knowledge follows on from it as a second stage of reflection. 'Orthopraxy' or right-doing must come before 'orthodoxy' or right-believing.

To those who object that this means that the needs of human society are setting the agenda for Christian doctrine, the liberation theologians point out that doctrines have always been shaped by their social context. Indeed even if they fail to realise it theologians have written from the perspective of one ideology or another, quite often that of the property-owning bourgeoisie. J. Miguez Bonino commends Freud and Karl Marx as 'masters of suspicion', sniffing out and unmasking the hidden ideologies that lie behind what purports to be 'pure' exegesis of the Bible. Our study of the doctrine of atonement has shown how greatly various models of interpret-ation have been influenced by the culture of their time. For all this, however, I believe it to be a little misleading simply to rank praxis and doctrine as first and second steps. After all, as the 'liberation theologians' themselves point out, we can only take the step of 'praxis' in the light of *faith*, and this has already been shaped by reflection on the scriptures. Moreover while we ought to be 'suspicious' of the praxis that lies behind traditional doctrines, we may also take this influence positively; we must take doctrine into account as being born from the experience of that people of God of which we are a part.

Thus we certainly know a good deal that is true about the meaning of the Christian faith before we have engaged in social and political action on behalf of the weak in our world. But we may say that we shall never *fully* or *adequately* know what our faith means, and in this case what atonement means, until we have become so engaged. Indeed if we reflect on the models of atonement which we have been exploring, we can see loose ends in them which can only be knitted up through political engagement. In the faith of ancient Israel, for instance, the sacrificial ritual was believed to cleanse a whole society from sin as well as individuals within it. When the death of Christ is portrayed as the final sacrifice, we are bound to ask *how* sins can be expiated by it here and now. If we say, as we have done, that the cross is a creative event which deals with sin by transforming sinful attitudes in the present, we must go on to speak of change on a social level too. It is not just individual sin that needs to be expiated through sacrificial self-giving, but the kind of structural sin that brought Jesus to the cross.

The image of *Christ the Victor* perhaps stands closest to political engagement, and we have already seen that the 'principalities and powers' and the 'idols' which Christ overcomes are corporate as well as individual. Some Christians, including some church leaders, will deny that we need to confront social structures directly, urging that society will be transformed when individuals are freed from sin. Only deliver the individual into the freedom of Christ, it is said, and he will go out from the church to make a free world. This is also a comfortable view for politicians, and we often hear even those who have no Christian faith chiding the church for forgetting about its 'main task' of 'saving souls'. Such a view ignores the massive injustices which many actually suffer at present, and which love demands be dealt with urgently. But, even if we think on the individual level, it is clear that people need to be liberated in several dimensions of their lives *at once*. While social revolutionaries who have no inner spiritual freedom will only end by putting others and themselves into new chains, it is true conversely that oppressive social conditions can prevent an individual from accepting an inner freedom. A person who suffers restrictions and discrimination socially acquires a 'slave mentality' in every part of his being.

This fact was discovered by William Knibb, an English Baptist missionary to the West Indies in the nineteenth century, who had set out to bring an inner spiritual freedom to the slaves working on British sugar plantations *despite* their outer slavery. He relates how he found the slaves' whole lives to be morally crippled by their situation, and concludes that 'the fact that a person could be happy in a state of slavery seemed to me to be one of its most accursed fruits'.[21] He was thus compelled by the gospel of freedom to protest and agitate for their emancipation;[22] 'Knibb the notorious' as the hostile plantation owners called him, came into conflict with a whole economic system.

By contrast, when the sort of legal model of atonement is adopted which understands the death of Christ as satisfying the demands of an eternal law, an unthinking obedience to all law is inculcated, and a 'civil service mentality' results. Structures of society are simply to be accepted. But if we understand the penal sufferings of Christ not as a 'commercial transaction'[23] but as a means of moving us to penitence, as I suggested above, then we are bound to ask about penitence for social sins as well as individual ones: how can a social penitence be expressed? Only an active movement to remove the cause of social sin is an adequate repentance. If we truly sorrow with the oppressed we will want to release them from their bonds.

In these ways doctrines of atonement which draw upon images of sacrifice, victory and judgement naturally lead us towards action in the world which is political. Our study of Abelard takes us in the same direction. If the revelation of the love of God is no mere pattern to be copied but an infusing of love into the human heart, we are bound to ask where God is revealing himself here and now. At least part of the answer is to find where his Spirit is active in the world, promoting freedom and wholeness. Again if the personality of Christ has a liberating effect we will want to know where we can find it. So we have Bonhoeffer's question, 'Where is Christ today?'

198

and this leads to a second major emphasis of liberation theology, seeing Christ in the 'unperson'.

The church begins to engage in politics when the humiliated and crucified Christ is 'recognised' among groups and classes who are discriminated against and unjustly treated. As the parable of the sheep and the goats comes alive in experience ('As you did it to the least of these my brethren, you did it to me'), there is momentum for action. A classical statement of this experience was made by the Dominican missionary Bartolome de Las Casas who tried and failed to get laws for the protection of the Indians established in the period of the Spanish Empire: he wrote, 'I left behind me in the Indies Jesus Christ our God, scourged, tortured, crucified, not once but a million times.'[24]

When Black theologians today speak of Christ as the 'Black Messiah' they know that they are not making a historical statement (though Christ, of course, was not white either). They mean that Christ, in his humility, takes the form of those who are treated as non-persons. James Cone bases the confession that 'Christ is black' upon the self-proclamation of Christ in Luke 4:18f as the bringer of good news to the poor: 'Christ is black, therefore . . . only because Christ really enters into our world where the poor, the despised and the black are, disclosing that he is with them, enduring their humiliation and pain, and transforming oppressed slaves into liberated servants.'[25] It is natural too that where women are discriminated against and denied their full human rights they should 'see' Christ as female. It is not that Christ is *identical* with any one group but that he *identifies* with them, so that we can find Christ 'with them'. Unless we remember this, we shall turn 'seeing Christ' into the nationalism of exclusively 'being Christ'. As Allan Boesak points out from his situation of courageous protest against the South African government, even a stress on a 'black nation' can lead to a new kind of apartheid and homeland policy.[26]

To say that the poor are 'mediations of God' is thus not to romanticise them, as if in their poverty they must be nearer to God and leading a more spiritual life. The point is that they confront us with the God of the cross; he invites us to move on the path from the silent cross to the eloquent resurrection by liberating them *from* their poverty. In the parable of the sheep and the goats Christ tells us that we can find him among those who are hungry, thirsty, naked and imprisoned; but the aim of the parable is to encourage those who follow Christ to release the victims from their situation. He is present, pleading for justice from those who can give it. Let us be specific. In our western world the characters in the parable will include the unemployed, the low-paid, those caring for elderly and handicapped relatives at home on low allowances or none at all, homeless families in bed and breakfast accommodation, and those with painful ailments classed as 'non-emergency cases' who have no private medical insurance. The cross, with its silence about God, breaks down our self-interest in constructing images of God. Here we will not find the God we want, the God who supports our desires and ambitions. Similarly people who are disadvantaged break down our self-interest; we cannot pursue our ambitions through them, and they raise the deepest questions about what it really means to be human.

Action and submission

As we have already seen, one aspect of the atoning work of Christ is his victory over the 'powers' that oppress and dominate humankind. Such powers, we observed, take form not only in 'personal idols' but also in social structures – for example in ideologies, political parties, economic theories and bureaucracies. If we hold a world view in which the powers have been placed under the lordship of Christ, then we have a right to resist powers when they are in rebellion against the divine intention for human life. Taking this as established, our task in this section is to ask whether the atoning death of Christ provides any clues as to the *way* that we might engage in resisting and breaking the powers when they become 'demonic'.

There is in fact a pattern disclosed in the death of Christ that is fundamental to all political engagement. It is a sequence that we have already seen as basic to forgiveness – that of action and submission. In his offer of forgiveness to sinners Jesus acts to bring the situation into the open, and then submits to what ensues. The provoking act in which repentance is awakened is followed by a suffering in which the hostility of the offenders is absorbed. Each side of the contrast needs the other, and since one is not merely swallowed up in the other we can speak of a 'dialectic'. This pattern of forgiveness is in fact typical of the whole ministry of Jesus, which is a dialectic of action and submission, or conflict and passion. Both moments of the dialectic are essential; we make the death of Jesus the basis for a spirituality of mere resignation, and even of wallowing in suffering for its own sake, if we forget that the cross was preceded by a ministry of action. Jesus calls us to follow him in unmasking all powers that seek to usurp the place of God; he calls us to break the idols, and then to accept the consequences.

The moment of submission within the dialectic is focused in the silence which Jesus assumes in the trial before Pilate. Three of the gospel writers record that at some point in his trial Jesus refuses to answer when questions are put to him. The evangelists do not present the same details about what Jesus *does* say, or *when* he is silent, but they all testify that the moment comes when Jesus confronts his judges with silence. Matthew underlines this fact, writing that 'he gave them no answer, not even to a single charge, so that the governor wondered greatly' (Matt. 27:14). The fourth evangelist relates that at a later stage of the interrogation 'Jesus gave no answer' (John 19:8), and it is this evangelist who has just portrayed Pilate as asking 'What is truth?' (John 18:38). The story is presenting an irony; the truth is in fact emerging through the reaction of the Roman and Jewish powers to the silence of Jesus. The power to crucify is faced by the power of silence, and it is a silence which is testing the truth. 'Silence makes room', as Paul Lehmann puts it, for the 'shock of recognition.'[27]

The silence is an opportunity for Pilate to take his own step forward into greater truth. The truth emerging is not only about himself but the Roman state, which can show an openness to the purpose of God by doing what is just. The state is not, of course, expected to act like the church, but it *can* stand for justice against the violent demands of the mob.[28] In this sense, as Paul affirms, it is ordained by God and carries out his mandate (Rom. 13:1–7). However, the weakness of silence has unmasked the weakness of power, exposing its inability to adapt to the new circumstances which Jesus' ministry has brought, anxious simply to restore order and the status quo. Instead of serving the truth Pilate first tries political manipulation and when this fails to pacify the crowds, washes his hands of Jesus.

201

Both sides of the dialectic are set out in Romans 13:1–7 which does not, as often supposed, command an unconditional obedience to governments. As Karl Barth has pointed out in his commentary on this letter, the merely 'negative' instruction to submit is set in the context of the 'great positive possibility', the command to 'owe one nothing except love'. In the end what matters is to recognise the claim of our neighbour upon our love: 'Inasmuch as we love one another, we cannot wish to uphold the present order as such, for by love we do the "new" by which the "old" is overthrown.'[29] This surely leaves open the possibility that love may require us, *in the last resort*, to resist and to disobey the authorities. Thus Paul's comment here upon the legitimacy of the state does not at all conflict with the Christian right to resist 'the powers', when they have become rebellious against God's purpose for them. When the powers have become demonic, failing to provide the framework in which human life can grow and develop in a healthy way, there is a positive duty to say 'we must obey God rather than men'.[30] When in the troubled month of March 1988 Archbishop Desmond Tutu was asked why he was disobeying an order of the South African government banning a demonstration against apartheid, he replied, 'I obey God every day.' Yet the command to submit is not altogether *replaced* by the command to love; the Christian reformer confronts the government not only with protest but with submission to the consequences of his actions.

Such a submission is no merely passive acceptance of the status quo, but an obedient waiting for the new order. As Lehmann sums up this stance, 'submission and silence become code words of revolutionary freedom' they are 'signs of a politics of confrontation that has arrived at the moment of truth and life'.[31] The desire to reconcile cannot avoid conflict, but then silence and submission are needed for the truth to emerge, for what is real to stand out. In partnership with the actions of love, submission and silence expose the truth of the situation, and this truth has the power to make free (John 8:32). That is, when the state reacts unjustly to Christian resistance and agitation for justice it only sows the seeds of its own downfall. Closed systems grow more violent as they approach their end. Amid the silence of those who were once protesting and are now suffering, they hasten to their destruction. So Christians may engage in political reform by a continual pattern of resistance and submission, although they may differ about the form that such resistance may take.[32]

In this process the way that power of weakness unmasks the weakness of power may be perceived by its effects upon the sufferer himself, upon the oppressor and upon the society as a whole. First, when someone suffers for the truth, submitting to unjust judgement, people throughout society become aware of what they had missed before or refused to see; the situation becomes unstable as the governing powers heap up mass resentment against themselves, so that either reform takes place or they are overturned. 'When Power crucifies truth it signals to all the world that it has come to its effective end' (Lehmann).[33] Second, when the sufferer for a just cause joyfully maintains his faith and hope in the coming kingdom of God, this attitude of freedom 'exasperates the agents of the system . . . it destroys their morale' (Boff).[34] Third, suffering actually keeps hope alive in the reformer himself, making all too plain his present captivity and creating the urgent desire for total liberation. Dreams of the new creation, as I have already suggested, build up a pressure to change the present together with a sensitivity to the new things with which God can surprise us here and now. Suffering, as Boff perceives, can provoke such disturbing dreams, and so 'can actually render our self-liberation more intense'.[35]

In these ways the silence which the reformer shares with the crucified Christ can be a powerful ferment, working towards freedom. But for anyone who engages in political action it is also something else – a means of guidance. To share in the silence and submission of Christ does not only open up the meaning of atonement as a doctrine, but enables us to find the meaning of reconciliation in our situation here and now. In submission the activist is waiting for the verdict of God upon the situation, which he does not presume to think is clear. Especially when we are taking up God's cause of justice there is the temptation to justify ourselves; the closer we stand to the action of God the greater the temptation to play God. So in the silence we wait for God to vindicate our actions, or else to be merciful upon our mistakes.

In his critical situation in Nazi Germany, Dietrich Bonhoeffer understood that he was following such a path. First he took the way of resistance in joining the bomb plot against Hitler, and then saw himself as submitting to the consequences. Writing of this twofold pattern in a letter of 21 February 1944 he calls the reality of a situation the 'disguise' of God (the supreme Thou) within the 'It' (the objective facts that befall us). This reality can only be found through an attitude of silence, waiting and surrender *after* the bold stroke of action against evil:

> We must confront fate . . . as resolutely as we submit to it at the right time. One can speak of 'guidance' only on the other side of that twofold process, with God meeting us no longer as 'Thou', but also 'disguised' in the 'It'; so in the last resort my question is how we are to find the 'Thou' in this 'It', or, in other words, how does 'fate' become 'guidance'? It's therefore impossible to define the boundary between resistance and submission on abstract principles; but *both of them exist and both must be practised*.[36]

The 'guidance' into reality for those of us who live in a western democracy will no doubt take a less dramatic form, but it will still be through the dialectic of resistance and submission. We may, for example, dare to speak the prophetic word which unmasks the powers. The Christian activist challenges myths which hold people bound, and breaks the idols which have gained power over them. When ideologies demand absolute devotion and bureaucracies have become merely self-preserving, then the word of judgement must be spoken, even if it means confrontation.

For the 'liberation theologians' of the Third World this has often meant the destroying of a sense of fatalism. Through reflection on their situation with the aid of study of scripture within the 'basic Christian communities' peasants and workers come to see that it is not the iron will of God that some people should be rich and others poor. They see that this is actually the result of sin, and that things do not have to be like this. For those of us in the West there are other myths which grip the mind, and which need to be shown up for what they are. At present, for instance, in both Britain and America a *laissez-faire* dogma is abroad which urges the pursuit of individual wealth to be a highly moral act. The argument runs that when an individual pursues his own interest in amassing wealth for himself, then inevitably, as if by the work of an 'invisible hand', this has a beneficial effect upon the whole of society. Not only will the affluent be able to relieve the distress of the poor through voluntary acts of charity, but successful individuals will make a successful economy in which jobs are created and welfare can be provided for the really needy.

That there is *some* truth in this analysis of the creation of wealth it would be rash to deny. But the 'invisible hand' becomes an idol when it is held as simple fact rather than as a theory, and when it is therefore allowed to exclude all other approaches, such as some redistribution of wealth from richer to poorer through a system of taxation. *Laissez-faire*, when made into an absolute, is a western kind of fatalism in which the reality with which people have to live is overlooked. A prophetic voice is needed to deflate the idols of *either* the left or right in politics, and to assert God's 'bias to the poor'. But then a kind of 'submission' is needed too. God's process of atonement is one of forgiveness and reconciliation, and in social terms this means seeking a consensus and common consent to what is right and just. We have to go on living together. When our own political ideal is not worked out fully by a government, though the substance of it has been taken account of, we must learn to forgive what has been left undone.[37] Such a compromise is not a betrayal of political vision, as long as it is held in the context of continual action and protest.

A still further step beyond direct action of protest is the method of 'civil disobedience' which Martin Luther King made famous in recent times in his struggle against racial discrimination in the United States. Following the example set by Mahatma Gandhi in his struggle for independence from British Rule in India, this kind of action refuses to use violence but is otherwise willing to break the laws of the state for the sake of a just cause. In the context of demonstration, this will mean a deliberate breaking of laws about public order, and where protests involve the symbolic cutting of security fences or 'sit-ins' in public buildings it may even involve charges of criminal damage. At another level it may take the form of refusing to pay taxes, or to cooperate with government agencies in filling in official forms. It may mean promoting strikes as a political protest rather than simply as part of a legitimate industrial dispute, and resistance to particular legislation may come to a head in the actual breaking of what is believed to be a bad law.

I believe it to be characteristic of Christian engagement to be more cautious in adopting these various forms of civil disobedience than in taking direct action within the law. A Christian's criterion is not just how much pressure can be exerted, or how much 'industrial muscle' he has as a worker. He will feel other claims upon him; there is the claim of the weak and vulnerable in society who are going to be hurt even by the refusal to pay taxes, let alone by strikes. Public disorder can create an atmosphere which will increase the fear of some as they go about their daily life. In a democracy there are parliamentary means to argue for a change in law and to try to persuade opinion. Moreover within the biblical perspective the Christian owes normal obedience to government as to Christ. In the last resort, however, the claims of justice and love may outweigh all other prior claims, and the Christian may find that obedience to Christ brings him into conflict with the law of his society. If so he must submit to the consequences because it is through the process of resistance and submission that the truth emerges. It emerges for the protester, who is not so arrogant as to think that he knows the whole truth of the situation, and it emerges to mobilise public opinion.

It is hardly surprising that a pattern for political engagement, following the pattern of the cross, should be the same twofold process as the act of forgiveness. Like personal forgiveness, social reform aims at reconciliation. Moreover forgiveness actually has a place in politics; reconciliation will only come about when the one who has gained the advantage through action does not press it in such a way as to repress the opponent. To hold back and seek a compromise in the very teeth of victory is to give the Spirit of God the opportunity to heal the breach and create a new social order. Forgiveness points to a more hopeful end to conflict than a merely oppressive victory.

10

The problems of suffering

Can there be theology after Auschwitz? How can we 'talk about God' in the same breath as the extermination camps in which over three million Jews were gassed and cremated in Hitler's 'final solution'? How can we think of God and such a suffering world together? The modern European mind keeps returning to Auschwitz, tracing in horrified imagination the track to its gates along which ran the trains carrying their human cargo; with the efficiency of a bureaucracy which had become demonic, the fare of each victim was scrupulously paid to the state railway company – third class, one way only, with children under four allowed to travel to death free.[1] When we reflect on the relevance of the atonement to the experience of suffering in general, the event which the Jews name *Shoah*, or the Catastrophe, sharpens the issues to a point where they are not only clear but almost unbearable.

Can God be justified?

In the face of the camps of death, no explanation which sets out to justify the goodness of the Creator will be entirely convincing. We may certainly *begin* a theodicy by affirming that God has passed over to his creation a radical freedom to be itself, and that he has limited himself in this way because he wants to make and enjoy fellowship with personalities who have, like himself, the ability to create. With their freedom to respond to God's purpose and to make their own contribution to his project, there also comes the risk that such personalities may slip away from the Good. Evil and suffering have thus emerged from creation as things strange to God, a disruption which he has not designed.

Even to begin to be convincing, this explanation will have to cover not only the human moral failure so viciously exhibited by the torturers of Auschwitz, but also the suffering caused by non-human agencies such as earthquakes, floods, hurricanes, genetic disorders and viruses. *Some* of what we tend to call 'natural evil' can no doubt be justified as an environment, arising from a mixture of natural laws and chance, within which human beings can develop a sense of morality and responsibility. As one philosopher claims, 'unselfishness would never be evoked in a situation in which no one was ever in real need or danger'.[2] But the shocking surplus of suffering to these requirements may be better understood as the result of a deeper kind of freedom than mere chance or random motion, granted by God to his whole creation. It is, I believe, consistent with the picture of a free universe that all levels of nature – not simply the advanced stage of human consciousness – should have some capacity in their own way to respond to, or resist, the urging of the Spirit of God. Since human personalities have emerged from the wider context of nature under the guidance of the creative Spirit of God, one would expect to find some family likeness throughout the whole. Though we scarcely have the language at present with which to describe it, we can envisage a relationship between God and his creation at every level, a bond which has some analogy to that between God and the human community.[3] Thus we can conceive of the natural world as also having slipped away from the aims and harmony that God desires for it. From this 'groaning' of the universe in frustration, as the apostle Paul puts it,[4] excessive damage can be inflicted upon human life.

The cross of Jesus assures us that God himself never directly inflicts suffering: a suffering God is to be counted among the victims and not the torturers. As we have explored the idea of atonement it has become clear that God does not even inflict suffering on himself; God the Father reconciles the world not by making the Son suffer, but by opening his triune being to a situation in which suffering *befalls* him as he accepts into himself the consequences which flow from sin and natural disorder. As I have argued extensively elsewhere,[5] if we affirm that God truly suffers with his world this must mean that suffering *happens to* him. In our experience the sting of suffering is the fact that it is outside our control; it has an unexpected, unknown quality before which we feel vulnerable. For

God to arrange and produce his own suffering as 'all his own work' would not be suffering as we understand it.

Even less then can we suppose that God sends suffering as punishment for sin. From our study of atonement it has become clear that the judgement of God is best understood, not as imposing a penalty upon human life from outside, but as his agonising consent, with deep pain of heart, to the outworking of sins into their natural results. This process is the dark side of our freedom, and *some* suffering may well be self-inflicted in this way; there is, by contrast, much other suffering in which we are the victims in a distorted world. However, if God is not the direct cause of any suffering, he still bears the ultimate responsibility for the situation since he has taken the risk of its happening, and it is precisely *at this point* that any theodicy falters. Suffering can certainly enrich the character of a sufferer and arouse acts of compassion and mercy in those who witness it, but confronted by an Auschwitz even these benefits fall short of convincing us that the risk of creating a free universe was justifiable.

Some philosophers have argued that if God exists he should have been able to make a different world in which beings would be safeguarded from committing evil while still remaining free.[6] However, since the kind of free beings we actually *are* requires there to be risks for the growth of personality, the real question is whether it was worth making *us*. Theodicy will always need a leap of faith to answer even the query (of Dostoevsky's Ivan)[7] as to whether it was worth the tears of one tortured child. We may, nevertheless, get a long way in 'justifying' God as a good creator, if we do believe *first* that his aim to create our free personalities was worth the risk, and *second* that he exposes himself as well as his creatures to the consequences.

My aim here is not to develop and defend an answer to *the* problem of suffering. Rather it is to explore ways in which belief in atonement shapes our experience of the *problems* of suffering. If the cross of Jesus stands at the centre of God's work of salvation it must be relevant to the damage caused by suffering. The affirmation that God himself shares the consequences of the risk he took is the most satisfactory theodicy we can achieve, and enables us to think of God and Auschwitz together, as long as we can speak of his transforming the effects of evil and suffering. Since this activity must be within the limits of the freedom he has granted to his creation, it cannot be imposed, but will call for response and cooperation. God's endurance of suffering will always, therefore, be balanced by something else – a struggle against it.

The protest and presence of God

In exploring the pattern of atonement as it is woven through the experiences of forgiveness and political engagement we discovered a sequence of action and submission. At the centre of both these experiences is a continual interaction of two movements – a passive moment of endurance and an active moment of protest and struggle. This dialectic we found to be rooted in the love of God incarnate in Jesus Christ, in his life and death. Since these experiences involve suffering, it is hardly surprising that we should find the relationship of God to suffering itself, and our own way of coping with it, to be marked by the same twofold dimension.

First we must affirm that God is present *in* suffering. This is the movement of divine endurance, of submission to the pain of the world. God was in Auschwitz. The theologian Jürgen Moltmann has rightly said that 'There could be no theology after Auschwitz had there been no theology in Auschwitz . . . anyone who comes up against insoluble problems and despair about suffering must remember . . . that the Lord's prayer was prayed in Auschwitz.'[8] We can think of God together with suffering, not as its cause, but *in* it. The theologians who wrote under the catchword that 'God is dead' were asserting that we no longer have any language with which to express the relationship of God to the world;[9] but we must surely reply that while the image of the cosmic monarch may be dead, God is not 'dead' to the world precisely because he experiences death. He is not irrelevant, even to Auschwitz, because he participates in its pain.

But second, God and the world as it is do not completely correspond to each other. We cannot argue for a proof of God from the visible things around us, and we cannot formulate a totally convincing theodicy, because God cannot be proved out of the evidence of a suffering world. But this is not because our reality contradicts God; rather God contradicts our reality. He is out ahead of the

210

world, protesting against what is imperfect and incomplete in its present state. From the viewpoint of the glory of the new creation he desires to bring about, he protests against the suffering and death that are an offence to love. As I have already argued, the resurrection of Jesus challenges our present understanding of what reality is. This is why, though an event in history, it cannot be verified with the tools of history. Moreover the cross also contradicts our view of how things should be; it is a scandal to accepted human views of what divinity might be like, that God should identify himself with a crucified man and show his glory by opening himself to death. In our world, power depends upon being able to escape death oneself and being able to inflict death on others. Thus in experiencing death God protests against our understanding of reality, making death serve him.

In this pattern of endurance and struggle lies the victory of God, for as he exposes his being to the alienating power of death, he overcomes it through his life. He absorbs its sting into his being and makes it serve his purpose. Though God is always confronting death in this way, he never goes further into its dark kingdom than in the cross. From the perspective of the Christian story, then, we may say that God was present in Auschwitz *and* protesting against it. He was not only sympathising but encouraging resistance to the machinery of death, even if that resistance could only take form in thought and attitude. It is this conviction that the Jewish philosopher Emil Fackenheim (himself a survivor of the camp at Sachsenhausen) expresses when he maintains that God's 'commanding voice' was heard in Auschwitz, speaking a new commandment – that 'the authentic Jew of today is forbidden to hand Hitler yet another posthumous victory'. Part of the content of that commandment is that 'we are forbidden to despair of the world as the place which is to become the kingdom of God lest we help make it a meaningless place in which God is dead or irrelevant and everything is permitted'.[10]

When Fackenheim speaks of a voice being heard in the camps he is speaking mythically. But in this dramatic style he draws attention to the protest of God, as well as to the actual resistance of many victims to having their human dignity stripped from them. The suffering most of us face is not of that magnitude, but any suffering poses practical problems to which this dialectic of endurance and struggle, and its location in the cross of Jesus, can be applied.

The problem of the acceptance of suffering

It has always been part of the Christian tradition to accept with faith the suffering that comes to us. This has sometimes been motivated by the hope of reward for virtue later on in this or some other life, or by awe-struck fear of a God who is more powerful than weak humanity. But the mystical writers who have urged followers of Christ to 'love suffering' as a means of communion with God have surely found something more healthy about the attitude of acceptance. The suffering that befalls us can be embraced as a means of dying to ourselves and our selfish preoccupations, of detaching ourselves from the possessions of life, and letting ourselves go into the 'calm' of being. To accept suffering in this sense is not merely passive; it is to enter upon a whole change in our existence, or as Kierkegaard expressed it, 'the highest action in inwardness'.[11]

But calmness can easily become apathy and indifference. There is a danger that acceptance of suffering may suppress the note of rightful protest against it. What then does it really mean in our experience to 'accept' suffering? How can it include an openness to the possibility that suffering can be overcome? In personal illness, for example, how shall we combine acceptance with trust in a God whose Spirit can promote healing processes through nature, in ways that we may not yet understand? Or again, since much suffering arises from the conditions that society imposes upon us, how shall we combine acceptance with a determination to change the situation so that needless suffering can be avoided in the future? Too often in the past people have been discouraged from questioning the status quo by being told that their Christian obedience was to 'accept' the lot that God had given them.

The question of 'acceptance' of suffering thus highlights the tension between the two dimensions of struggle and endurance we have been exploring. There *is* a kind of acceptance that is mere fatalism, expressed in such popular phrases as 'these things are sent to try us' or 'you've got to put up with it' or 'that's life', or even 'someone up there doesn't like me'. Christian fatalism is a resigned submission before the decrees of a God who is portrayed as a stern unmoving monarch; this view of acceptance corresponds to the concept of a God who cannot suffer, and who can have no feelings in the sense of undergoing any change in his consciousness. Thus his love cannot involve passion and sympathy, and can only be a charity of doing good – or what seems good to him. As Dorothée Soelle rightly perceives, an a-pathetic (un-feeling) God makes apathetic believers: 'ethically that means the Stoic concept of suffering triumphs over the Christian one'.[12] Moreover those who have steeled themselves to be aloof to suffering become hard and impatient towards others who are not so resigned. By contrast we remember the portrait of Job who was in a healthy revolt against a God who laid down inflexible decrees and could not be moved:

> I would speak to the Almighty,
> and I desire to argue my case with God.[13]

Since, however, God does suffer with his creation, and himself protests against suffering, our acceptance of suffering cannot be mere resignation. What then is its character? First true acceptance is *a facing up to the fact* of suffering. Our society tends to hide suffering away, to tidy it into safe compartments of life. The children are kept from funerals, and people look askance when mourning and grief goes on too long. Televised charity events raise money for handicapped people; they are safely defined as objects of pity but are not given proper employment to work beside the 'healthy' in the office or the factory. Great publicity is given to success in war, but the presence of those badly wounded or mentally disturbed through their experience is not allowed to disturb the neatness of the victory parades. Those who refuse to accept the presence of suffering will finally become insensitive to it; because they do not allow themselves to be exposed to suffering at close quarters, the death and suffering exhibited twice nightly on the television news has no reality for them, and hardens them still further. A symptom of the refusal to face the reality of suffering is the way that people urge others to look for compensating factors, and so to 'accept' their lot (in the sense of being resigned to it). The Christian psychologist Paul Tournier observes wisely that:

If an old person complains of losing his sight, many well inten-
tioned people reply: 'But you still have good hearing.' To a man
who bewails his loneliness since he lost his wife, they say: 'But
you have the children, and good friends.' Such remarks do more
harm than good. A privilege never wipes out suffering. 'Nothing
replaces anything,' one of my patients said to me only
yesterday.[14]

Telling the story of the cross means that we have to face the fact of
suffering. Living through its details in imagination, through gospel
reading and liturgy, will not allow us to evade the brute facts of
loss, torture and death. This does not mean that Christianity is a
'religion of misery', since the doctrine of atonement affirms that
suffering is not a *necessary* dimension of love. As we have seen, the
cross was inflicted upon Christ in human reaction to the identification of God with his creation; it is the indwelling of God, his
making of himself at-one with his rebellious creatures in love which
is atoning and saving. The deepest entrance of God into his creation
inevitably took the form of a cross, given the state of the world and
its evil. But if that past event is to have a creative power upon
human lives the doctrine must also be connected to the reality of
suffering in the present. As Kenneth Surin puts it, 'all theological
affirmations – including that of a God who suffers with those who
suffer . . . must be 'interrupted' by the narratives of those who are
victims'.[15] So the story of such places as Auschwitz must interact
with the story of Golgotha. As Elie Wiesel, himself a survivor of the
death camps, urges us: 'Let us tell tales . . . all the rest can wait. . . .
Tales of children so wise and so old. Tales of old men mute with
fear. . . . Tales of immense flames reaching out to the sky, tales of
night consuming life and hope and eternity.'[16]
    To face the facts of suffering and evil is the first step in acceptance.
Beyond this an 'accepting' of suffering which avoids apathy means
choosing the suffering as one's own. This does not mean choosing to
suffer in the first place, but taking it on when it has befallen us and
making it ours. It then ceases to be something from outside that
we are powerless before, since 'what I take belongs to me in a
differing sense from something I only bear' (Soelle).[17] Once we have
accepted suffering in this way, recognising it as ours and an alien
force no longer, then there is room to promote change where this

214

is possible. We affirm our suffering only in the context of affirming the *whole* of life; 'to accept is to say yes to life in its entirety' (Paul Tournier).[18] On behalf of life we struggle against death when it is untimely and cruel. We strive to change the conditions that cause death and all that is destructive of health; but moments also come when we accept what cannot be changed and the fact that healing will not come, or will come *as* death. The balance between protest and endurance will be different for each person, each dimension taking its meaning from the other; but we will only find the balance through active acceptance, love of the whole of life, and not resignation.

This kind of acceptance is characteristic of God's own life, who both endures suffering and protests against it. Indeed if God was not like this, but was a dictatorial ruler who sent suffering as punishment and corrective, we could dethrone him by making the suffering our own. Defusing it of its power over us, we would defeat its author. Religious people sometimes commend an attitude of thanking God *for* everything that happens to us; but the Christ who 'offered up prayers with strong cries and tears'[19] could hardly be misconstrued as giving thanks for the cross. Nevertheless, in communion with his Father, he said yes to the sacrifice he was asked to make, so that the apostle Paul can describe prayer as a participation in the 'Amen' (yes) which Christ himself speaks, and the author of the letter to the Hebrews conceives of prayer as a sacrifice of praise made 'through' Jesus.[20] Sharing in the acceptance of the cross which was characteristic of Christ, and which has meaning *only* because of the movement of protest and action that surrounds it, we can say yes to the whole of life and, loving it, want to change it.

The problem of isolation in suffering

The sting of suffering is loneliness. It cuts the sufferer off from the healthy and prosperous, and he feels deserted and abandoned. Of Jesus Christ in Gethsemane we read that 'they all forsook him and fled' and that on Golgotha he cried 'My God, why have you forsaken me?' Moreover the person who suffers tends to desert himself as well, to despise and even hate himself. He finds strange things happening to him, and he cannot relate to his own body which was once so familiar to him. Out of a loathing for themselves in their condition, sufferers often project morbid ideas that God is punishing them for particular sins, and this can account in part for the feeling that they have been abandoned by the God who once seemed so close to them. So the poet William Cowper laments in one of his frequent bouts of depression, 'Where is the blessedness I knew?' and pleads:

> Return, O holy Dove, return,
> Sweet messenger of rest!
> I hate the sins that made thee mourn
> And drove thee from my breast.

A further reason for the sense of desertion in suffering is no doubt the failure of expectations that God will intervene to put things right, since it is taken for granted that the presence of God must involve intervention on behalf of the sufferer. But the God who gives freedom to his creation does not coerce it. He works persuasively from within, drawing out a response not only from his human creatures but from all levels of the natural world, luring on his creation and being thwarted by it in ways that we do not yet have the tools of perception to comprehend. So the sense of being forsaken by God is at least partly a sense of the weakness of God. The cross of Jesus shows us that a God who submits to weakness will seem to be a hidden God; his divinity is veiled as he shares in the suffering of the world. But hiddenness is not absence, and veiling is not desertion.

In the poem of Job the sufferer rightly denies that his plight is caused by his sin. So far he refuses to confine God within a strict law of retribution as his friends do. But he returns to a legalistic view when he insists that, since he is innocent, God must vindicate him. Job's deep sense of isolation, his cry to be allowed into the heavenly court to meet God, and his complaint that God keeps avoiding him, frame a demand to be restored to health and prosperity.[21] His repentance at the end is not a cowering before a God who thunders louder than any other being, but a recognition that he cannot demand that God should act in a certain way, and that it is enough to know that God is with him:

216

> I had heard of thee by the hearing of the ear,
> but now my eye sees thee.

> (Job 42:5)

The poem leaves us with the mystery of suffering, sketched against the backdrop of a creation so vast and complex that it eludes our grasp.[22] We may, in the light of the cross, interpret this as meaning that God fails to release Job from suffering, not because he has some better 'plan' for him that he alone knows, but because he does not work in the world in the simple unilateral way that Job wants. The fact that the poem ends with encounter and conversation between Job and God is witness that suffering love can itself be a form of communication, overcoming isolation.

A similar conversation ends the historical novel *Silence* by Shusaku Endo, which relates the cruel dilemma of a Jesuit missionary in seventeenth-century Japan who has to watch members of his peasant flock being tortured and killed; he only has to make a formal gesture of apostasy – treading on an image of Christ laid on the ground – to save them. In his agony of spirit he appears to receive no answer from Christ when he prays; there is no intervention to stop the massacre. Finally out of sheer love he treads on the image:

> The priest raises his foot. . . How his foot aches! And then the Christ in bronze speaks to the priest: 'Trample! Trample! I more than anyone know of the pain in your foot. Trample! It was to be trampled on by men that I was born into this world. It was to share men's pain that I carried my cross.[23]

Later the priest complains, 'Lord, I resented your silence,' and hears Christ reply, 'I was not silent. I suffered beside you.'[24] The hidden Christ was not absent, and was calling for a response which was a human step of freedom, shrouded as all human acts are in the ambiguities of guilt and betrayal. As the priest treads upon the face of Christ, 'Dawn broke. And far in the distance the cock crew.'

As a matter of doctrine we can affirm that God has not in fact forsaken us, that he is veiled in weakness, and that (in Bonhoeffer's phrase) 'only a suffering God can help'. But we must still recognise a mysterious depth in the sense of forsakenness that exceeds either a morbid sense of sin, or mistaken expectations of how God acts, or even the way that divine weakness must inevitably be perceived from the human side. There is an overplus, a dark night witnessed to in the agony of Job, of Endo's priest, of the millions in the death camps and of the crucified Christ, which cannot be reduced to a rational concept. Again we need to listen to the witness of the martyrs of the Holocaust; as Elie Wiesel writes in his first-hand account, 'Theirs was the kingdom of the night. Forgotten by God, forsaken by him, they lived alone, suffered alone, fought alone.'[25] Thus if we are to learn how to protest against suffering and to change the conditions that cause it, we must first simply be present (as God is present) to those who are the victims. Either by listening to their stories or by actually sitting in fellowship – probably without speaking – with those who are suffering now, we accept them and their suffering. The healthy and the prosperous are full of advice for those who are 'worse off than themselves' (the phrase itself has a patronising ring to it); but we can only act when we endure. This is the divine dialectic of presence and protest.

It is part of the creative power of the cross to assure the sufferer that isolation can be overcome in new relationships, though it behoves those who are not afflicted not to say this easily and glibly to those who are. At the cross the relationships within the being of God himself were broken; that is, we can begin to express the belief that God stood in the place of alienation by saying that God experienced what it was like for a Son to be forsaken by his Father and for a Father to lose his Son. As we say this, we remember the stories – of children torn from the arms of their mothers, of fathers and sons driven by the gnawing demon of starvation to fight each other for a scrap of bread, of the parents who lose their children to the slavery of drugs. But the cross assures us that because the love of God is stronger than death, the relationships within his being did not only survive, but emerged from death as altogether new. If God did indeed expose his being to death in the cross, as the doctrine of atonement affirms, then he himself encountered what was strange; this too is part of the reason why those who share his cross enter a kingdom which cannot be mapped by human explanations. The creative power of the cross heals our relationships, but also plunges us into the Golgotha of the Spirit (Hegel's

218

phrase). Or, as Bonhoeffer says daringly, 'Christians stand by God in the hour of his grieving.'[26]

We can, then, take up the struggle against untimely death together with God, witnessing to the coming glory of God when death will be no more. Then, when death comes, we can trust in God to maintain our relationships with himself and each other; nothing will be lost, but there is something unknown about the new for which we have to trust.

Conclusion: the problem of silence in suffering

Suffering not only isolates but numbs. The one who suffers is left speechless, silent in grief, and that very silence contributes to his isolation. To put this suffering into words will be the first stage towards accepting it (in the sense outlined above), and those who sympathise can help to give the words, leading the sufferer out of the isolation of dumbness. Those who care must learn to allow for the half-formed cries of protest and the hostile words of resentment against friends, relatives and God. To express shock, to rebuke, or to argue is to drive a person back to a brooding within himself. These are only the first words out of the silence; once he or she is in converse with God and others there will be time to reach a balance of protest and endurance.

The most numbing suffering is that which appears to be completely meaningless. Suffering which befalls us with no obvious cause or ideal to inspire us to endure it is the kind that drives us deepest into silence. There seems no way to speak of it. This may be true of the most horrific events, such as a multitude of individual deaths in the Holocaust which offered no opportunity of being embraced as martyrdom for the faith. It is also the character of much of the suffering we endure day by day, even if we do not feel as keenly as Macbeth that:

> it is a tale
> Told by an idiot, full of sound and fury,
> Signifying nothing.[27]

But we can put alongside this senseless tale of suffering other stories of suffering which *do* have a meaning, through which a purpose was being fulfilled. They supply words through which the sufferer can begin to articulate his own experience. Of course we should never urge another person to find this or that purpose within his suffering; that would be to suppose that there is a final answer to the mystery of suffering. But to place another story alongside is to enable the sufferer to find a meaning *for himself*, to form words for suffering and so to discover a way towards the place of both acceptance and healthy protest.

The Christian doctrine of atonement affirms that the story of the death of Christ has universal meaning, an inexhaustible relevance for the human condition. There is, certainly, a point when meaning is lost within this story; despite the context of his purposeful actions as the faithful Son of God, there still comes the moment when Christ cries out, 'My God, why have you forsaken me?' But all loss of meaning is overcome with the resurrection of Christ to new life from the dead. God *gives* the cross meaning, as he reveals himself to have been present there, making the furthest journey of discovery into his creation. He makes this story, written in human flesh and history, available so that all other human stories can acquire meaning also. This past event has a creative power upon the present; as it grasps our imagination we find that we are being grasped by the living God.

Notes

pages 3–12

1 INTRODUCTION: ATONEMENT AND THE HUMAN PREDICAMENT
1 1 Cor. 2:2 Jerusalem Bible.
2 *katallage*, as in 2 Cor. 5:18; Rom. 5:11.
3 *kipper*: see further below, pp. 69, 71–3.
4 Walter Hooper, ed., *They Stand Together: the letters of C. S. Lewis to Arthur Greeves (1914–1963)* (London, 1979), p. 427.
5 C. S. Lewis, *Mere Christianity* (London, 1952), pp. 44–5.
6 J. A. T. Robinson, *The Human Face of God* (London, 1973), pp. 14–16.
7 Jean-Paul Sartre, *Being and Nothingness* (ET, London, 1957), p. 90.
8 J. A. W. Bennett, *Poetry of the Passion* (Oxford, 1982), p. 32.
9 e.g. R. T. Davies, ed., *Mediaeval English Lyrics: a critical anthology* (London, 1963), pp. 117, 84.
10 So Reinhold Niebuhr, *The Nature and Destiny of Man*, vol. I, *Human Nature* (London, 1941), p. 194. Similarly Tillich speaks of a tension between 'freedom and destiny' and Macquarrie finds a polarity between 'possibility and facticity'. See Paul Tillich, *Systematic Theology*, combined volume, II (Welwyn, 1968), pp. 36–7; John Macquarrie, *Principles of Christian Theology*, rev. edn (London, 1977), pp. 62–3.
11 Macquarrie, op. cit. pp. 71–2, 259–61.
12 Albert Camus, *The Myth of Sisyphus*, tr. J. O'Brien, New York, 1955.
13 Jean-Paul Sartre, *Existentialism*, tr. B. Frechtman (New York, 1947), p. 28.
14 Tillich, op. cit. II, pp. 54–5.
15 Niebuhr, op. cit. pp. 176, 198. Macquarrie also stresses the nature of sin as idolatry, op. cit. pp. 259–61.
16 Tillich analyses the nature of 'the demonic' in the individual and society, op. cit. III, pp. 108–13.
17 Karl Marx, *Capital I*, tr. E. Mandel (Penguin, Harmondsworth, 1976), pp. 164–5, 772, 990.

221

2 SALVATION AS EVENT AND PROCESS

1 Shakespeare, *Love's Labour's Lost*, Act V, Scene 2, 780–1.

2 See D. E. H. Whitely, *The Theology of St Paul* (Oxford, 1964), pp. 156–65.

3 H. R. Mackintosh, *The Christian Experience of Forgiveness* (Welwyn, 1927), pp. 190–1.

4 See the study by John Day, *God's Conflict with the Dragon and the Sea: echoes of a Canaanite myth in the Old Testament*, Cambridge, 1985.

5 See also such texts as Gen. 1:2–10, Pss. 29; 33:7–8; Prov. 8:24–29; Jer. 31:35.

6 The Wisdom strand of literature in the Old Testament also presents creation in another mode than conflict, argued from the regularities of human experience. See, for example, Pss. 8, 19, 104 written under the influence of wisdom modes of thought. On this whole theme see G. von Rad, 'The theological problem of the Old Testament doctrine of creation' in *The Problem of the Hexateuch and Other Essays*, tr. E. W. Trueman Dicken (Edinburgh and London, 1966), pp. 131–43.

7 This is still rather a contentious issue in Old Testament scholarship. For a classical account see Aubrey R. Johnson, *Sacral Kingship in Ancient Israel*, 2nd edn (Cardiff, 1967), pp. 54–72, 103–28.

8 See, for example, Gustavo Gutierrez, *A Theology of Liberation*, tr. C. Inda and J. Eagleson (London, 1974), pp. 155–60. I develop this theme further in Chapter 9.

9 This is well expressed by Jürgen Moltmann, *The Trinity and the Kingdom of God*, tr. M. Kohl (London, 1981), pp. 108–14.

10 For a more detailed account see Paul S. Fiddes, *The Creative Suffering of God* (Oxford, 1988), pp. 25–31.

11 e.g. Luther, *Confession Concerning Christ's Supper* (1528) in *Luther's Works*, American edn, vol. 37 (St Louis, 1961), p. 210.

12 See Abraham J. Heschel, *The Prophets* (New York, 1962), pp. 221–31.

13 See Franz Rosenzweig, *The Star of Redemption*, tr. W. W. Hallo (London, 1971), pp. 409–10; cf. Ps. 78:61; Isa. 63:9; 42:14; Ezek. 36:30–31.

14 Elie Wiesel, *Night*, Foreword by François Mauriac, tr. S. Rodway (Penguin, Harmondsworth, 1981), pp. 10–11.

15 See Mark 4:35–41; Matt. 14:25–17; Rev. 21:1.

16 'The Wreck of the Deutschland' in *Poems of Gerard Manley Hopkins*, 4th edn, ed. W. H. Gardner and N. H. Mackenzie (Oxford University Press, London, 1967), p. 53.

17 Gustav Aulen, *Christus Victor: an historical study of the three main types of the idea of atonement*, tr. A. G. Hebert (London, 1930), pp. 20–3, 160–76.

18 The idea of the 'focus' of God's saving act in Christ has been most

helpfully developed by John Macquarrie, op. cit. pp. 300–3; cf. pp. 324–7.

19 See e.g. Rom. 13:11; 1 Thess. 5:9; 1 Pet. 1:5; cf. Rom. 8:22–25; Phil. 2:9–11.

20 1 Cor. 11:26; cf. Luke 22:16. On the eschatological hope in the Eucharist see J. Jeremias, *The Eucharistic Words of Jesus*, tr. N. Perrin (London, 1966), pp. 237–55.

21 A well-known example is Alvin Toffler's *Future Shock*, London, 1970.

22 Jürgen Moltmann, *The Future of Creation*, tr. M. Kohl (London, 1979), p. 55. He also calls it the difference between 'eschatological extrapolation' and 'eschatological anticipation', ibid. pp. 41–8. See further Moltmann's earlier book *Theology of Hope*, tr. J. W. Leitch (London, 1967), pp. 15–36.

23 James Cone, *God of the Oppressed* (London, 1977), pp. 11–13.

24 ibid. p. 22; cf. pp. 29ff.

25 Harvey Cox, *The Feast of Fools: a theological essay on festivity and fantasy* (New York, 1970), pp. 74–6.

3 FAITH AND HISTORY

1 Acts 26:26.

2 e.g. Rudolph Bultmann, 'New Testament and theology in *Kerygma and Myth*, vol. I, ed. H. Bartsch, tr. R. Fuller (London, 1964), pp. 34–8; John Knox, *Myth and Truth* (London, 1966), pp. 61–4.

3 Albert Schweitzer, *The Quest of the Historical Jesus*, ET, London, 1910.

4 ibid. p. 399.

5 See below, pp. 190–2, 196–7.

6 Wolfhart Pannenberg, *Jesus – God and Man*, tr. L. Wilkins and D. Priebe (London, 1968), p. 98.

7 e.g. 1 Cor. 15:20.

8 E. P. Sanders, *Jesus and Judaism* (London, 1985), pp. 274–81, 290–3.

9 Sayings that stress the presence of the kingdom include Matt. 12:28/ Luke 11:20; Matt. 11:5; Luke 17:20; 10:18; sayings that point to a future kingdom include Matt. 8:11; Luke 13:8–29; Matt. 16:18; Mark 14:25; Matt. 19:28/Luke 22:28–30. Mark 1:14 catches the double meaning. For the compatibility of these meanings of kingdom see Norman Perrin, *The Kingdom of God in the Teaching of Jesus* (London, 1963), pp. 159ff.

10 Matt. 16:27/Luke 9:26/Mark 8:38. My summary of the situation agrees with Pannenberg's stress upon the authenticity and centrality of the saying of Jesus in Luke 12:8f. See Pannenberg, op. cit. pp. 60–2.

11 This point is made by Sanders, op. cit. p. 184.

12 For the foregoing see Matt. 11:28; Luke 4:18; Mark 10:31; Matt. 20:12; Luke 18:25.

13 e.g. Luke 15:1–2; Mark 2:15; Matt. 21:31.

14 Sanders, op. cit. pp. 202–3.

15 See Joachim Jeremias, *New Testament Theology: Part One*, tr. J. Bowden (London, 1971), pp. 109–10.

16 See Luke 7:36–50; Luke 10:38–42; Mark 15:40f; John 4:27; Mark 10:14; Matt. 18:3.

17 Mark 2:23–28; Matt. 12:9–14/Mark 3:1–6. Sanders however, op. cit. p. 266, maintains that the scribes would not have regarded the latter as work.

18 Mark 3:4.

19 Luke 6:35. This positive version was also known in the Diaspora: see Jeremias, op. cit. p. 212 n. 3.

20 Matt. 5:33–39.

21 Matt. 8:21ff./Luke 9:59f.

22 Matt. 6:17.

23 The phrase is from Eduard Schweizer, *Jesus*, tr. D. Green (London, 1971), pp. 30–9.

24 Matt. 26:65/Mark 14:34.

25 With Mark 14:58/Matt. 26:61, compare Mark 13:1–2; John 2:19.

26 Here I follow the argument of Sanders, op. cit. pp. 71–6, 302–5.

27 Dan. 7:13–14. This is, of course, a highly contested subject. M. D. Hooker, *The Son of Man in Mark* (London, 1967), pp. 182–98, traces the majority of the sayings to Jesus.

28 See the essays by J. P. M. Sweet and E. Bammel in *Jesus and the Politics of His Day*, ed. E. Bammel and C. F. D. Moule, Cambridge, 1984.

29 This point is well made by John Knox, *The Death of Christ* (London, 1959), pp. 27–9.

30 Josephus, *Jewish Antiquities*, 18:116–19, Loeb Classical Library, tr. L. H. Feldman (Harvard and London, 1965), vol. IX, p. 83.

31 John 11:50. In this section I am indebted to the argument of the Jewish scholar Ellis Rivkin, *What Crucified Jesus?* (London, 1984), pp. 49–55.

32 So E. Schweizer, *The Good News According to Mark*, tr. D. Madvig (London, 1971), p. 244.

33 cit. James D. G. Dunn, *Christology in the Making* (London, 1980), p. 15.

34 Ps. 2:7.

35 Isa. 1:2.

36 John 5:19; Mark 1:11.

37 Rom. 1:4.

38 Dunn, op. cit. p. 25.

39 ibid. pp. 26–7.

40 Col. 2:3; 1:16–17.

41 Pannenberg, op. cit. p. 336.

42 Jürgen Moltmann, *The Crucified God: The cross of Christ as the foundation and criticism of Christian theology*, tr. R. Wilson and J. Bowden (London, 1974), pp. 240–1.

4 THE POINT OF SACRIFICE

1 T. S. Eliot, 'Burnt Norton', V, from *Four Quartets* in *The Complete Poems and Plays of T. S. Eliot* (Faber, London, 1969), p. 175.

2 Gifts included not only holocausts of animals, but also burnt-offerings of flour, oil, incense and wine: e.g. Exod. 29:38–42; Lev. 23:9–14; Num. 15:1–12; 2 Sam. 6:18; Ps. 50:1–12. See R. de Vaux, *Ancient Israel: its life and institutions*, 2nd edn., tr. J. McHugh (London, 1965), pp. 415–16, 421–2, 451–2.

3 See the discussion by Frances M. Young, *The Use of Sacrificial Ideas in Greek Christian Writers from the New Testament to John Chrysostom*, Patristic Monograph Series, No. 5 (Cambridge, Mass., Philadelphia Patristic Foundation, 1979), p. 12f.

4 e.g. Pss. 51:1–10; 40:6–7; cf. 24:3; 32:5. See H. H. Rowley, *Worship in Ancient Israel: its forms and meaning* (London, 1967), pp. 251ff, 261ff.

5 e.g. Amos 5:21–24; Hos. 6:6; Jer. 7:21–23; Isa. 1:11–17; Mic. 6:6–8. For a discussion of the prophetic criticism of sacrifice see R. E. Clements, *Prophecy and Covenant*, SBT 43 (SCM Press, London, 1965), ch. 5.

6 cf. Rom. 12:1; Phil. 4:18.

7 Early examples are Col. 1:24; Martyrdom of Polycarp 14:1–3. See Frances M. Young, *Sacrifice and the Death of Christ* (London, 1975), p. 56.

8 Origen, *Homilies on Leviticus*, 2:3.

9 For a discussion, see G. von Rad, *Old Testament Theology*, vol. I, tr. D. M. G. Stalker (Edinburgh, 1962), pp. 262ff; cf. de Vaux, *Institutions*, pp. 418–21.

10 Lev. 16; 23:27–32; cf. Num. 29:7–11. For a discussion of the origin of 'The Day' see de Vaux, *Institutions*, pp. 508–10.

11 This classification was popularised by G. B. Gray, *Sacrifice in the Old Testament* (Oxford, 1925), pp. 64–5.

12 Von Rad, op. cit. p. 255.

13 See Joachim Jeremias, *The Eucharistic Words of Jesus*, pp. 225–31.

14 In this contentious issue I follow Jeremias, ibid. pp. 15–26, 82.

15 See n 4 above; also G. von Rad, op. cit. pp. 270–1. Rowley, op. cit. p. 134, quotes the important sentence from the Talmud: 'Sin offering

and guilt offering and death and the Day of Atonement all put together do not effect atonement without repentance.'

16 C. G. Montefiore and H. Loewe, *A Rabbinic Anthology* (London, 1938), pp. 430–1.

17 4 Macc. 6:28 (Hadas), cit. Young, *Sacrificial Ideas*, p. 68.

18 Lucan, *Pharsalia*, 2.304–9, cit. Martin Hengel, *The Atonement: the origins of the doctrine in the New Testament*, tr. J. Bowden (London, 1981), p. 24.

19 ibid.

20 For an extended discussion see Young, *Sacrificial Ideas*, pp. 15–23.

21 See H. Wheeler Robinson, *Inspiration and Revelation in the Old Testament* (Oxford, 1946), pp. 226ff.

22 cf. W. D. Davies, *Paul and Rabbinic Judaism*, 2nd edn (London, 1955), p. 235.

23 Chrysostom, *Homilies on Hebrews*, 29.

24 Athanasius, *De Incarnatione*, 8.

25 Calvin, *Institutes of the Christian Religion*, Book II, 16.3–5.

26 See Gen. 1:14. On the priestly theology see Peter R. Ackroyd, *Exile and Restoration: a study of Hebrew thought of the 6th century BC* (London, 1968), pp. 95, 99–101.

27 e.g. Lev. 18:25,28; Ps. 51:1ff. See von Rad, op. cit. pp. 273–5.

28 See Num. 5:2–3; cf. Lev. 13:15–17; Luke 7:21–23.

29 Lev. 16:8–10. For the word 'Azazel' see de Vaux, op. cit. p. 509.

30 *Epistle of Barnabas*, 7.6–11; Justin, *Dialogue with Trypho*, 40. In Origen, *Contra Celsum* 6.43, Christ is the person who leads away the scapegoat (the devil). Frances Young makes this image of atonement a main theme of her study, *Sacrifice and the Death of Christ*, op. cit.

31 This is the view taken, for example, by John Whale, *Victor and Victim: the Christian doctrine of redemption* (Cambridge, 1960), p. 50; cf. Vincent Taylor, *Jesus and his Sacrifice* (London, 1937), p. 50.

32 See, for example, Origen, *Contra Celsum* 4.71–72; *De Principiis* 3.1:10–12; Clement of Alexandria, *Stromateis* 7.15.

33 Hengel, op. cit. pp. 49–55.

34 In Rom. 4:25, however, Paul uses the form 'he was given up'. For the infrequency of sacrificial terminology in Paul, see Davies, op. cit. pp. 230ff.

35 Patrick White, *Riders in the Chariot* (Penguin, Harmondsworth, 1964), p. 418.

36 The rituals are outlined in Lev. 3 and 7. See de Vaux, *Institutions*, pp. 417f, 427f.

37 Virginia Woolf, *Mrs Dalloway* (Panther, London, 1976), p. 109.

38 George Herbert, 'Love (III)', in *The Poems of George Herbert*, ed. Helen Gardner, World's Classics (Oxford, 1961), p. 180.

39 Young, *Sacrificial Ideas*, p. 170.
40 Paraphrase by Young, ibid., p. 169.
41 See above, n. 17.
42 Claus Westermann, *Isaiah 40–66: a commentary*, tr. D. M. G. Stalker, Old Testament Library (London, 1969), p. 262.
43 *Poems by John Wilmot, Earl of Rochester*, ed. Vivian de Sola Pinto, 2nd edn, The Muses Library (London, 1964), p. xxxvi.
44 Wilmot, Satire LXVII, 'Consideratus, Considerandus', ibid. p. 126.
45 Westermann, op. cit. p. 268.

5 THE DEMANDS OF JUSTICE

1 pp. 41–8.
2 See above, pp. 49–50.
3 G. Schrenk, in G. Quell and G. Schrenk, *Righteousness: Bible key words from G. Kittel's Theologisches Wörterbuch*, tr. J. R. Coates (London, 1951), pp. 45, 61. The Old Testament forbids the justification of the wicked, Exod. 23:7; Prov. 17:15; Isa. 5:23.
4 See e.g. Deut. 19:15–19; 25:1; 1 Kgs 8:31–32; Prov. 17:15; R. de Vaux, *Institutions*, pp. 155–7 The aspect of fellowship and community is emphasised by D. E. H. Whitely, op. cit. pp. 159–60.
5 Job 9:3; Pss. 72:2–4; cf. 71:2–4.
6 e.g. Augustine, *De Trinitate* 13.10: Christ pays the debt to release the debtors.
7 *Commentary on Galatians* (1535) in *Luther's Works*, American edn, vol. 26, ed. J. Pelikan and W. A. Hansen (St Louis, 1963), p. 277.
8 Wolfhart Pannenberg attempts to argue this case, in *Jesus – God and Man*, pp. 259–60.
9 Rudolph Bultmann makes clear that for Paul the judgement 'which factually already takes place' is equivalent to the 'wrath' of God; see *Theology of the New Testament*, vol. I, tr. K. Grobel (London, 1952), p. 288.
10 e.g. Ps. 81:12: 'I gave them over to their stubborn hearts, to follow their own counsels'; cf. Ps. 27:9; Isa. 59:2; Jer. 33:5; Ezek. 39:23; Mic. 5:3. For the idea of God's 'hiding his face' see Samuel E. Balentine, *The Hidden God: the hiding of the face of God in the Old Testament* (Oxford, 1983), pp. 143–51.
11 See Jer. 12:7–11; 31:20. H. Wheeler Robinson speaks of Jeremiah's sense of the 'tragedy of God's defeated purpose', *The Cross in the Old Testament* (SCM, London, 1955), p. 184.
12 Tillich, *Systematic Theology*, II, p. 201.
13 See above, and G. von Rad, *Old Testament Theology*, vol. I, p. 266.

14 So C. H. Dodd in his influential comments on Rom. 1:18–32, *The Epistle of Paul to the Romans*, Moffat New Testament Commentary (London, 1932), pp. 21–9.

15 Moltmann, *The Crucified God*, p. 151.

16 The phrase is that of John Robinson in *The Body: a study in Pauline theology*, SBT 5 (London, 1952), p. 42.

17 Anselm, *Cur Deus Homo?* 1.11.

18 ibid., 1:7–8.

19 Calvin, *Institutes*, Book II, 16.5.

20 ibid.

21 ibid. 12.3.

22 ibid. Book III, 21.5.

23 This development was opposed by the Lutherans, especially in the *Formula of Concord*.

24 Centuries of conflict between Protestant and Roman Catholic theologians on this matter have now apparently been resolved by *Salvation and the Church: an agreed statement by the Second Anglican–Roman Catholic International Commission, ARCIC II* (Church House Publishing and Catholic Truth Society, 1987), pp. 17–19: 'God's declaration of forgiveness and reconciliation does not leave repentant believers unchanged.'

25 Abelard is a good representative of this tradition; see Chapter 7 below. This way of thinking relied upon Rom. 5:5 as a proof text, and stemmed largely from Augustine; see *On the Spirit and the Letter*, 3.5, 9.15, 32.36.

26 See *Augsburg Confession*, Article IV; Luther, *On the Twofold Righteousness* (Sermon, 1519); Calvin, *Institutes*, III, 11.2.

27 Calvin, *Institutes*, Book III, 11.10.

28 Anselm, *Cur Deus Homo?* 2.18a; cf. Calvin, *Institutes*, Book III, 12.1: 'It was not simple or absolute necessity, but flowed from a heavenly decree.'

29 Tillich, *Systematic Theology*, II, p. 203.

30 R. C. Moberly, *Atonement and Personality* (London, 1924), p. 65.

31 The whole phrase is 'a perfect Amen in humanity to the judgement of God on the sin of man', J. Mcleod Campbell, *The Nature of the Atonement*, 4th edn (London, 1873), p. 118; cf. the similar phrase 'Amen to the mind of God in relation to sin' (p. 119).

32 P. T. Forsyth, *The Work of Christ: lectures to young ministers*, Uniform reissue (London, 1938), pp. 150, 164.

33 Moberly, op. cit. p. 80.

34 F. Schleiermacher, *The Christian Faith*, tr. H. R. Mackintosh and J. S. Stewart (Edinburgh, 1928), pp. 431–8.

35 This idea of our participation in the Trinity is worked out further below, pp. 166–8.

36 This is worked out in Chapter 8, below.
37 See further below, pp. 158–60.
38 Jean-Paul Sartre, *Altona, Men Without Shadows, The Flies* (Penguin, Harmondsworth, 1962), pp. 305, 311.

6 THE DECISIVE VICTORY
1 Gustav Aulen, *Christus Victor*, p. 176.
2 See above, pp. 17–19.
3 John 12:31; Rev. 12:9; Heb. 2:14.
4 Gustav Aulen, *The Faith of the Christian Church* (London, 1961), p. 226.
5 e.g. Rom. 5:14; 6:6,17,20; 7:11,14; Gal. 3:22; 1 Cor. 15:56.
6 See above, pp. 11–12.
7 Rom. 1:25.
8 Macquarrie, *Principles of Christian Theology*, p. 319.
9 Rom. 7:12.
10 Gal. 3:15–29; cf. Rom. 4:1–17.
11 See Rom. 2:14–15; Gal. 3:23–26; Rom. 10:4.
12 Rom. 7:7–8.
13 Rom. 3:2; 4:13ff.
14 So Jürgen Moltmann, *Theology of Hope*, op. cit. pp. 121–4.
15 Rom. 7:10 NEB.
16 1 Cor. 15:26.
17 Heb. 2:15 NEB.
18 Job 1:9–12; Zech. 3:1–2.
19 G. B. Caird, *Principalities and Powers* (Oxford, 1956), p. 37.
20 Luke 10:18; John 12:31; Rev. 12:10.
21 Walter Wink, *Unmasking the Powers: the invisible forces that determine human existence* (Philadelphia, 1986), pp. 15–20.
22 See Matt. 4:1–7; cf. Wink, op. cit. p. 19.
23 John 8:44.
24 Rom. 8:35–59.
25 H. Wheeler Robinson, *Inspiration and Revelation in the Old Testament*, pp. 70–1, 81–2.
26 Wink, op. cit. p. 24.
27 Mark 3:22–27.
28 Ps. 96:5 NEB.
29 Ps. 82:1–7.
30 1 Cor 2:6–8; Eph. 6:12.
31 Rom. 13:1–2. For further on this passage, see below, pp. 201–2.
32 2 Thess. 2:6–7

33 Gal. 3:19; Acts 7:53; Heb. 2:12; cf. Jubilees 1:27; Josephus, *Jewish Antiquities*, 15:5.
34 Caird, op. cit. p. 53.
35 Also see Phil. 2:10, Col. 1:16–20; Eph. 3:10.
36 Col. 1:16.
37 e.g. Rev. 16:5 (the angel of water); Rev. 7:1 (angels of wind); Rev. 19:17 (angel of the sun); Heb. 1:7 (angels of wind and fire); John 5:4 (angel of water). See Wink, op. cit. p. 158.
38 Rom. 8:22–3; 1 Cor. 6:3; cf. Heb. 1:13, 2:6–9.
39 Rom. 8:20; Heb. 2:8; cf. Ps. 8:4–6.
40 Friedrich Nietzsche, *Thus Spoke Zarathustra*, tr. R. J. Hollingdale (Penguin, Harmondsworth, 1969), Prologue 3: 'I teach you the Superman. Man is something that should be overcome.'
41 Heb. 5:2,7.
42 Mark 14:36; Luke 22:42.
43 See above, pp. 40–1.
44 Gregory of Nyssa, *Great Catechism*, 24.
45 cit. Aulen, op. cit., p. 119.
46 *The Gospel of Nicodemus*. XX-XXIII, in New Testament Apocrypha, vol. I, ed. E. Hennecke and W. Schneemelcher, tr. R. McL. Wilson (London, 1963), pp. 472–4. The tradition persists in Langland, *Piers Ploughman*, passus XVIII (B Text)
47 See above, p. 73. In the Ethiopian book of Enoch, 9:6; 10:4–8, Azazel is described as the Prince of Demons.
48 Origen, *De Principiis*, 3:2.1; *Contra Celsum*, VI.43.
49 Tillich, *Systematic Theology*, vol. II, p. 198.
50 Rom. 7:19.
51 Irenaeus, *Adversus Haereses*, 5:1.1.
52 Origen, *Homilies on Leviticus*, 9.9.
53 Ps. 95:8–11; Ezek. 16; 20:1–20.
54 Athanasius, *De Incarnatione*, 7.
55 See above, pp. 118–19.
56 Aulen, op cit. pp. 72–6, 128–30.
57 ibid. pp. 136–8, 172–5.
58 cit. Aulen, p. 136.
59 *Lectures on Galatians* (1535), *Luther's Works*, op. cit. vol. 27, pp. 4–5.
60 ibid. vol. 26, p. 281 (on Galatians 3:13).
61 See above, pp. 91–3.
62 Irenaeus, *Adversus Haereses*, 4:40.3
63 Barth, *Church Dogmatics*, IV/I, ed. G. W. Bromiley and T. F. Torrance (ET, Edinburgh, 1936–77), p. 253.
64 ibid. However in Barth's view sinners have not brought 'nothingness'

into existence; God has given it a kind of reality by saying no to it in creation. See *Church Dogmatics*, III/3, pp. 77, 361–5, and my critique of this idea in *The Creative Suffering of God*, pp. 216–21.

65 Barth, *Church Dogmatics*, III/3, 363–8.

66 ibid. IV/1, p. 254.

67 ibid, III/3, p. 367.

68 Caird, op. cit. p. 97.

69 Macquarrie, *Principles of Christian Theology*, op. cit. p. 324.

70 R. Bultmann, 'New Testament and mythology', op. cit. p. 36.

71 Heb. 2:10; 10:19; 12:2.

72 Macquarrie, op. cit. p. 325.

73 Col. 2.15; Gal. 4:9.

74 1 Cor. 2:8–11.

75 Macquarrie, op. cit. p. 326.

76 Caird, op. cit. pp. 89–91. For a similar argument see J. A. T. Robinson, *The Body*, op. cit. p. 40.

77 Robinson, *The Body*, p. 43, translating Col. 2:20.

78 Aulen, *Christus Victor*, pp. 150–1.

79 Macquarrie, op. cit. p. 321.

7 THE ACT OF LOVE

1 Peter Abelard, *Commentary on the Epistle to the Romans*, II. 3:26, in *A Scholastic Miscellany: Anselm to Ockham*, The Library of Christian Classics, vol. X, ed. and tr. E. R. Fairweather (London, 1956), p. 283. In citing Abelard's commentary on Romans, reference is made where possible to these excerpts (LCC); otherwise the reference is to *Petri Abaelardi Opera Theologia, Corpus Christianorum Continuatio Mediaevalis*, XI, ed. E. M. Buytaert (Turnholt, 1969) (CCCM). References to the *Ethics* are from the edition by D. E. Luscombe, Oxford, 1971. Other works of Abelard are cited from J.-P. Migne, *Bibliotheca Patrum Latina*, CLXXVIII (1855) (PL).

2 This thesis is ably expounded by G. R. Evans, *Anselm and a New Generation* (Clarendon Press, Oxford, 1980), see especially p. 154f.

3 Abelard, *Romans*, II.3:27 (CCCM, pp. 118–19).

4 Abelard, *Romans*, II.3:26 (CCCM, p. 116; LCC p. 282).

5 ibid.

6 Abelard, *Theologia Scholarium*, iii: v. (PL 1101b).

7 Abelard, *Expositio in Hexaemeron*, PL 765a. The other marks of the image are power and reason.

8 Richard E. Weingart, *The Logic of Divine Love: a critical analysis of the soteriology of Peter Abailard* (Oxford, 1970).

9 Abelard, *Romans*, II.3:26 (LCC, p. 284, tr. slightly emended; CCCM, p. 118).
10 Abelard, *Romans*, II.3:25 (CCCM, p. 112).
11 Abelard, *Romans*, II.5:7–8 (CCCM, p. 155).
12 op cit. (n. 9 above); my italics.
13 Bernard, *Letters*, 190, tr. L. W. Grensted, *A Short History of the Doctrine of the Atonement* (Manchester, 1962), p. 106.
14 Bernard, *Sermons on the Song of Solomon*, XV, tr. S. J. Eales in *On Loving God*, ed. Hugh Martin (London, 1959), p. 84.
15 Abelard, *Sermons*, 3 (PL 396b).
16 *The Letters of Abelard and Héloïse*, tr. Betty Radice (Penguin, Harmondsworth, 1974), p. 151 (letter 4).
17 ibid. p. 154.
18 1 Cor. 1:23–24. Reinhold Niebuhr, *The Nature and Destiny of Man*, vol. II, pp. 59–64.
19 ibid. pp. 103–4.
20 ibid. vol. I , pp. 201–20.
21 ibid. vol. II, p. 113.
22 ibid. p. 100.
23 R. S. Lee, *Freud and Christianity*, Penguin, Harmondsworth, 1967.
24 ibid. p. 162.
25 ibid. p. 163.
26 Athanasius, *De Incarnatione*, 20.
27 See Vladimir Lossky, *The Mystical Theology of the Eastern Church* (Cambridge, 1957), pp. 148–55, 126–7.
28 Athanasius, *Contra Arianos*, 3.33.
29 Abelard, *Ethics*, ed. op. cit. pp. 5–9, 54–7.
30 ibid. p. 29.
31 1 Sam. 5:29.
32 Athanasius, *Contra Arianos*, 2.59.
33 Lossky, op. cit. pp. 164–6.
34 Abelard, *Sermons*, 5 (PL 423c); cf. Abelard, *Romans*, III.3:15 (CCCM, p. 217).
35 Abelard, *Theologia Summi Boni*, 1:6, cit. Weingart, op. cit. p. 158.
36 Abelard, *Romans*, II.3:26 (LCC, p. 284; CCCM, p. 116).
37 Abelard, *Expositio in Hexaemeron*, PL 770d–771a, cit. Weingart, op. cit. p. 166.
38 *Romans*, II.3:26 (LCC, p. 279; CCCM, p. 113).
39 e.g. *Romans*, II.3:25 (LCC, p. 279, CCCM, p. 112).
40 For Abelard's use of these traditional models see his *Romans*, II.1:1 (CCCM, p. 54), II.4:11 (CCCM, p. 141), III.7:4–5 (CCCM,

pp. 188–9), II.4:24 (CCCM, p. 153), II.5:7–12 (CCCM, pp. 156–7), II.3:25 (CCCM, p. 112, LCC, p. 279), *Sermons*, IX (PL 446d).

41 *Expositio symboli apostolorum*, 625a.
42 Barth, *Church Dogmatics*, II/1, p. 306.
43 ibid. II/1, p. 472.
44 ibid. IV/1, p. 186.
45 Abelard, *Romans*, III.7:13 (CCCM, p. 202).
46 Thomas Traherne, 'First Century', 43.
47 Barth, *Church Dogmatics*, II/1, p. 281.
48 Tillich, *Systematic Theology*, II, pp. 202–3; III, pp. 239–43.
49 Barth, *Church Dogmatics*, I/1, pp. 132–6.
50 Abelard, *Romans*, III. 8:9 (CCCM, pp. 213–14).
51 *Sermons*, 4, PL 404d.
52 *Sermons*, 32, PL 575a.
53 Schleiermacher, *The Christian Faith*, p. 433.
54 Dietrich Bonhoeffer, *Lectures on Christology*, tr. E. Robertson (London, 1978), p. 445.
55 ibid.
56 John D. Zizioulas, *Being as Communion* (London, 1985), pp. 36–41.
57 ibid., p. 107.
58 Doris Lessing, *The Making of the Representative for Planet 8* (Granada, London, 1983), p. 159.
59 Bonhoeffer, *Christology*, op. cit. p. 59.
60 ibid, p. 107.
61 ibid. p. 58.
62 Dietrich Bonhoeffer, *Letters and Papers from Prison*, ed. E. Bethge (London, 1971), p. 360.
63 ibid. p. 391.
64 2 Cor. 1:20–21. See further below, p. 215.
65 e.g. Ezek. 37:9; Isa. 40:7; Gen. 2:7; Isa. 61:1; 4:4; 44:3; 1 Cor. 12:13; Acts 2:2–3; Luke 1:35; Gen. 1:2; Luke 3:22.
66 Rom. 8:19–27.
67 John 3:8, Ecclus 11:5.

8   THE COST OF FORGIVENESS

1 Caliban, the half-human creature of the island, makes another who refuses to join the charmed circle of harmony, Act I, Scene 2, 365.
2 W. H. Auden, 'The Sea and the Mirror', II, in *W. H. Auden: Collected Longer Poems* (Faber, London, 1974), p. 212.
3 *The Tempest*, Act IV, Scene 1, 148–58.
4 See above, pp. 15–17.

5 H. R. Mackintosh, *The Christian Experience of Forgiveness*, p. 191.
6 ibid. p. 211.
7 Mark 2:1–12; Luke 7:36–50. Jeremias, *New Testament Theology*, I, p. 114, refers also to pictures of forgiveness: debt remitted, the stray brought home, the lost found, the child accepted into the father's house.
8 See above, pp. 43–50.
9 See above, p. 44.
10 Luke 15:1–7.
11 Mackintosh, op. cit. p. 211.
12 Luke 19:1–10. Even after his repentance Zacchaeus does not make an offering as the law required.
13 Luke 7:36–50.
14 Heb. 12:3.
15 This lies at the heart of the temptation narratives: see Matt. 4:1–10.
16 See above, pp. 48–9.
17 Paul Tillich, *The Courage to Be* (Fontana, London, 1962), pp. 159–71.
18 William Golding, *Free Fall* (Faber, London, 1959), p. 47.
19 ibid. p. 131.
20 ibid. pp. 234–6.
21 Paul Tournier, *Guilt and Grace: a psychological study*, tr. A. W. Heathcote (London, 1962), pp. 63–4.
22 David Jenkins, 'Responsibility, freedom and the Fall' in E. W. Kemp, ed., *Man: Fallen and Free* (London, 1969), p. 28.
23 F. Dostoevsky, *The Brothers Karamazov*, tr. D. Magarshack (Penguin, Harmondsworth, 1958/1962), p. 287.
24 Rabbi Dr Albert Friedlander, speaking in the BBC programme 'The Heart of the Matter', 21 February 1988.
25 cit. R. L. Rubenstein and J. K. Roth, *Approaches to Auschwitz* (London, 1987), p. 260.
26 Dostoevsky, op. cit. p. 288.
27 U. Simon, *Atonement: from Holocaust to paradise* (Cambridge, 1987), pp. 49–50.
28 T. S. Eliot, *Complete Poems and Plays*, op. cit. p. 360.
29 Daniel Day Williams, *The Spirit and the Forms of Love* (Welwyn, 1968), p. 212.
30 F. W. Dillistone, *The Christian Understanding of Atonement* (Welwyn, 1968), p. 266.

9 POLITICAL ENGAGEMENT

1 XIth thesis against Feuerbach. See Karl Marx, *Early Writings* (Penguin, Harmondsworth, 1975), p. 423.

2 cit. Guttierez, *A Theology of Liberation*, p. 152.
3 Leonardo Boff, *Passion of Christ, Passion of the World* (Maryknoll, New York, 1987), p. 11.
4 So J. Miguez Bonino, *Revolutionary Theology Comes of Age* (London, 1975), p. 27.
5 ibid. pp. 29–30.
6 Leonardo Boff, *Church, Charism and Power* (London, 1985), pp. 40, 5.
7 Rubem Alves, *Protestantism and Repression* (London, 1985), p. 19.
8 See above, pp. 47–8, 102.
9 Moltmann, *The Crucified God*, pp. 244, 241.
10 Boff, *Passion of Christ, Passion of the World*, p. 114.
11 Moltmann, *The Crucified God*, p. 246.
12 ibid. pp. 207, 217, 243.
13 Boff, op. cit. p. 51.
14 ibid. p. 114.
15 Barth, *Church Dogmatics*, IV/1, pp. 186–7.
16 Jon Sobrino, *Christology at the Crossroads: a Latin American approach*, tr. John Drury (London, 1978), pp. 219–22.
17 ibid. p. 227.
18 ibid. p. 196.
19 ibid. p. 227.
20 Final Declaration of the First Assembly of Ecumenical Third World Theologians at Dar-es-Salaam (1976). Printed in *The Emergent Gospel*, ed. S. Torres and V. Fabella, New York, 1978.
21 J. H. Hinton, *Memoir of William Knibb* (London, 1849), pp. 50–1.
22 Though he was careful to plead the abolition of slavery only to the white population in England, and avoided preaching 'temporal freedom' to the slaves, he had doubts about this policy: 'we did not attack slavery [in the island], though perhaps it was our duty to do so', ibid. p. 184.
23 Alves, op. cit. p. 40, quotes this phrase from a teaching document of the Protestant church in Brazil.
24 cit. Theo Witvliet, *A Place in the Sun: an introduction to Liberation Theology in the Third World*, tr. J. Bowden (London, 1985), p. 12.
25 James Cone, *God of the Oppressed* (London, 1977), p. 136.
26 Allan A. Boesak, *Black Theology, Black Power* (London, 1978), p. 14.
27 Paul Lehmann, *The Transfiguration of Politics* (London, 1975), p. 64.
28 So Rudolph Bultmann, *The Gospel of John: a commentary*, tr. G. R. Beasley-Murray (Oxford, 1971), p. 660: 'the state stands over against the world'.
29 Karl Barth, *The Epistle to the Romans*, tr. E. C. Hoskyns (Oxford, 1933), p. 493.

30 Acts 5:29.

31 Lehmann, op. cit. pp. 270, 68.

32 Christians may differ about whether violence is ever justified as part of resistance. I have not directly discussed this issue, although it is a key one in the 'Southern' and 'Third' worlds, since here I am confining my attention to modes of political engagement that are appropriate to western democracies today.

33 Lehmann, op. cit. p. 66.

34 Boff, op. cit. p. 123.

35 ibid. p. 126.

36 Bonhoeffer, *Letters and Papers from Prison*, p. 219.

37 Haddon Willmer suggests that every act of consent to government is an act of forgiveness: see 'The politics of forgiveness', *The Furrow*, 30 (Maynooth, 1979), p. 214.

10 THE PROBLEMS OF SUFFERING

1 Raul Hilberg, *The Destruction of the European Jews*, rev. edn (New York, 1985), vol. 2, p. 411.

2 John Hick, *Evil and the God of Love* (London, 1968), p. 361.

3 Process theology is a notable attempt to work out a metaphysic for this picture. See David R. Griffin, *God, Power and Evil: a process theodicy* (Philadelphia, 1976), pp. 275–310.

4 Rom. 8:22.

5 Paul S. Fiddes, *The Creative Suffering of God*, esp. pp. 61–3.

6 See e.g. J. L. Mackie, *The Miracle of Theism* (Oxford, 1982), pp. 174–5. Alvin Plantinga, *The Nature of Necessity* (Oxford, 1974), pp. 173–89, argues in opposition that theodicy only requires it to be *possible* that God could not have created any conceivable world containing no moral evil. My own argument does not depend on deciding this point.

7 Dostoevsky, *The Brothers Karamazov*, op. cit. p. 283.

8 Moltmann, *The Crucified God*, p. 278.

9 Representative of this movement of the 1960s are Thomas J. J. Altizer and William Hamilton, *Radical Theology and the Death of God*, Penguin, Harmondsworth, 1968.

10 cit. Rubenstein and Roth, *Approaches to Auschwitz*, p. 319.

11 S. Kierkegaard, *Concluding Unscientific Postscript*, tr. D. F. Swenson and W. Lowrie (Princeton, 1941), p. 386.

12 Dorothée Soelle, *Suffering*, tr. E. Kalin (London, 1975), p. 43.

13 Job 13:3.

14 Paul Tournier, *Learning to Grow Old*, tr. E. Hudson (London, 1972), pp. 179–80.

15   Kenneth Surin, *Theology and the Problem of Evil* (Oxford, 1986), p. 162.
16   Elie Wiesel, 'Art and culture after the Holocaust' in Eva Fleischner, ed., *Auschwitz: beginning of a new era?* (New York, 1977), p. 403.
17   Soelle, *Suffering*, op. cit. p. 103.
18   Tournier, op. cit. p. 178.
19   Heb. 13:15. See above, p. 166
20   2 Cor. 1:20; Heb. 13:15.
21   Job 9:1–24, 13:14–28.
22   See Job 38–41.
23   Shusaku Endo, *Silence*, tr. W. Johnston (Sophia University, Tokyo, 1969), p. 271.
24   ibid. p. 297.
25   Quoted by Susan Shapiro, 'Hearing the testimony of radical negation' in *The Holocaust as Interruption*, ed. E. Fiorenza and D. Tracey (Edinburgh, 1984), p. 3.
26   Bonhoeffer, *Letters and Papers from Prison*, p. 349.
27   Shakespeare, *Macbeth*, Act V, Scene 5, 26.

Index